KU-249-866

Sybil Kenton
'Folly Cottage'
53 West Drive
Harrow Weald
Middx. HA3 6TX
Telephone: 01-954-3817

An Illustrated Handbook of Machine Knitting

Janet Nabney

An Illustrated Handbook of
Machine Knitting

B.T. Batsford Ltd, London

ISBN 0 7134 5338 9

Typeset by Servis Filmsetting Ltd, Manchester
and printed in Great Britain by
The Bath Press Ltd,
Bath, Somerset
for the publishers
B.T. Batsford Ltd
4 Fitzhardinge Street
London W1H 0AH

To John, of course!

Contents

Acknowledgements

Firstly, I would like to register my great debt of gratitude to the people who have put domestic machine knitting on the map: Mary Weaver, Kathleen Kinder, and many others. Thanks are due also to all the avid machine knitters I have met who are anxious to broaden their knowledge. I have always been lucky enough to find them full of enthusiasm and keen to trade tips and techniques.

I would like to acknowledge the inspiration of Kaffe Fassett and John Allen. They led me to see knitting as an art form and not just making 'people-shaped-tea-cosies'.

Many thanks to Kathryn Hobbes for her unlimited enthusiasm and encouragement. I would like to thank all my students who taught me a great deal while I was teaching them. Thanks also to Dorothy who showed me how to be generous with my knowledge.

I must also pay tribute to the many foreign textile, knitting and craft magazines. They are an unlimited source of ideas and techniques.

My chapter on the use of the garter bar was originally written for Jones/Brother and appears by their kind permission.

Abbreviations

Alt. = alternate
Beg. = beginning
Carr./C. = carriage
cm = centimetre
C/O. = Cast-off
C.O.B.H. = Cast on by hand.
    ('E' wrap method.)
C.O.L./C.O.R. = Carriage on left/
    right
Col./Con. Col. = Colour/Contrast
    colour
Cont. = continue
Dec. = decrease
Ev. = every
F.A./F.B. = Feeder A/B
F.F. = Fully fashioned
F.N.R. = Full needle rib
Foll. = following
H./H.P. = Hold/holding position

H.C.L. = Holding cam lever
Gms. = grams
K. = Knit
Kg. = kilos.
K.H./K.R. = Main bed/ribber bed
Lps. = loop
M.C. = machine
M.T. = Main tension
M.Y./M.Col. = Main yarn/main
    colour
N(s)/Nds./Ndls. = needles
N.W.P. = Non-working position
    (A position)
Opp. = opposite
Patt. = pattern
Pos. = position
R.C. = Row counter
Rem. = remaining

Rept. = repeat
Ret. = return
R.S. = right side
Rws. = rows
St.(s) = stitches
S.S. = stitch size
st.st. = stocking stitch
T./T.D. = Tension/tension dial
Tog. = together
Transf./trs. = transfer
T.U.H. = Turn up hem.
U.W.P. = Upper working position
    (Knitmaster = C pos. Jones/
    Brother = D pos.)
W.P. = Working position
W.S. = wrong side
W.Y. = waste yarn
X's = times

How to use this book

I would recommend that you start at the beginning of the book and work through the techniques methodically. You will find simple skills, which are carefully illustrated early on in the text, relevant as the techniques become more complicated and demanding. This will save you from hopping about trying to find a simple technique later on. Also, never begrudge that little extra time spent when making your own knitted garments. It will pay dividends in originality in the long run.

This book is for all knitters who want to produce a garment which is more than just a 'people-shaped-tea-cosy'. This book will introduce you to the elements of 'knitmanship'. It's up to you to use them.

Introduction:
The Machine Knitter's Progress

1 Buying a knitting machine

When you see knitting machines in a store or at an exhibition you may have overheard comments like: 'It looks so complicated – do you need a degree to operate it?' or 'Does it get all four T.V. channels on the antennae?'

Contrary to hand knitting where you have only two needles for lots of stitches, on a knitting machine, you have lots of needles, one for every stitch. Each needle is really just a small latch hook, very like a rug hook, and the needles are placed side by side in the needle bed. They are numbered from 0 in the middle outward symmetrically. The tension mast at the top of the machine does the same job that your fingers do when you hand knit, controlling the tension of the yarn to make the stitches even. The number of needles on a machine and the size of the stitch dictates the width of fabric that you can produce. The carriage moves across the needle bed, moves the needles and feeds the yarn thus making the stitches.

Pros and cons of acquiring a knitting machine

The pros
(1) A knitting machine can free you from having to buy knitting patterns. This means that you can:
  ● 'copy' expensive garments that you see in the shops;
  ● knit a garment to fit you exactly no matter what shape or size your are;
  ● knit a garment in the right colour to fit in with your existing wardrobe;
  ● alter or modify the design to suit you;
  ● personalize your garment by knitting in club emblems, motifs or names.
(2) The yarns available for knitting machines are often less expensive than those for hand knitting. They are often also the ends of lines from industrial designer-knit ranges. The initial cost of the machine can favourably be set against the money you save, often in less time than you think, by knitting for your family needs.
(3) The time factor: it takes considerably less time to machine knit a garment than it does to hand knit one.
(4) You gain a great deal of self satisfaction from having knitted an expensive looking garment, which is the shape, size and colour you designed and at a fraction of the cost you would have to pay if you could even find it in a shop!

The cons
(1) The initial outlay is very great but the expense of buying a machine is a 'one off' as the machine will last for many years. Over a period of time you can save a lot of money as shop-bought garments are more expensive than those made on a domestic knitting machine.
(2) The time required to learn may be seen as a drawback. It does require some time to acquire the necessary skills. The more adventurous your designs, the more skill you need. Fairly simple garments, however, can be knitted quickly.
(3) Concentration required: having a knitting machine does not mean that you can push a button, and a completed designer-knit garment will fall off the machine. With all crafts you get out of it what you are prepared to put into it. You must have patience and common sense! The rewards, however, are enormous in terms of satisfaction and achievement.
(4) You may think that machine knitting is no substitute for hand knitting.
  ● The quality of the fabric produced by machine-knitting is much more even and professional – like 'shop bought' garments – than hand knitting.
  ● You may not think that machine knitting has the same therapeutic value, but it is a different 'ball game'. Machine knitting can supplement hand knitting: it bears the same relation to hand knitting that hand embroidery or hand sewing bears to the sewing machine. Each discipline serves its own purpose.
(5) The time factor: although it often takes very little actual knitting time at the machine to make a garment, it still requires time to assemble and finish off the garment. Just because you can start and finish knitting a garment in a morning this doesn't mean that the garment will put itself together!
(6) A knitting machine is bulky. The width of the machine determines the width of your finished fabric, therefore, to knit garments of a useful size you will require a machine of a standard width. Most modern knitting machines, however, can be assembled and taken down within

minutes. They fold flat and can be stored in a cupboard, taking up the same room as an ironing board.

(7) A knitting machine can be an absorbing pastime, (not to say a passion or obsession) and can take you away from the company of your family. It is not a hobby that can be indulged in while you watch television as it requires concentration. However, you wouldn't do dress making while watching T.V., and the time actually spent working at the machine is limited because it is so quick that you can save the hand finishing for doing with the family later.

Buying your machine new or second-hand

The following problems are some of the pit-falls you ought to consider before buying a second-hand machine.

● The machine might be obsolete – that is spare parts (like needles) would be impossible to replace, instructions might not be readily available and modern patterns not easily applicable.

● Why is it being sold? If the person who bought it found difficulties in learning how to use it, where will you go for instruction? A reliable dealer, however, will always be pleased to help you over any problems or difficulties that may arise.

● A novice to machine knitting cannot judge the condition of the machine. It may be damaged, and then when you experience difficulties in learning how to use it, it may be the fault of the machine and not you. The machine may just be dirty, gummed-up with old oil or badly maintained, or it may be broken.

● A second-hand machine that seems to be a bargain may discourage you from machine knitting for life!

Unless you can get expert advice and help, a second-hand machine can be a very risky proposition. You might be better advised to go to your local dealer where you can rely on ongoing advice and help when things go wrong. (This advice relates to buying a machine from a mail-order catalogue as well.) Having said that, it is wise to shop-around as prices (and willingness to help can vary a great deal). You might remember that the price can also include valuable assistance, without which the machine could be useless.

Generally speaking the more you pay for a machine – the more 'advanced' it is likely to be. A good machine is likely to be:

(*i*)   more versatile in stitch patterning ability;

(*ii*) more automated, doing boring chores like remembering which line you are in in your stitch garment pattern and selecting the right needles to do your stitch pattern automatically;

(*iii*) able to do a wider stitch pattern repeat. That is when the machine makes a pattern across more needles before it begins to repeat itself. (There is no limit to the length of the pattern repeat.)

Which gauge machine should you choose?

Not all machines knit all yarns. In hand-knitting the diameter of the needle determines the size of your stitch. You use thin needles for fine yarn and thick needles for chunky yarn. On a knitting machine you cannot change all your needles when you want to change the type of yarn you are using but you can alter the size of loops the needles make to get big stitches or little stitches (within limits). Just as you wouldn't consider hammering a carpet tack with a sledge hammer, you wouldn't knit very chunky yarn on a fine gauge machine. The standard gauge machine is 4.5mm – that is, each needle is 4.5mm away from its neighbour. On this type of machine you can knit from a fairly fine industrial yarn to a double knit-

ting yarn, but you cannot knit very knobbly yarn on these machines.

The standard chunky machines now available are 9mm gauge – that is, the needles are exactly twice as far away from their neighbours as the standard gauge machines. These machines will deal comfortably with the chunkier yarns, mohairs, dishcloth cotton and even thin fabric strips. They are not, however, suitable for very fine yarns, and because the needles are twice as far apart, they have half the number of needles and consequently half the number of stitches as a standard gauge machine. This is not a disadvantage if you are using thick yarns as you will need fewer stitches to achieve your required width. Other gauge machines available are: the fine gauge machine (3.5mm), some European manufactured machines (5mm) and older machines (which may be 8mm). You must decide what type of garments you wish to knit and what sort of yarn you wish to use.

Stitch patterning facilities

This is the ability to knit some sort of variety of stitch to give the fabric interest. All machines will knit plain stocking stitch automatically, but if you wish to knit a coloured pattern or a textured pattern some machines make this easier than others. Of course you must remember that nowadays yarns are so interesting that you can often just knit a plain fabric and produce a very attractive garment. These are some of the alternatives available.

Manual These are the simplest machines available. They are designed to use chunky yarns and often rely on the yarn to give the garment interest. Some are very basic indeed (and therefore much less expensive), but creating any stitch patterning can be a long and tiresome chore – or a challenge, depending on your viewpoint. Most manual machines are designed to use thicker yarn. The yarn becomes the design feature of the garment. These are usually 8mm or 9mm gauge machines.

Push button These machines are standard gauge machines, so you can use quite fine yarns on them. In terms of patterning facilities they might be considered as semi-automatic. The needle selection for the patterning is done by pushing a set of buttons and pulling a lever for each row to set the needles. The advantages are that they are quite reasonable in terms of cost and are fun to 'play around' on. There are two main disadvantages. Firstly, they require concentration because you must remember the row of your stitch pattern repeat as well as the row of your garment pattern. Secondly, they have only an 8 or 12 stitch repeat, which means you can only do small stitch patterns automatically. (The Toyota 12 stitch repeat 858 model combines a punch card facility with the push button facility, but the needle selection in both cases is made row by row manually with a set lever.)

Punch card machines These are the sort of machines which are most widely available today. They are mainly 4.5mm or standard gauge machines (although some manufacturers have recently developed punch card facilities for the 9mm gauge machines – both have 12 and 24 stitch repeats). All Japanese manufactured standard gauge, standard punch cards are interchangeable, (except for the Toyota 858) and will also fit the new 9mm gauge machines. However, not all machines produce their patterns in the same way. Although the card will fit another machine, the machine will not be able to produce the same pattern. These machines all produce a 24 stitch repeat pattern totally automatically. There is no limit to the length of the pattern. The advantages of these machines is that they are very readily available, and it is easy, once you have done your ground work, to knit a finished garment very quickly.

There are a great number of attachments available for these automatic punch card machines such as colour changers, intarsia carriages and casting-off attachments that simplify various tasks.

There are disadvantages, however. You do have to do your planning in advance and choose your stitch pattern punch card, etc. If you are planning to punch out your own cards, they must be long enough to feed through the machine automatically (18cm minimum). On some machines it is difficult to over-ride the automatic needle selection.

European machines with the punch card facility have a bigger stitch repeat of 40 sts., enabling you to knit wider patterns.

The electronic machine This machine is basically a very sophisticated version of the punch card machine. Mechanically it works in exactly the same way as the manual machines. It forms stitches and knits stitch pattern variations. However, it is programmed to read the stitch pattern information from the Mylar sheet and transmit this information to the needles. It is an extremely versatile machine, whose full potential has yet to be explored. Some of the more immediately obvious advantages are that only one repeat of the pattern need be recorded on the Mylar (pattern) card; this information can be a 60 stitch repeat and can be manipulated electronically before it is transmitted to the needles. The drawback with this machine is the high initial cost.

The double bed machine These machines are manufactured in Europe and are basically not designed to be as portable as the Japanese machines. They tend to be 5mm gauge, which means that the needles are slightly further apart than the standard gauge Japanese machines. They have various attachments available, but each machine has its own punch card system. Some of them will do selective patterning on both beds but not automatically on the second bed. They are much heavier machines: the Passap is the only double-bed machine to produce ribbed fabric without weights.

Accessories

Not all accessories are available for all machines and these must be checked out before the initial decision to buy a machine is made. This is very impor-

tant, even if you are planning to space out the buying of accessories.

Garment shaping attachment By far the most important accessory available is the garment shaping attachment. This device literally frees you from patterns. You choose the yarn, the stitch pattern and the garment shape. You give the measurements of your tension square and garment shapes to the attachment and it writes your knitting pattern for you. Not only does it tell you how many stitches and rows to knit to make a garment to fit you but it follows you along as you knit to remind you exactly where you are in the garment pattern. This means you can leave the machine and go away for six months and return to find the machine still knows where you were in the pattern!

Each machine has its own attachment, some being added on and others built into the machine. The advantage of those that are added on is that you can transfer them from a 9mm gauge machine to a 4.5mm gauge machine if necessary. They range from full size – full scale attachments (which are large but easy to see; they can be used to trace out garment shapes, to the exact dimensions even if they are not symmetrical; and can be used as an aid to picture knitting) through half size–full scale, to half size–half scale attachments, which are very neat and the patterns, being smaller, are easy to store. There is also a computer available, but it is not easy to design your own patterns on this attachment. On the full scale patterning attachments you can trace ordinary dress patterns out to give you your garment shape.

Ribbers This is often the attachment that people choose to buy after mastering the basic machine. Some very simple machines do not have ribbers available. The job of the ribber is to produce plain and purl stitches in one row. Ribbers themselves vary from machine to machine, offering different facilities – for example 1 × 1 automatic needle selection, plaiting, pile knitting, drive lace, 'simulknit' and so on.

Colour changers These are necessary if you wish to knit Fair Isle patterns with the ribber, in order to produce a much thicker firmer fabric than a single bed fabric. One advantage is that your don't have any 'floats' as you would do in a single bed Fair Isle fabric. With these double bed colour changers you can produce single bed fabric, but only if you have a ribber. You can obtain a single bed colour changer which makes some multi-coloured stitches much easier to produce. There is also a colour changer that may be used with either the ribber or the single bed on its own. A ribber is not required with this colour changer but it also works with one.

Intarsia carriage This is used to produce picture knitting on the more sophisticated punch card machines (unnecessary on simpler machines).

Transfer carriage This tool enables you to transfer stitches from the ribber to the main bed automatically. On Passap and Pfaff machines the transfer attachment will move stitches from either bed to the other one; on Japanese machines the transfer carriage will work in only one direction.

Linker This is an automatic casting-off device that you can also use to help you assemble your garments.

Garter carriage This is an electronic device that knits plain-purl stitch patterns and moves across the machine automatically. It can be left to knit by itself, although it is very slow compared with ordinary machine knitting. Its main advantage is that it is totally independent and requires no supervision as it has a number of built in fail-safe devices. It can knit your garment overnight while you sleep, but it only does straight knitting and no shaping (increasing and decreasing).

2 Using your machine

Beginners' blues – don't be put off

O.K. – You've made your decision and you've got the machine home.

'This machine has got it in for me! There's something wrong with it. Every time I try to cast on the carriage jams. When I try to knit all the stitches drop off. All I do is make a pile of spaghetti!'

Don't be nervous; don't be frightened; don't be scared. Everyone goes through beginners blues and you mustn't lose heart. There are some simple golden rules to be observed.

(1) Go slowly. The machine knits fast enough – you don't have to move the carriage quickly too – so take your time.

(2) Read the instruction book *carefully* without skipping any bits that you don't think look important. They probably are the most important bits.

(3) Go through the instruction book *again* with the machine carefully step by step. Again don't be tempted to try to knit a lace wedding dress just because you have mastered step one of the casting-on! Just because you have watched Stirling Moss change gear that doesn't mean you can race your new electronic knitting machine around Brand's Hatch circuit! The magic word is *practice*.

(4) The last but possibly most important and most difficult rule to follow is *never work at the machine when you are overtired*. So often you can be tempted to try 'just once more' and you're sure it will come out right this time. Even though you've been knitting for four hours, it's nearly one o'clock in the morning and everyone else in the house has been in bed for hours! This is exactly the time when if nothing went wrong before, by Murphy's law, something's sure to go wrong now. Leave it for the morning after and what took you two hours the night before will probably take 15 minutes the following morning.

Making a garment

Once you have mastered the basic principles of machine knitting you

come to the next hurdle, the garment. You can now produce a nice knitted fabric, but ultimately the object of the exercise is to make this fabric up in a garment that you or your beloved or your customer can wear – and preferably one that will fit just one of you at a time. Your idea when you purchased the machine was that you would be free to knit garments of your choosing quickly and easily. You may perhaps find it difficult to find a pattern for a garment that you like. There are several alternatives. Sources for patterns for machine knitting can be any of the following.

- Popular magazines obtainable from newsagents such as *Pins and Needles*, *World of Knitting* and *Machine Knitting News*.

- Some good hand-knitting magazines include instructions (although rather rudimentary) for machine knitting, such as those produced by Pingouin.

- Hand-knitting patterns can be adapted to machines if you can either get your tension swatch to measure the same as the one specified in the pattern or you are prepared to adapt the hand-knitting pattern so that you can achieve the same shape on your machine.

- Provided you are prepared to invest a little time and effort, you can write your own simple patterns, (if you use very basic shapes) with the help of a calculator.

- If you have a patterning attachment the world is your oyster and as source material you can use: diagrams from any knitting patterns – even ones in Italian or Japanese; measurements you get from one of your favourite garments; or commercial dress patterns.

Measurements

You have knit your garment and you feel cheated as it doesn't fit properly. You must be very careful and check your measurements exactly. Have you measured your tension square accurately? Or more precisely is the measurement of the garment really the correct measurement for you? If the garment makes the model look like a film star that doesn't mean it is going to do the same for you. Fashion photos are designed to relay an impression, not necessarily convey accurate information! You must also be honest with yourself when you are taking your own measurements and avoid the sin of wishful thinking.

Always knit your tension square very carefully. Treat it as you will eventually treat the garment. Allow it to rest before measuring. If in doubt about it make a tension square twice as big as you need. Take your measurements carefully then divide them by two. Large tension squares are always more accurate and never a waste of yarn. Knitting a garment that will not fit is just wasteful. Remember, you cannot accurately measure your knitting while it is under tension on the machine.

You must also remember that your design must be a happy blend of:
- shape;
- stitch pattern;
- yarn;
- colour.

Acquiring more skills

Once you have mastered the basic techniques of using the machine and can produce wearable garments you will want to spread your wings. Perhaps you may want to knit 3 D sculptures or artistic wall hangings or make individualistic and exclusive garments that won't be seen anywhere else. Think of knitting as you would a child's colouring book:

(*a*) The outline: the garment shape.
(*b*) The filling in: the stitch pattern and the yarn.
(*c*) The finishing off: put your picture, or your garment, into a frame, e.g. the neckline, the hem and so on.

Any design you make is basically a combination of these three elements.

Sources of inspiration (as opposed to copying) can be: fashion magazines: e.g. *Vogue, Harpers and Queen,* etc; hand knitting magazines: e.g. *Phildar, Pingouin, Laines Anny Blatt, Vogue Knitting Book, Rakam, Benissimo, Cent Idees,* etc; and stores. Keep an eye out for fashion trends. Do go into shops and try garments on. See if they fit you and if they suit you. Take a tape measure to make sure of the measurements.

Inspiration for designs

Ideas for designs can be taken from: books on embroidery and cross stitch patterns; patterns for weaving and books on related crafts; or even fabric or wall paper patterns. In addition look at designs in museums, e.g. the Victoria and Albert Museum (for both fashion and fabric designs), the Commonwealth Institute and the Museum of Mankind. Also craft shows and craft shops (e.g. the British Craft Centre) are inspirational, as are degree shows and art/textile college shows, e.g. the Royal College of Art. (These passing out shows take place in early spring.) Lastly, don't forget dealers' and clubs' fashion shows – these are often advertised in knitting magazines.

Colour and texture

Another important element in your design is colour and texture – that is, the yarn you use. When you buy yarn always make sure you buy enough to experiment and finish your garment. Too little yarn is always false economy. Also keep a record of the yarn you have in stock by tying samples of the yarn into holes punched along the side of a stiff piece of card. Note on the card next to the yarn the quantity, source, price, etc. Keep separate cards for different types of yarn – e.g. lambswool, shetland, acrylics, cotton, mixtures and fancy yarns, etc. Keep your cards up to date and remember to:
- have your cards with you when you plan to go on a wool buying expedition;
- take samples of fabrics you wish to match when you go on wool buying expeditions;
- try to buy yarn in matching groups – that is buy different colours or textures that you think will complement one another or a yarn you may have already, rather than just buying an isolated cone which you think is attractive and then finding that you have no idea how you are going to use it!

Most important for all your design endeavours is to keep extensive notes. Keep note books in which you have cut out pictures from magazines that have inspired you to new ways of thinking. Keep note books in which you have pasted pictures of colour combinations that you find attractive. If possible take these with you when you go yarn hunting. Careful colour matching can make or break a garment and this is often far more important to the finished result than all the fiddly little bits and pieces of technique tacked onto your garment.

When you see a garment in a shop that appeals to you or gives you inspiration, it is often a good idea to go home quickly and knit up a small swatch or sample in the correct yarn or colourway. A sketch or diagram with colour notes can be helpful. Even if you don't have time to design and knit the garment immediately, it forms part of your most important store of ideas which you can draw upon at a later date. The more meticulous your record of ideas, the easier it will be to use them at your convenience at a later date.

Machine knitter's mania

As an experienced machine knitter have you contracted this mysterious ailment?
The symptoms:
(*1*) An enormous collection of machine knitting books.
(*2*) An equally enormous collection of patterns.
(*3*) An equally enormous collection of magazines of all descriptions – British and foreign.
(*4*) Membership of every knitting club you can reasonably get to and several postal clubs as well!

(5) An unerring instinct to encourage your family to take their yearly holiday in healthy areas of natural beauty like the Lake District in the North of England (near the mills) or the north of Italy in the mountains (near the mills).

(6) Shelves, nay cupboards, nay rooms full of yarn (usually in one or two favourite colours).

(7) An almost overwhelming desire to rush up to a complete stranger and rip off their garment because it is knitted in a stitch pattern you find interesting or intriguing and you want to dissect it on the spot.

(8) A collection of *knitted tea cosies*– that is, garments which are hideous but you have had to knit them because you found the stitch pattern or technique involved irresistible, even though the final result was unwearable.

(9) Finally, a glazed look and a total inability to make a decision about actually tackling a project, much less knitting a garment.

The cure: Make a list of all the ideas that you find appealing and attractive and do little samples. Put your sample in a book with detailed and extensive notes and then *work through your book idea by idea*.

1 How the Knitting Machine Works

1 Single bed machines

Let's look at knitting machines more closely. They may look complicated, but once you understand how they work, using them becomes child's play.

The needles

There are a number of needles set in channels side by side in the needle bed. Each needle represents a stitch.

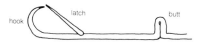

Needle

These needles consist of 3 important parts:
- butt
- hinged latch
- hook

If any of these parts are faulty or damaged the needle won't work properly. The needles can easily be removed and replaced. The carriage moves across the needle bed and as it does it pushes the needles. They run forwards and backwards in their channels, thus making the stitches.

The stitches

The stitches are made in the following manner.

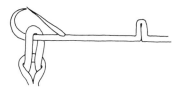

Stitch in the needle

(*1*) There is a loop of yarn (a stitch) in the hook of the needle. The needle butt is in working position.

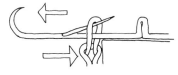

Needle comes forward and stitch is pushed back behind the latch

(*2*) The carriage is pushed across the needle bed and in turn it pushes the needle forward so that the loop of yarn (the stitch) is pushed back behind the latch.

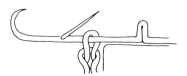

Stitch behind the open latch

(*3*) The carriage feeds the free end of yarn into the empty hook.

Yarn placed in the needle hook

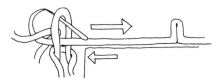

Needle pulled back pulling new loop of yarn through the old stitch

(*4*) The carriage then pulls the needle back again so that the latch closes over the new loop of yarn and pulls it through the stitch that is behind the latch. Now you have the new stitch in the needle hook.

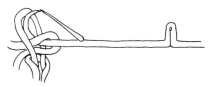

Formation of the new stitch

This is basically how all knitting machines produce knitted fabric.

The tension mast

All machines except the Bond have a tension mast (also called a yarn brake). The tension mast does the same job as your hand when you do hand knitting. You can also compare it with threading up a sewing machine except you must remember that wool for a knitting machine is much thicker than sewing thread, therefore, the device you thread it up on must be bigger.

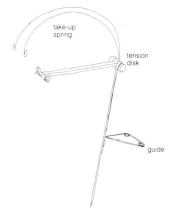

Brother tension mast

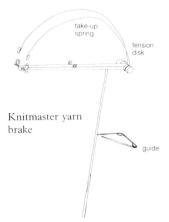

Knitmaster yarn brake

The tension mast does two jobs.

(*1*) The yarn is kept under tension when it passes through the adjustable tension disks, thus helping it to flow freely and evenly through the machine. These disks have a finger between them to catch and hold the yarn under tension. This means that the stitches are all very even.

Close-up of a tension disk

(*2*) The yarn then passes through a 'take-up' spring. This spring takes up the slack in the yarn when the carriage passes the end needle in the row and then turns to come back. This prevents loops forming at the edge of your work and also prevents the yarn from dropping down below the carriage and getting caught in the wheels and brushes, causing jamming of the carriage and dropped stitches. The take-up spring is not adjustable but it is replaceable.

The hand does the same job as a tension mast/yarn brake

The tension mast, therefore, is really an enlarged hand. That is, it does the same job on a knitting machine that your hand does when you are hand knitting: The yarn wound around the little finger controls the speed of the yarn flow, and the index finger takes up any slack in the yarn.

The needle bed

This is the body of the machine that holds the needles in channels. The position of the needle in the bed dictates:

(*a*) how may stitches you are using; and

(*b*) the stitch pattern or type of fabric you are producing.

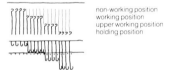

Needle-bed positions on Japanese machines

When you push or select your needle butts to different places in the bed this positioning will affect what the carriage does with the needles as it passes across the machine. (The position of the needles refers to position of the needle butts not the needle hooks.) On all knitting machines there are basically *four* possible positions. (The exception on currently available machines is the Jones/Brother KH 710 which has two upper working positions.)

On all machines, if you have stitches on the needles but do not wish to knit these stitches, you may push the needles to holding position (H.P.). Then, if you set the carriage properly, it will pass across the needle bed and 'ignore' these needles, leaving them to remain in H.P.

The Bond machine – This has two positions where the needles do not work at all. The carriage passes the needles by and completely ignores them: (*i*) right at the back of the needle bed; and (*ii*) all the way forward in the needle bed.

There are two other needle positions on the Bond. In both cases the needles can be moved to form new stitches by the carriage: (*i*) mid-way forward, far enough to enable the hooks to reach the edge of the bed where the stitches can hang straight down and (*ii*) a bit further forward where the latches of the needles line up with the edge of the bed when they are open. Then the stitches are on the needles just behind the open latches and the knitting hangs straight down at the edge of the needle bed.

The Knitmaster Zippy 90 – With this machine the needles right at the back of the machine and all the way forward in the bed do not knit. Needles in working position will knit unless the side levers on the carriage are manually held forward as the carriage passes across the bed. Needles in the forward position (the bed is marked with little dots to help align the butts so that the open latches would be in line with the edge of the needle bed) always knit.

The Japanese single bed machines (Brother/Jones, Knitmaster and Toyota) — If we look at the end of the needle bed we can see a number of letters imprinted in the metal there. These letters correspond to the position of the needle butts in the bed. When the positions are clearly marked on the bed it is much easier to position the needles. Needles all the way back in the needle bed (A position) correspond to needles in resting or non-working position. Needles all the way forward (D position Knitmaster, E position Toyota, Brother/Jones) correspond to needles in holding position. Needles selected to positions in between these two positions, whether automatically by machine or manually, correspond to working position and upper working position. Needles in this position are 'available' for the carriage to knit and pattern.

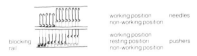

Positions of needles and pushers on a Passap/Pfaff machine

The Passap knitting machine – has a totally different sort of needle bed. There are two identical beds set opposite each other. In each of these beds there appear to be two sets of needles in the channels. They are separated by a bar. There is also another bar at the bottom edge of the needle bed called a 'blocking rail'. This bar at the bottom of the needle bed is spring loaded and can be operated manually by a knob at one end. The second set of 'needles' with butts but not hooks sit in the channels below the needles and can be taken out of use by 'locking' them away behind the blocking rail.

(*1*) One set of needles looks very like ordinary working needles – that is, there is a butt, a hook and a hinged latch. These needles can be selected to resting/non-working position with the butts resting on the needle bed rail.

(*2*) Needles are in working position when needles are lined up with the heads of the hooks in a line with the edge of the needle bed. (On the Passap machine these are the only two positions the needles can be in.) Below this set of needles there is another set of 'blind' needles. These are called *pushers*. The pushers 'push' the needles, thus helping the carriage to knit and pattern with the needles. The pushers can be locked away behind the blocking rail and in this position they do not work. If the pushers are released from the blocking rail they can be selected (up or down) manually or by the patterning device (Deco) or manipulated by setting the carriage. They tell the needles and the carriage what to do.

NB On all knitting machines stitches are only formed by needles which are selected to working position by you. The remaining needles rest at the back of the machine and to all intents and purposes they do not exist until you call them forward.

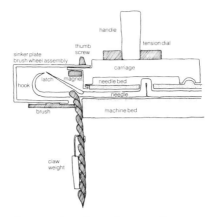

Cross-section of a carriage on a Japanese machine

The carriage

The carriage has two parts. The main body is called the carriage, cam box or lock and moves across the needle bed directing the movements of the needles, pushing them backwards and forwards. As the carriage is pushed across the needle bed the needle butts pass through grooves or pathways on the underside of the carriage; you can see this happening quite clearly if you pass the Bond carriage across the bed with the key plate in but without the handle. If you turn your carriage upside down and press the various pattern buttons or turn the pattern dial you can see alterations in the tracks through which the needle butts will be directed.

The second part of the carriage is called the sinker plate (fabric presser, brush assembly or connecting arm). It connects to the main part of the carriage. The primary function of this part is to push the stitches first behind the latches, then to push the stitches down over the needle hooks.

First we must look at the main part of the carriage more closely. The carriage has four jobs to do.

(*1*) *Stitch size* – In patterns the size of stitch is often referred to as T.D. or tension dial number. It refers to the large round dial in the middle of the carriage that determines the size of the knitted stitch. A big number results in a

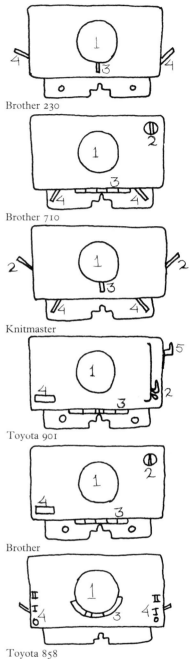

Brother 230

Brother 710

Knitmaster

Toyota 901

Brother

Toyota 858

Comparative carriage settings on Japanese machines
1 Tension dial for stitch size
2 Side levers, change knob for automatic needle selection
3 Pattern lever, buttons, indicator – for automatic pattern knitting
4 Holding cam lever, Russell levers for knitting when needles in H.P.
5 Carriage release lever

big stitch and a small number a small stitch. On the Bond machine plates inserted into the carriage do the same job. On the Knitmaster Zippy 90 there are coloured circles on the stitch size dial that correspond to the diameter of hand knitting needles. The size of your stitch can vary greatly from one machine to another even though they are identical in make and model – just as two hand knitters samples can vary in size although they use the same size needles and the same yarn.

The factors that affect the size of the stitch are numerous:

(*a*) The even feeding of the yarn: if you have wound your yarn on a wool winder and then taken the yarn from the centre of the ball you may find that it is very tight. Alternatively, if you are using a hand-knitting ball the ball may 'bounce' around while you are knitting and the yarn will not feed at an even speed onto the machine.

(*b*) If you alter the setting of the tension discs on the tension mast you will affect the stitch size.

(*c*) If you knit quickly or slowly your knitting speed will affect the feeding of the yarn into the machine, thus altering the stitch size.

(*d*) Weights: if you hang more weights on your work the result will be larger stitches. (This also happens if you forget to remove your ribber weights!)

(*e*) On the Bond machine there is no 'Dial' but there are four 'key plates' that give you a choice of stitch size.

(*2*) *Needle selection for subsequent patterning* – By setting the carriage, the patterning information is conveyed from the punch card to the needles. This facility is only on the carriages of the automatic machines. To aid in selection on the manual Zippy 90, the needle butts are coloured in groups of five. On semi-automatic machines needle selection is done by pushing buttons and pulling a lever on the body of the machine.

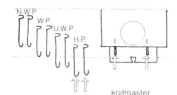

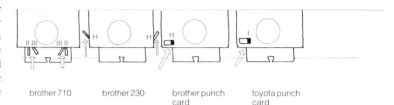

brother 710   brother 230   brother punch card   toyota punch card

(*3*) *Knitting either plain or patterned fabric* – Once the needles have been selected to working and upper working position the carriage must then be instructed as to what kind of stitch pattern you wish to produce.

(*4*) *Ignoring or holding needles* – The carriage can also be told whether to knit (either plain or pattern knitting) or to ignore or hold needles with stitches. This facility for having work in the hooks of all your needles but not actually forming stitches with selected needles is very important. It enables you to carry out both simple and complex shaping within your garment pattern – for example knitting necklines, shaping the hemlines of skirts and knitting shaped skirts sideways. It also helps to carry out stitch patterning on simple machines as well as adding to the stitch patterning facility on more complex machines. The hold function is a combination of needle position (see section below on needle bed) and carriage setting on all machines except the simplest.

THE BOND

There are no carriage settings on the Bond machine and all needles brought by hand selection to holding position *never knit*. You can bring them back into work by pushing them back slightly in their channels so that the open latches are aligned with the edge of the machine. The stitches are still behind the latches, but the

Comparative carriage settings for H.P. (hold position) on Japanese machines

needles will then knit on the following row. There is no need to replace the stitches in the needle hooks manually.

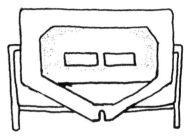

Bond carriage

Chunky manual machines

Jones/Brother KH 230 – This is a chunky machine with a pattern facility on the carriage but no automatic needle selection. One holding-cam lever is located on each side of the carriage. The holding-cam levers are directional and control the carriage when it moves in the direction of the lever. There are two settings.

N: All needles are working when the carriage moves in the same direction as the lever in this position. When doing stocking stitch, all

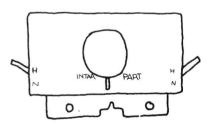

Jones/Brother KH 230 carriage

needles knit. When doing patterned knitting, all needles in hold position and upper working position knit and needles in working position pattern.

H: Needles in hold position *never knit* when the carriage moves in the same direction as the lever in this position. When doing stocking stitch, needles in holding position *never knit*. Needles in working position and upper working position knit. When doing patterned knitting, needles in holding position *never knit*, needles in upper-working position knit and needles in working position pattern.

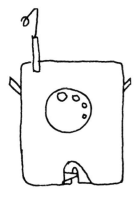

Knitmaster Zippy 90 carriage

Knitmaster Zippy 90 – There are no special settings on the carriage for holding stitches on this machine and all needles pushed to Hold Position will not knit.

Push button machines

The *Jones/Brother KH 710* and the *Toyota 858* – The holding-cam levers are on the front of the main carriage on the Jones/Brother and on the side on the Toyota. There are three positions.

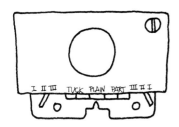

Jones/Brother KH 710 carriage

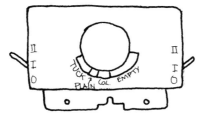

Toyota 858 carriage

I (on the Jones/Brother) **O** (on the Toyota). In this position needles are never ignored by the carriage. If you are doing plain or stocking stitch knitting, no matter what position the needles are in, they will knit. If you are doing pattern knitting, those needles selected to any position other than working position will *knit*.

II (on the Jones/Brother) **I** (on the Toyota). In this position the carriage will ignore any needles in hold position. If you are doing plain or stocking stitch knitting the carriage will knit *all* needles *except* those in holding position. If you are doing pattern knitting: needles in working position *pattern*; needles in upper working position *knit*; and needles in hold position *do not move*.

III (on the Jones/Brother) **II** (on the Toyota). The carriage will ignore any needles in hold position and it will select (push) any needles in upper working position to hold position and leave them there. If you are doing plain or stocking stitch knitting the carriage will knit only the needles in working position. All other needles (in upper working position) will be pushed up to hold position. If you are doing pattern knitting: needles in working position *pattern*; needles in upper working position are selected by the carriage to hold position and do not knit; needles in hold position *do not move*.

Automatic patterning machines

There are two types of machines and the controls differ in the way they do the job of ignoring the needles in Hold Position.

Knitmaster – There are two levers at the front of the machine called russell levers. They each have two

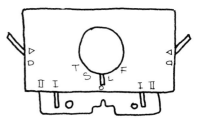

Knitmaster punchcard and electronic carriage

settings: I and II (levers forward and levers back.) When the carriage is moving to the right, the right-hand lever controls whether the carriage will knit needles in hold position or not. The same is true of the left-hand lever.

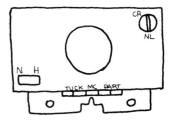

Jones/Brother punchcard and electronic carriage

Jones/Brother and Toyota 901 – There is only one control on the carriages of these machines called a holding cam lever. This control is not directional, and the carriage either holds or knits, no matter what direction it is travelling in. There are two settings on these machines.

1 The holding cam lever or russell levers on:

N (*Jones/Brother*)

O (*Toyota*)

II (*Knitmaster-directional*)

If the carriage is set to stocking stitch *all needles knit*.

If the carriage is set to patterned knitting needles selected to upper

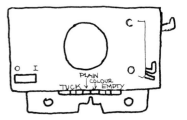

Toyota 901 carriage

working position and hold position *knit*. Needles in working position pattern.

2 The holding cam lever or russell levers on:

H (*Jones/Brother*)
I (*Toyota*)
I (*Knitmaster-directional*)

If the carriage is set to stocking stitch needles in hold position *do not knit*. Needles in working and upper working position knit.

If the carriage is set to patterned knitting needles in hold position *do not knit*.

Needles selected to upper working position knit.

Needles selected to working position pattern.

In other words the carriage is a very versatile part of your machine and is capable of doing quite a few jobs. This means that you must pay particular attention to how you set your carriage. Each knob or button gives the carriage another job to do, and if it is not set properly it will not work properly. Get into the habit of checking all the settings on your carriage often. In this way you can avoid making errors that waste both time and effort.

The sinker plate

The other part of the carriage is called the *sinker plate* (or fabric presser or connecting arm) and it helps to deal with the actual formation of the stitches. It works on the hooks, the latches and yarn, feeding into the needle hook to form the new stitch. In our diagrams of how stitches are formed you will note that, as well as the needle moving forward, the loop on the needles must be pushed back so that it pushes the latch of the needle open and then falls behind this latch. There are two ways of doing this: one is a brush, wheel or 'presser' attached to the carriage itself; the second is the use of weights on the fabric as it is knitted.

The Bond has the simplest device called a *fabric press*, which is a simple wire that clips onto each side of the carriage. This device together with a

weighting system helps to pull the loops already on the needles behind the latches, then down over the new stitches. Unless the fabric is well weighted this method is not efficient. Weighting can be supplemented with additional small claw weights.

On all Japanese machines the latches are controlled by a series of small magnets located on the underside of the carriage. These machines also have a separate part, which is screwed onto the front of the carriage, called a *sinker plate*. There are a number of round brush wheels located on this sinker plate that help to push the existing loops back behind the latches on the needles. These brushes must be unscrewed and removed from time to time to clean out any yarn that may have become tangled up underneath them which may stop them from moving freely.

On a double bed machine there is not enough room between the beds to fit brush wheels like the ones located on the bottom of the Japanese sinker plates on the single bed machines so a different method of pushing the stitches behind the latches must be used. On these machines there are straight brushes and what are called *strippers* (Passap Pfaff) or *pressers* (Brother/Jones KR230). These are small removable devices which slip into each side of the lock and they act like little fingers that help push the existing loops on the needles over the new loops being formed. They push down on the fabric as the carriage pushes the needles up towards the yarn. They work most efficiently when doing double bed work. There are two machines that use these fingers, the Passap and the Brother/Jones KH230/KR230 (as below) chunky machine with the ribber. The Brother/Jones machine uses a weighting system in addition. Passap

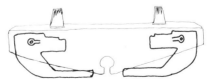

Pressers in the KH 230 connector arm

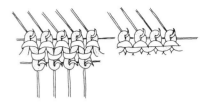

Stitches on a ribber and stitches on the single bed

claim that because of the way the strippers work you don't need to use weights to pull the stitches off the needles. In practice, however, with some stitch patterns weights can prove very useful.

The carriage thus helps to form stitches. On all knitting machines the pushing process of wires, brush wheels, brushes and strippers can be helped by *pulling down* on the knitted fabric as new stitches are being formed. On some of the double bed machines and the single bed machines with ribber attachments weights are the most important means of forming the stitches as there is no room to fit any brush assembly system in between the needle beds. There are various types of weights available: claw weights, cast on combs, etc.

2   The ribber

At some point you may decide that you need a *ribber*. In order to produce a knitted fabric that has knit stitches adjacent to purl stitches you must have another set of needles to pull the yarn through in the opposite direction. Not only is it a very large item – nearly as big as your main bed and in fact another machine, although it may not have all the patterning facilities your main machine has – but there are different principles governing its formation of stitches. Unless you have a thorough understanding of the principles of how your machine works, you may find some difficulty in using the ribber and you will not be able to take full advantage of its potential in creating stitch patterns.

Most ribbers do not have a needle selection system. Any pattern options you choose are normally carried out on all working needles on the ribber. There are two exceptions to this: the Jones/Brother KR 850, which has a setting for alternative needle selection automatically; and the Passap, where a more elaborate needle selection system is available. The Passap system, however, is only semi-automatic (in other words some manual selection is needed). At present Jones/ Brother have, as an alternative (or supplement) to a ribber, a *separate carriage* called a garter carriage, which operates on the latest models of their standard gauge machines (both the punch card and the electronic versions). It will produce both knit and purl stitches in the same row in a pattern automatically controlled by the pattern card. This is not a separate needle bed but in fact a single needle in the carriage itself that is operated as the carriage passes across the needle bed in response to the information fed into the machine by the punch card. The way this carriage forms stitches is based on single bed principles.

When you use the ribber you are still forming stitches in the same way

Sample from the KG88 Brother garter carriage

by pushing the needles forward and backward, forcing the loops in the hooks of the needles back behind the open latches, catching a new loop of yarn in the hooks of the needles and then pulling this new loop through the old loop (stitch), which then passes over the closed latch and settles down below the needle hook.

On a single bed machine there are *brushes* on the sinker plate that perform two functions. Firstly, they help to push the stitches behind the latch when the needle comes forward. Secondly, they help to push the old stitches down off the needles when the needles pull the new loop of yarn back and through.

As you can see, with a ribber set up on the front of your machine, there is no room to attach your sinker plate onto the front of your carriage. In fact you are provided with a connecting arm, which attaches the main carriage to the ribber carriage (the ribber carriage duplicates the job of the main carriage on the ribber). If there are no brushes to help the carriages form the stitches then something else must be substituted for them.

On most machines a system of

weighting is used. Weights are used to help the machine work when producing single bed fabric, but with the ribber weighting is much more important as it is the main method of forming stitches.

There are two exceptions: the Passap uses strippers, and the Ribber KR 230 (for the Jones/Brother Chunky Machine) combines a weighting system with pressers, which operate in a similar way. These strippers or pressers are like little fingers that are inserted into the connecting part of the carriage next to the yarn feeding unit. They press down on the work between the two beds in a similar way to the brushes on the sinker plate. Weighting is also used on the chunky machine.

Weights

If the weights are to operate efficiently they must be distributed correctly. This is of *vital importance*. One of the difficulties of using a ribber is that you cannot see your work as it comes off the machine. It disappears between the two beds and, short of crawling underneath the machine with a torch or transferring all the stitches to one bed in order to drop the other one to view your work, it is something you must just put up with.

Weighting enables the machine to form stitches but the system must be designed so that *all* stitches are pulled down off the needles equally, not just some of them.

Initially the weights are distributed evenly across your work by hanging a cast-on comb onto the first row and then hanging the weights onto the comb. As your work progresses and lengthens an interesting phenomenon occurs. The weights on the comb still pull the work down in the centre, but the edges of your knitting begin to curl in; even though the comb hangs from all your stitches at the bottom, it loses its effectiveness at the edges of your work as it gets further from the needle bed. In other words, after several rows there is no weighting system pulling the stitches

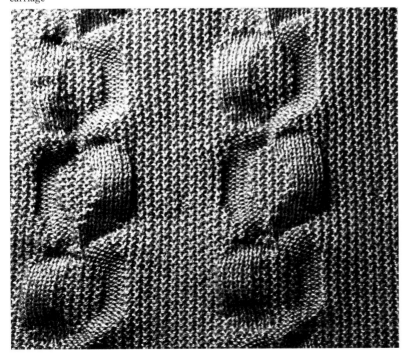

down off the edge needles. Putting more weights on the comb will only increase the pull on the central needles and will have no effect on the formation of edge stitches. You must add weight at the edges where it is needed and remember to move these weights up frequently.

In addition to weighting the edges of your work very carefully, you must pay particular attention to the formation of the edge stitches. If the needle doesn't completely pull the new bit of yarn through the old stitch, you must push the needle butt back manually. You will notice that the needle butts are not properly aligned when you have finished knitting a row, and a few needles at the edge adjacent to the carriage may be pulled forward slightly. A little time spent watching your work carefully can save you hours of frustration and unravelling later. When you wind up with a mass of spaghetti on your central needles the fault usually lies at the edges where the stitches have not been properly formed.

Tension dial or stitch size

On single bed knitting the yarn travels horizontally from needle to needle passing only around the gate peg in between. When you are using a ribber, the yarn does not travel directly to the adjacent needle but passes across the gap between the two needle beds to the needle across the way. In other words there is lot more yarn available between the stitches. This spare yarn is 'absorbed' into the stitches as the knitting 'relaxes' after it is removed from the machine. The more frequently the yarn passes from bed to bed the smaller your stitch size must be. The more your needle arrangement resembles single bed knitting – that is, the less the yarn passes from bed to bed, travelling instead from needle to adjacent needle on the same bed – the *larger* your stitch size (or tension dial number) must be.

The gravity pull on a Japanese machine with a ribber occurs at a point nearer the ribber than the main bed. The ribber needles, therefore, are shorter. The tension dial on a ribber is often set to a *higher* number than the main bed to compensate for the ribber stitches tending to be smaller.

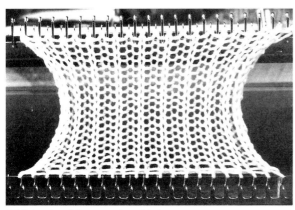

Additional weights must be added at edges to compensate for ribbed kintting curling

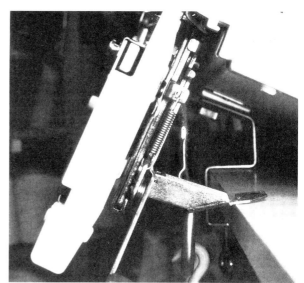

Ribbed knitting hangs closer to the ribber than to the main bed

II How the Patterning Works

1 Needle butt positions

It is essential to know how most generally available domestic knitting machines actually work. That is, what happens when you push various buttons and pull various knobs and what the effect will be on your knitting. Unless you want to know how to convert a stitch pattern from one machine to another, you need to read only the information that pertains to your particular machine. Once you become familiar with the operation of your own machine, the directions for the use of other machines may make more sense.

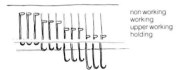

non working
working
upper working
holding

Needle bed positions on a Japanese single bed machine

If we look at the needle bed more carefully we can see that the needle butts (the handles of the needles) travel through channels on the underside of the carriage as it passes across the bed forming new stitches. These butts can be located in several positions in the needle bed. On most machines there are basically four needle butt positions. The needles can be 'selected' to these positions manually or automatically. The different positions of the needle butts enable the carriage to do different jobs with these needles, and thus allow you to make patterns in your knitting rather than just plain stocking stitch fabric. On some machines these positions are marked in the bed at the end.

The *Passap/Pfaff* knitting machine needles have only two positions: non-working position and working position. Needles on both beds of these double bed machines are capable of patterning. But the patterning is not done by positioning the needles themselves. In the needle bed there are *pushers* in the channels below the needles. These pushers can be positioned manually on the back bed and automatically on the front bed. Once they have been selected they, in turn, select the needles.

The four needle butt positions

(*1*) **non-working position** The needles are pushed right back in the needle bed. In this position they cannot have stitches in the hooks as they are too far back from the edge of the machine. They do not exist as far as the carriage is concerned.
(*2*) **working position** The needle butts are pushed slightly forward and the needle hooks are aligned with the edge of the needle bed. This is the main working position on all knitting machines. Some machines label this position at the end of the needle bed **B**. When needles are in this position the machine can produce stocking stitch fabric.
(*3*) **upper working position** The needle butts are pushed a little further forward than working position and the hooks of the needles protrude out beyond the edge of the needle bed. If the latches of the needles are opened, they will line up with the edge of the needle bed. (The needles are not pushed as far forward as they can go.)
On the Jones/Brother push button machine KH 710 there are two upper-working positions for

the needle butts. These positions are labeled 'D I' and 'D II'.
On the Passap and Pfaff machines the needles cannot be positioned manually but the pushers in channels below the needles can.
(*4*) **hold position** The needle butts are pushed as far forward as they will go in the needle bed. When the needles are in hold position the carriage may pass across the machine and ignore these needles completely. They are effectively locked away in a cupboard for the time being. In other words the needles are treated in the same way as the needles in non-working position but in hold position they can have stitches on them, whereas in non-working position they cannot. On most machines the carriage must also be *set* not to knit needles in hold position.

When the needles have been selected to working and upper-working position the carriage can be set to 'pattern'. That is, it can do one job with the needles in W.P. and another job with the needles in U.W.P.

2 Needle positioning – how do the needles know where to go?

Basically the needle selection system depends on the type of machine you have.

Manual – The Bond and some of the more simple machines in the Japanese manufactured range do not have an automatic needle selection system and needles have to be selected manually to upper working position or hold position.

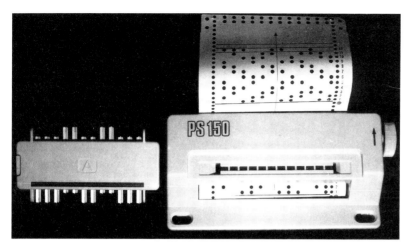

Semi-automatic pattern selector

Semi-automatic attachment – For 9mm gauge machines Knitmaster do an attachment called a P.S.150. This consists of a separate device that can sit on the back of the machine. You insert a standard punch card into this pattern selector which reads the pattern information for every other needle (instead of every needle) thus giving you a 12 stitch repeat patterning possibility. You then insert the needle selector into the pattern selector which houses the punch card. The fingers or feelers of the needle selector read the pattern information from the punch card and are then set. The selector is then used to select the needles manually to upper working position so that the machine can knit a patterned fabric. This device will only work on a 9mm gauge machine.

Push button selection system – This system is currently available on the *Jones/Brother KH 710* and on the *Toyota 858*. It may also be found on

some older models in the Jones/ Brother and Toyota range. On the KH 710 and the 858 it provides a method for semi-automatic selection of needles to upper working position with an 8 (on the 710) and 12 (on the 858) stitch repeat across all needles in working position. The sequence of the repeat can be moved from right to left across the needle bed and once the needles have been selected by the set lever, they can be manually rejected

(pushed from upper working position back to working position) before the row is knit. This can be important if you wish to create single motifs etc. This machine is a half-way house between the punch card and manual machines. The knitter must remember what row of the stitch pattern sequence they have reached as well as the row for the garment pattern. However, the needles may be selected for the pattern across the whole needle bed at one fell swoop.

The mechanical punch card machine – On these machines the pattern is punched out on a card. Most cards are a standard size and can be used interchangeably. The exceptions are, the *Toyota 858 machines* (12 stitch repeat) and the *Knitmaster 270/370* series (30 stitch repeat.) On all other punch card machines the size and shape of the card is identical, *but* the way the machine patterns means that punched patterns cannot always be transferred from one machine to another.

Blank punch card for Japanese machines

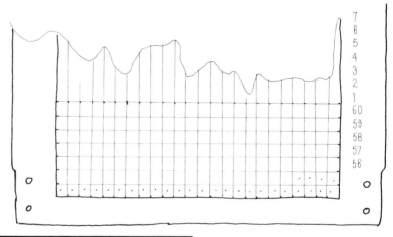

The needles and the punch card

Now let's look at the correlation between the information on the card and the needles. If we look at the card closely we can see that there are only two alternatives for positioning the needles – that is there are either *blanks* or *holes* on the card. The needles can be sent to only one of two positions

A push button selection system

Mechanical knitting machine

automatically. This is a very important factor in constructing a stitch pattern.

On mechanical Japanese knitting machines the squares or holes on the card will match up exactly with the needles on the bed (on 4.5mm gauge machines). If you hold the card against the needles, the centre of the card corresponds to the centre of the needle bed and the pattern repeats outwards symmetrically.

Normally the card is set to move forward every row. On some machines it can be set to move forward every alternate row thus doubling the length of the pattern. The card can, of course, also be locked so that the same needle selection takes place on every row. The movement of the carriage triggers the movement of the card. (If you are using two carriages simultaneously the lace carriage *always* triggers the movement of the card and the selection of the needles.)

Knitmaster, Jones/Brother and Toyota all do lace in a different way and the lace card for one machine may not be used on another. The other difference is the marking of row one. The number your eye sees printed on the card refers to a line punched out *below* eye level which is the row the machine sees. In other words the printed number is not adjacent to the punched line of the pattern. The distance between the row the machine is reading and the row your eye is reading varies from machine to machine so if you lock a card on what you think is row one, the machine may, in fact, be reading two rows later or earlier in the pattern sequence, depending on the card and the machine. On the Jones/Brother and the Toyota 901 machines there is a seven line difference; on the Knitmaster, the difference is five lines.

3 Different types of mechanical punch card machines

There are two types of machine in the Japanese manufactured range.

Pre-selected punch card

The machines which have a **pre-select** row work as follows. The punch card is inserted into the machine, and the information is read by feelers feeling the holes in the card. The carriage is connected to the patterning mechanism by your moving a lever or knob on the carriage. Then the carriage as it passes across the needle bed leaves behind the needles selected to working and upper working position, ready to knit a pattern on the following row. The needle selection system and the card reading mechanism are both locked away in the body of the machine. By looking at the needle set up you can see how the pattern will be knit on the following row.

There are two types of machines that have pre-select rows (the needles are selected to working and upper working position on the row *before* the pattern knitting is done). These are the fully automatic machines and machines with a set lever which are semi-automatic.

In order to get the pattern information from the card to the knitting needles you must do the following.
(1) Insert the card into the card slot on the back of the machine. Lock the card.
(2) On the row *before* you wish to knit in a *pattern*, connect the card to the needles by turning a knob or moving a lever on the carriage on the automatic machines. This is,

Punch card in a Japanese machine

your eye reads a number

the machine reads some rows below

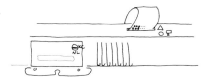

Carriage setting to set needles for patterning on a Jones/Brother machine

the K.C. knob on the Jones/ Brother Machines, which is moved from N.L. to K.C./S.M., (on mechanical machines) K.C.I./K.C.II (on electronic machines). On Toyota machines the pattern levers at the side of the carriage must be moved from forward (O) to backward (I).

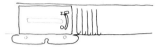

Carriage setting to set needles for patterning on a Toyota machine

(3) Pass the carriage across the needles leaving them selected according to the information on the card or pull the set lever manually on the semi-automatic machines.

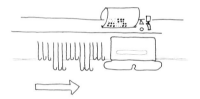

Machine set to begin patterning

You are then ready to begin your pattern knitting. Unless the needles are selected to working (W.P.) and upper working position (U.W.P.), your machine will not knit in a pattern.

The important advantage of a machine with a pre-select facility is that you can *manually* override the needle selection system *before* you knit the row. This means that you are always in complete control over the patterning on your machine and you can bring additional needles into U.W.P. or push other needles back to W.P., according to your design requirements. This may be time-consuming, but it does mean that you have more scope for creative potential when designing your knitted fabric and creating stitch patterns.

(4) Push the patterning buttons on the carriage to tell the carriage what kind of stitch pattern you want to knit, e.g. tuck etc.

Memory drums

The machines where the memory drums are located in the carriage have a pattern card that is read by feelers in the card reading mechanism on the back of the machine. This information is transmitted to the patterning drums in the carriage automatically when the carriage passes across in front of it. As the carriage passes across the needle bed it automatically selects to W.P. and U.W.P. and knits the row at the same time leaving the needles behind in W.P. The needles are selected needles to U.W.P. only as the carriage passes over them; therefore, to see what patterning information you are passing on to the needles you must set the card reading mechanism so that the feelers on the front of it reflect the row it is currently reading on the punch card. Working needles always remain in B or working position unless manually selected.

On these machines with memory drums there are several steps required to get the pattern information from the card to the needles. The feelers will show the line currently read when the card is locked. Feelers that are back show where the holes are in the card, feelers that are forward show the blanks on the card.

(1) The card is inserted into the card reading mechanism.
(2) The feelers of the card reading mechanism transmit the pattern information to the pattern drums in the carriage.
(3) The pattern drums transmit the pattern information to the

needles selecting the needle butts to working and upper working position as the carriage passes across the needle bed. (To connect the information from the pattern drums to the needle butts, the side levers on the carriage must be pushed back to *Δ*.)

4 Movement of the punch card

The other factor that can affect your patterning on automatic machines is the movement of the card. On automatic machines the card may be locked and the machine will read the same pattern line repeatedly. However, once you unlock the card it will move automatically every time the machine is 'triggered'. Once the carriage is connected to the pattern mechanism the movement of the carriage triggers the movement of the card. On the most recent models you have the choice of moving the card every row or every other row. Again, the trigger for the card movement differs according to whether you have a pre-select machine or a memory drum machine

Card movement in pre-select systems

On machines with a pre-select pattern system, the carriage is connected

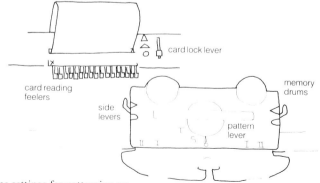

Machine settings for patterning on Knitmaster punch card machines

to the card reading mechanism by a belt at the back of the carriage. The lace carriage is automatically connected to the patterning mechanism at all times. Every time the carriage changes direction, the card moves on one row. (If you were to move the carriage from L. to R., remove the carriage from the machine bed, replace it at the L. and move L. to R. again, the card would *not* be triggered to advance one row.) This is important if you are using the lace carriage *and* the pattern facility on the main carriage at the same time – e.g. lace/tuck, lace/slip, lace/weaving etc.

The Jones/Brother Electronic machine is mechanically identical with its punch card counterpart but instead of having the punch card read mechanically by feelers, the card is read electronically by a chip. All marks on the mylar sheet must be opaque to infra-red light and non-reflective. These marks normally correspond to the holes on punched cards. Two separate patterns may be programmed simultaneously and then placed anywhere across the width of the fabric produced, providing these two patterns are on the same horizontal plane on the pattern card so that the chip can read the information as it passes across the card. This factor must be taken into consideration when adapting patterns from the mechanical punch-card machine. Card patterning information can be altered (doubled in length, width etc.) by flicking a switch. The programming of the patterning can be complex but because of the programming potential this is one of the most versatile machines on the market. Once the pattern information is read by the machine, it transmits the information to the needles in the same way as the mechanical machine.

There is a difference in the way the card is triggered to move on the electronic machine. The change in the direction the belt moves does not advance the card. It is only when the carriage (main carriage set to K.C.I, K.C.II or lace carriage) passes the *centre* of the needle bed that the card is triggered to advance, even if *both* carriages are moving in the same direction.

Card movement in machines with memory drums

On machines with Memory Drums, the card advances when a lever is triggered by the passing of the carriage when knitting a row. As the carriage must always pass the card reading mechanism completely in order to transfer the pattern information to the memory drums, this lever is always triggered. You can only use one carriage at a time on this machine so you cannot combine the lace patterning facility with tuck, slip, Fair Isle, weaving, etc.

On the electronic Knitmaster the mylar sheet or pattern card is similar in appearance to the Jones/Brother machine but the patterning potential is much more limited. Only one pattern at a time can be read by the machine. But the pattern can be doubled in length, width, reversed, etc by flicking a switch similar to that found on the Jones/Brother Electronic.

Card movement in double bed machines

The Passap/Pfaff machines are double bed machines. They are engineered in such a way that the needle beds are the same, working in the same way and taking identical needles (unlike the Japanese machines that have two different beds and require different size needles for each bed). Because it is possible to select needles for *both beds* simultaneously these machines can do some stitch patterns that cannot be carried out on other machines. This needle selection, however, can only be done with pre-punched cards automatically on the front bed. The *card reader* or *deco* is attached onto a bar located at the bottom of the front bed. The small pusher selector is attached onto the side of the front lock (front needle bed carriage). As the lock passes across the bed, the pattern information is passed from the card reader to the

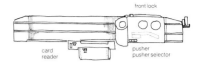

Machine settings for patterning on a Passap/Pfaff machine

pusher selector. The pusher selector then selects the pushers so they may select the needles. The pusher selector can be disconnected from the front lock and passed across the card reader separately in order to register the patterning information and select the pushers. A dial on the selector regulates the advance of the pattern card which can be adjusted to move every two rows, or every four rows depending on the type of stitch pattern.

5 Selection of stitch patterns

When the needles have been selected how does the carriage use this information to produce fabric in a stitch pattern? What are stitch patterns? It is important to understand your machine. If we deal with stitch patterning on Japanese single bed machines we can see that they consist of two parts:

- selecting the needles to two positions;
- doing different jobs with the selected needles.

Pre-selected machines

Machines with a pre-select row
The *Jones/Brother* machines have sets of pattern buttons and the patterning is directional. You can push one pattern button at a time and the instructions to the carriage only apply when the carriage is moved in the direction of the pushed button. So you can, in fact, knit one kind of patterning in one direction and another kind of pattern in the other direction. These sets of pattern buttons are found on the push button machines as well as the punch

card and electronic machines. This machine is the only machine which will provide you with the facility to do two different types of stitch patterning automatically simultaneously. For example it can tuck when the carriage moves from R. to L. and part (slip) when the carriage moves from L. to R.

The *Toyota* machines have a dial that gives you the option of patterning in one direction or both directions after the needles have been selected. However, you cannot combine different types of patterning alternating directions automatically. You can only combine pattern knitting in one direction with plain knitting in the other.

Machines with pattern drums
These machines will not combine two alternative pattern facilities automatically. When you instruct the carriage to pattern it does so automatically in both directions. In order to pattern in one direction and knit plain knitting in the other direction you do not transfer the pattern information from the pattern drums in the carriage to the needle butts – the needles are not then selected to upper working position. This means putting one side lever to △ (towards the back of the carriage) which will connect the pattern drums to the needle butts when the carriage moves in that direction, and leaving the other side lever on ◠ (towards the front of the carriage); the pattern drums will then not transfer pattern information to the needle butts when the carriage moves in that direction.

Double bed machines
The Passap/Pfaff machine – The card information is transferred to the pushers through the Deco system, which, in turn, relays this information to the needles as the lock (carriage) passes across the bed. There are a number of pattern options on the lock that can be chosen to allow the machine to combine patterning rows with plain knitting rows. There are additional settings on the lock that enable the knitter to alter the setting of the pushers automatically without using a pattern card. These are the arrow buttons. With these, patterns can be achieved automatically without the deco or pattern card reader.

6   General procedure for starting pattern knitting

It is wise to develop regular habits when doing pattern knitting to save time, material and patience.
(1) Insert the pattern card, clip it in a circle with the card-clips and *lock it* on row 1 or the chosen row. You don't want it flying around until you have transferred the information to the needle butts and started your pattern knitting.
(2) Set the machine to transfer the pattern information from the card to the needles.
(3) Set the carriage to execute the desired patterned knitting, e.g. tuck etc.

If you are doing a stitch pattern which requires two yarns (such as Fair Isle, weaving or plaiting) don't forget to put your second yarn in the appropriate place!
(4) Unlock the card: proceed with your pattern knitting.

Word of caution
Unless your needles are selected to working position and upper working position (that is, you have transferred the pattern information from the card to the needles) no matter what you tell the carriage to do with the needles (what sort of patterning you wish to knit) the carriage will do the same thing with *all* the needles in the same position.
- On machines with a pre-select row you can *see* the needles positioned in working position and upper working position before you start knitting your pattern. If all the needle butts are aligned, the carriage will do the same thing with all the needles in the same position.
- On Knitmaster machines (machines with pattern drums in the carriage) all needles always return to working position at the end of the row even though the machine is knitting a stitch pattern. *Therefore*, you must remember to complete the transfer of pattern information from the card to the needle butts by pushing the side levers back to △ before you start your pattern knitting! Because needles are always in working position at the end of the row you will not have a visual check on this before you start your pattern knitting.

III Pattern Possibilities

1 How patterns are produced

With punch cards to make automatic patterning much easier there are many opportunities to produce interesting fabrics. All knitting machine companies produce books of stitch patterns showing you how to punch cards out. It is an easy matter to produce your own Fair Isle cards from other sources such as hand knitting patterns because what you see is what you get (in two colours). To produce tuck, slip or lace patterns, however, is more difficult and it is important that you understand how the machine mechanically produces a patterned fabric.

On a single bed machine the needles are all lined up identically in the bed, in the same plane and they always pull the yarn through the previous stitch *in the same direction*. All knitting, therefore, is always stocking stitch on one side and purl

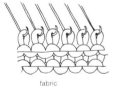

fabric   stitch diagram

Stocking stitch fabric and stitch diagram purl side facing

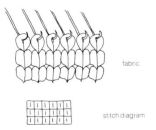

fabric

stitch diagram

Stocking stitch fabric and stitch diagram plain side facing

stitch on the other. You would need another set of needles facing the opposite direction to be able to form plain and purl stitch in the same row.

There are only a limited number of possibilities open to you when patterning on a domestic machine, and all automatic stitch patterns are variations of these possibilities. As the carriage moves across the needle bed the following process occurs.

Plain – The needle pulls the yarn through the stitch as it passes by.

Tuck stitch

Tuck/AX – The needle keeps the stitch and pulls an additional loop of yarn onto its hook as it passes by selectively, according to the punch card pattern. There are then two loops on some of the needle hooks.

Slip/Part/Empty/BX – The needle ignores the yarn passing by selectively, according to punch card pattern.

Fair Isle – There are two separate yarns in the carriage feeders. The two yarns are pulled through the previous stitches separately, according to the

Slip stitch

Fair Isle

pattern. The needle is instructed to pull the yarn from one feeder or the other through the stitch as they pass by.

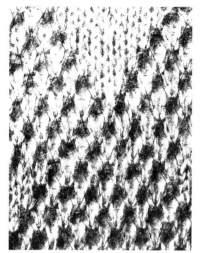

Punch lace

Punch lace – There are two separate yarns in the carriage feeders. The needles pull the yarn in the main feeder through the stitch according to the pattern (some needles pull the yarn through the stitch, others ignore it). *All* needles pull the yarn in the second feeder through the stitch. (On some needles you only have the loop of the second yarn in the hook, on other needles you have *two* loops simultaneously in the hook.)

Weaving

Weaving – As the carriage knits plain knitting and the needles pull the yarn through, a supplementary yarn is woven over and under as the needles form new stitches.

Lace – The stitches are moved from needle to needle in a separate mechanical process done by a lace carriage. This carriage has no feeder and carries no yarn. The job can also be done along with the knitting, in which case there is a feeder to carry yarn, and after the stitches are transferred, the needles will pull the yarn through the stitches in their hooks.

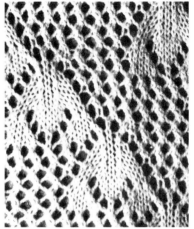

Lace

On Jones/Brother machines there is an additional facility which allows the stitches to be *shared* between two needles instead of actually being transferred or moved from one needle to the needle next door. This is called *fine lace*. On double bed machines a transfer carriage/lock moves stitches from one bed to the other.

Plaiting – This is a special system for feeding the yarn into the needles. There are two yarns in the plaiting feeder. They pass by the needles in sequence. One yarn always passes by first, the second yarn always follows. This results in one yarn always being dealt with first by the needles followed by the second yarn, giving a two sided effect to the fabric. This plaiting feeder may be used to good effect in combination with other patterning possibilities such as *tuck*.

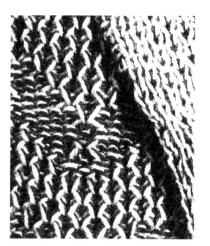

Plaiting

2 Tuck stitch

The appearance of tuck stitch

Tuck stitch can give a very sculptured effect to your fabric. Because you are only knitting some stitches and looping the yarn up over the needles on the remaining stitches you are distorting the fabric. In fact you are selectively gathering little lumps of it across the surface. People often think that tuck stitch looks better on the 'wrong' side, or the purl side. There is, in fact, no wrong side to fabric, only the side you like and the side you don't.

Tuck stitch has a most notable effect on the tension swatch or the number of stitches and rows you need to knit to get a given shape as compared with stocking stitch. Because you are 'holding' and 'gathering' some stitches you will need to knit more rows to achieve a given length of fabric. But this technique also results in your fabric being pushed out or expanded sideways so you will need fewer stitches to achieve the desired width of fabric. In other words the same number of stitches and rows done in tuck stitch will result in a short wide piece of knitting as compared with a similar piece of stocking stitch knitting.

How the stitch is formed

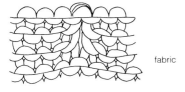

fabric

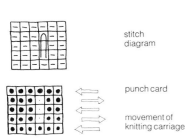

stitch
diagram

punch card

movement of
knitting carriage

Tuck stitch diagram: fabric, stitch
diagram and punch card showing
carriage movement

Look at the fabric on the machine
closely and note that some needles
knit while others keep the stitch they
have and grab another loop of yarn
onto the needle. This can be accomplished in two ways.

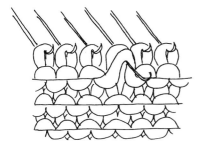

Tuck stitch achieved by manually
pushing needle to H.P.

(*1*) **Manually:** a pull-up stitch
  (*a*) Needles are selected to H. P.
  (*b*) The carriage is set not to knit
      needles in H.P.
  (*c*) The required number of rows
      are knit. The carriage can be
      re-set or the needles can be re-
      selected.
(*2*) **Punch card:** automatic pattern-
    ing. Consider the correlation be-
    tween the card, the needles and
    the fabric produced. Instead of
    selecting needles that you do not
    wish to knit, you are by means of
    the card, selecting needles you *do*

wish to knit. *All holes correspond
to needles which knit.* The blanks
correspond to needles which grab
an additional loop of yarn but *do
not knit.*

Tuck stitch fabric can be difficult
to visualize just by you looking at a
pattern card. A tuck stitch card is
easily recognizable because most of
the card has punched-in holes – that is
most of the needles are pulling
through loops of yarn and knitting.
Because needles that correspond to
the blanks only make loops, you cannot have more than *two needles next
door to each other making loops at the
same time* – thus you cannot have
more than two blanks adjacent on
your pattern card. You will have two
blanks following each other in con-
secutive rows on the card. Because
there is a limit to the number of loops
any one needle can cope with, this will
limit the number of rows where
blanks occur before you will find a
hole. (A hole means that the needle
will knit the stitch – pull the loop of
yarn through all the loops it has
accumulated in its hook.)

3 Slip stitch

How the stitch is made

The way the machine forms this
stitch is to select needles for knitting.
The carriage then 'ignores' the
needles that are not selected. This
kind of stitch pattern is most difficult
to achieve manually on any machine
without slip stitch facility. As we
know only needles in N.W.P. or
needles in H. P. (with the carriage set
not to knit these needles) *do not knit.*
In the first case, if there are stitches in
the needle hooks they cannot be
pushed back to N.W.P. In the second
case, if the needles are pushed out to
H.P. the yarn will gather up on the
needle stems and when the needle
finally does pull the yarn through you
will get a tuck stitch effect.

Again, there is a correlation between the card, the needles, and the

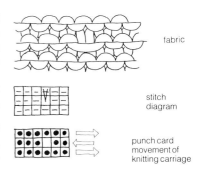

fabric

stitch
diagram

punch card
movement of
knitting carriage

Slip stitch diagram: fabric, stitch
diagram and punch card showing
carriage movement

fabric produced. *All holes correspond
to needles that knit.* The blanks represent needles that are passed by. There
is (unlike tuck stitch) no limit to the
number of needles adjacent or con-
secutive that do not knit.

When to use slip stitch

Slip stitch patterning can be used to
great effect to achieve a **three dimensional quality** to the fabric
without being limited in the way tuck
stitch is by the number of loops
gathered together *into* the stitch. Instead the yarn loops pass by the
stitches and 'hang loose' on the surface of the fabric. This type of patterning is also used to introduce a
number of **colours** in a knitted row.
What happens is that each colour is
threaded through the carriage and
carried across separately. Only the
stitches required in that particular
colour will be knit. Thus if you wish
to knit a row with three colours you
would take the carriage across three
times, each time carrying a different
coloured yarn. When you have completed the row, all the stitches will
have been knit but three different
yarns will have been used. In practice
the yarn is usually changed on the
same side so you would move the
carriage across and back: two knitted
rows would mean six movements of
the carriage. On machines which do
not have a facility for knitting two
colours in one row simultaneously
(i.e. Passap) this is how multicoloured
knitting is done.

There are no rules about the effect different patterns will have on your tension swatch. It depends very much on the number of needles ignored in the pattern. If you leave a long gap between the needles that are forming stitches, the yarn may pull across the surface of the fabric and thus make it narrower, but measurements are very much a question of trial and error and depend on the type of yarn and stitch size as well as the pattern.

You can combine the slip stitch facility with manual selection (by disconnecting the punch card from the needles) and selecting the needles to U.W.P. by hand. (Remember needles in U.W.P. correspond to the holes in the punch card.) Then those needles will knit while the remaining needles will be ignored.

Special effects of slip stitch

Some less explored special features of this particular type of stitch pattern are as follows:

Mock cable effect – This is a way of using groups of floats together in a mass to achieve an interesting effect.
(1) Cast-on the required number of stitches and knit several rows.
(2) Insert the card illustrated and set the machine to slip/part/empty.
(3) Commence pattern knitting. You will notice that it takes (on this version of the pattern card) *eight* passes of the carriage to complete

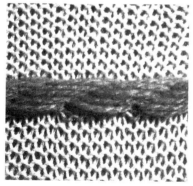
Mock cable

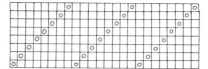
Punch card for slip stitch special effect (o = holes punched). Mock cable

the knitting of all the stitches in *one* row.

Once you have grasped this technique you can use it to make up your own variations of the cable effect. Because you are not knitting adjacent needles, there are gaps between the needles that will knit in any one pass of the carriage. You will also find that you will be able to knit a much thicker yarn than you might have had you been doing hand knitting.

Purl hems

Purl hems – You will also find that you can 'lock' one row into the patterning mechanism and repeat this row in a slip stitch, piling-up the stitches from the working needles and achieving some very interesting hem effects on the purl side of the fabric.
(1) Cast-on and knit several rows.
(2) Insert a card which will result in alternate needle selection (e.g. card 1). Lock the card on any one row.
(3) Set the machine to slip/part/empty and commence pattern knitting. You should be able to knit about ten rows in a pattern. Be careful to weight the work well.

Punch card for slip stitch special effect (o = holes punched). Lumps and bumps

(4) Then do several plain rows before recommencing the pattern. It might be interesting to see what effect a change of yarn between or in the middle of patterns would have.

Lumps and bumps – A variation on the previous 'hems' would be to 'hold' sections of needles by not knitting them while you knit quite a few rows on other sections of needles. The achievement of this effect relies on:
● the grouping of the working and non-working sections; and
● the changing of yarn (i.e. a contrast in colour or texture).

(1) Cast on and knit several rows in M.Y.
(2) Insert the card and lock on row 1. Set that machine for slip/part/empty pattern knitting. C.O.R. Thread up with M.Y.
(3) Unlock the card and commence pattern knitting. Change the yarn in the main feeder every 12 rows.

Lumps and bumps

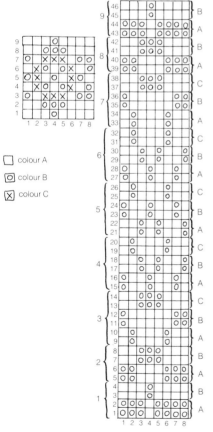

- [ ] colour A
- [⊙] colour B
- [✕] colour C

Punch card for slip stitch special effect
(o = holes punched)

This new view of slip-stitch effects can give a sadly neglected pattern facility a new lease on life!

Three (or more) colours in a row – The principle behind this technique is that you must change the yarn in your feeder and then when you take the carriage across the needle bed you knit only the stitches required in that particular colour. You also return with the carriage and can re-knit the same stitches. So when you complete one pattern sequence you will have *two* rows knitted. If you require three colours in a row you will make six passes of the carriage to complete two rows of knitting. This will also mean that you will have more floats and the fabric you are producing will be a third thicker than ordinary Fair Isle. When you are punching out your card you will punch out two identical rows for each colour required. Six rows on the card will result in two knitted rows.

4   Fair Isle

This is one of the easiest types of patterning to recognize. What you see is what you get. There is no mistaking Fair Isle patterns.

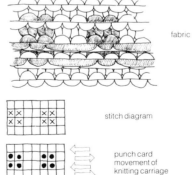

fabric

stitch diagram

punch card
movement of
knitting carriage

Fair Isle stitch diagram: fabric, stitch diagram and punch card showing carriage movement

Automatic machines

Most single bed automatic punch card knitting machines have two feeders. You thread up two yarns, putting one in feeder A on the sinker plate and the other one in feeder B. The machine will knit all needles corresponding to the blanks on the card in the main yarn (in feeder A) and all needles corresponding to the holes on the card in the contrast yarn (in feeder B).

All the patterning is done automatically by the machine. The pattern repeats across all the working needles. On more recent models it is extremely simple to isolate the pattern by placing cams or markers on the needle bed. The machine will then only reproduce the pattern within these markers – that is, needles are only selected to U.W.P. between these markers. What you must consider when planning your single motif or pattern repeat is the fixed interval of the pattern repeat in relation to the needle bed. You may have either to:

- move your garment horizontally on the needle bed to get the single motif to appear in the correct position, or
- punch your card so the pattern will appear on the correct needles at the correct position.

Problems can arise if you are dealing with such things as a monogram that must be carefully placed – you may find it either disappearing into the neckline or the armpit. Also be careful when you are making a cardigan. An animal carefully punched out might be cut in half by the button band.

On electronic machines you needn't worry about the pattern repeating at a fixed interval on the needle bed because you can place the pattern at the desired position horizontally on your needle bed.

On push button machines (Jones/Brother 710)

On these machines there is no two colour feeder facility. You must set the change knob on the carriage to M.C. and the M.C. change lever on the machine to M.C. before you begin. After selecting the needles with the set lever, two colours may be knitted automatically and simultaneously. The main colour is threaded into the yarn feeder and the second colour is laid across the needles. Alternatively you can manually lay more than one colour across the needles. The part buttons are pushed in and the row is knitted. You are limited to an eight stitch repeat, but you have the option of adjusting the sequence of the repeat by moving the slide lever. This, in effect, slides the pattern across the needle bed.

On manual machines

To knit more than one colour in a row you would use the part or slip facility described in a previous section. Alternatively, push the needles not required to knit into holding position for one row while knitting the remaining needles in the required colour yarn; then push those needles already knitted to H.P. whilst pushing the un-knitted needles back to U.W.P.; then bring the carriage across again with the second colour yarn. Thus each colour knitted requires a separate pass of the carriage.

Some special considerations involved in Fair Isle knitting

Because you are knitting *two* yarns in one row, of necessity, one yarn is always being carried across behind where the other yarn is being formed into a stitch. This means one of the following.

(a) you are knitting a fabric of *double thickness*.

(b) your fabric has less elasticity because the yarn being carried across is straighter (not zigzagged as it would be if it were forming stitches). Therefore it has less stretchability.

(c) If there is a large gap between needles knitting one of the yarns and these yarns are not woven-in as they might be in hand knitting it is caused by one of the following.

- **Floats**–that is loops of yarn lying loosely between one knitted stitch and the next.
- **Ladders** – that is gaps between a stitch knitted in one colour and the next-door stitch knitted in the second colour. This problem occurs less commonly. It is most noticeable when your pattern involves straight vertical lines, or when you are knitting single motifs.

5   Problems in Fair Isle knitting

Edges in single motif knitting

When you are knitting only a small area in a Fair Isle pattern, the contrast yarn will pull away from the main fabric at the edge of the patterning. This may cause unsightly holes and ladders at the edges of your patterns.

A. Tying In Edges with Spare Yarn

(1) Cut two spare lengths of M.Y. Make a slip knot at one end of each length.

(2) Program your machine to begin knitting the Fair Isle single motif.

(3) Attach each length of spare M.Y. to a needle adjacent to the Fair Isle Single Motif. C.O.R.

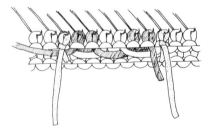

Attaching ties of background yarn

- On machines *with a pre-select row*, you will place the yarn on the first needles at each edge in W.P. next to the needles selected to U.W.P.
- On machines *without a pre-select row*, you will place the lengths of yarn on the two

needles that correspond to the edge of the pattern where you have the S.M. cams on the needle bed.

(4) Knit one row, C.O.L. Take the length of yarn *between* the knitting and the carriage and place it onto the hook of the needle knitting in the M.Y. at the edge of the single motif.

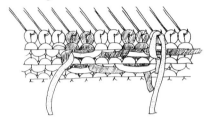

Neatening the edges of a single motif

(5) Knit one row, C.O.R. Repeat step (4) at the right hand edge of the motif. This technique will prevent untidy edges in single motif knitting.

B. Tying In Edges Using Contrast Yarn

This technique is more rapid but does not give as good a result. Hook the contrast yarn over the hook of the last needle knitting in M.Y. between the motif and the carriage on every row, first on one side, then on the other. Unfortunately, the contrast yarn may show through the fabric on the stocking stitch side and then look untidy.

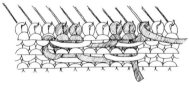

Neatening the edges of a single motif with the contrast yarn

Combining Fair Isle fabric with stocking stitch

When knitting garments you may wish to have only a section of the garment knit in a Fair Isle pattern. Often a strip of Fair Isle knitting is inserted at one point in an otherwise plain garment. However, it is rather difficult to combine the two types of fabric. Stocking stitch fabric is often shorter and wider than fabric with the same number of stitches and rows in Fair Isle. Also, when you are knitting Fair Isle you are knitting a double thickness fabric because you are using two yarns simultaneously. To achieve a similar fabric in texture but with a plain pattern the solution is to knit a standard basic card such as a 1 × 1 card (usually the number 1 card in the basic punch card pack included with the machine is suitable) but use two strands of main yarn and knit the fabric in Fair Isle patterning.

Floats

Floats can be a big problem in single bed Fair Isle fabric. There are several ways of dealing with them:

Altering the pattern – Look carefully at your pattern and see if a crafty hole punched (or left unpunched) here or there cannot break-up a large area and shorten very long floats without distorting your pattern too much.

Tying in floats – Hook long floats up on your needles while you are knitting. You will see the floats forming as you knit and you may be able to tie them in by hooking them onto needles where they will be knit-in on the following row.

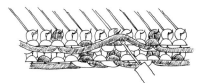

Hooking-up floats

Adding yarn – Add a piece (or pieces) of supplementary yarn at the beginning of your knitting at strategic

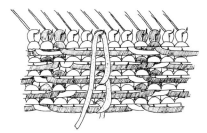

Using a separate strand to tie in floats

points, attaching them to the needles with a slip knot. As you progress you can tie in your floats by carrying these lengths horizontally up your fabric and hooking them over your needles as required.

Latching – When you have finished your knitting, before you knit the last row to remove your work from the machine, you may use your latch tool to latch up the floats, hooking the last one onto one of the needles. Then, when you knit the last row, the last float will be caught. The disadvantage of this technique is that you will find the floats pull across the work causing the fabric to pucker. This

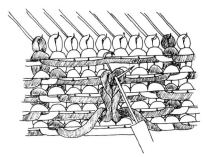

Latching up floats

technique of latching up the floats can also be done manually after the work has been removed from the machine. In this case the last float is sewn in.

Sewing – Sew the floats in by hand after the completion of the knitting. Use M.Y. and carefully catch-stitch the longer floats in.

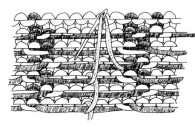

Sewing in floats

Patching – It is possible, when knitting small areas of Fair Isle patterning, such as a single motif, to knit, in a matching fine yarn, a piece the same size as the motif. This can then be attached to the knitting while the

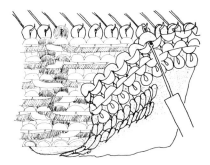

Attaching a lining to cover floats

work is on the machine, by picking the edge up onto the appropriate needles before the pattern begins, and then picking up the opposite edge of the lining piece onto the same needles after the patterning is finished. Alternatively, sew the lining by hand onto the reverse side of the knitting after it has been removed from the machine.

Lining – When knitting a garment with extensive patterning over the whole garment it is also possible to line the knitting thus removing the problem of floats.

- Knit another garment in a fine yarn to line the first garment. If only one section of the garment has a float problem you may find it easier to just knit a lining for one section.
- Line the garment with a fine fabric, either woven or jersey.
- If knitting a single motif you can knit a lining for only the motif.

Whichever solution you use, the lining can be a design feature. You might even emphasize it by adding a thin layer of padding between the two layers and quilting them on your sewing machine.

'Stitch-in-a-Ditch' – This is a most effective way of dealing with floats for those who have a sewing machine. Upon completion of the knitting, you may sew the floats down by using a straight, small-to-medium sized stitch on your sewing machine.

(*a*) Stabilize your floats on the wrong side of the piece of knitting by temporarily sticking them down with self adhesive tape.

(*b*) Thread up your sewing machine

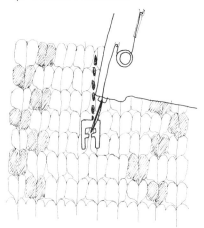

Stitch-in-a-ditch

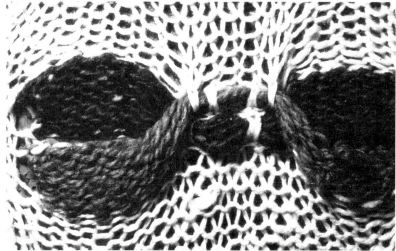

with polyester thread matching as close as possible, the colour of the M.Y.

(*c*) Place the knitting onto the sewing machine and stitch carefully down the 'valleys' between the rows of stitches.

The stitching will not show and the effect on the stretchability of the fabric will be surprisingly minimal. As well as minimizing and disguising the floats, you can also make a design feature of them!

Fringing – Use long floats by cutting them and making them into fringes. If you use self adhesive tape to block off areas of patterns on cards with small, all-over patterns you can achieve very interesting results. The purl side of the fabric would be the right side.

Decorative floats – Use long floats twist them, or bind, pick-up, and tuck them behind stitches to make decorative fabric.

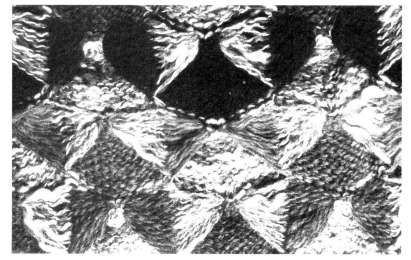

Fringing

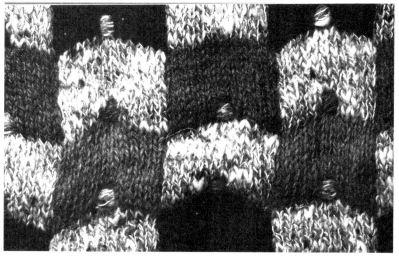

Pick-up floats

Manual introduction of third colour

(*1*) Push needles to H.P. and then knit them manually in the third colour. Follow this procedure:
  (*a*) C.O.R. set the machine to begin Fair Isle patterning;
  (*b*) set the carriage not to knit needles pushed into H.P.;
  (*c*) select the needles you require to knit in the third colour to H.P.

Three colours in a row

On machines with a *pre-select row* you can see the needles selected to knit the pattern are in U.W.P. Within a pattern repeat you can manually select similar needles to H.P. After knitting the row in the two Fair Isle colours, C.O.L., manually knit those needles in the third colour and then repeat the needle selection procedure. If you wished the pattern on this area to be different as well. You would have to select the needles by hand from a chart.

On machines with *memory drums* you will have to select the needles from a chart making sure that you are pushing to H.P. those needles that would have been knitting the second colour. On this machine if you wanted the pattern to be different you would have to isolate the whole pattern repeat with your single motif cams, thus making all needles not selected to H.P. knit in the background colour.

(*2*) Alternatively, use two single motifs or Fair Isle areas of pattern separated by a number of stitches, which will enable you to hand-feed the yarn in the second feeder and thus change it between the two motifs. On machines with a *pre-select row* you can push back any needles to W.P. you do not wish to knit in the second colour yarn. If you leave a wide enough gap between the needles in U.W.P. you will find that if you hand-feed the contrast yarn in feeder B you can swap over after you have passed the first group of needles and before you have come to the second group of needles. Alternatively, you can use your single motif cams to isolate the groups of patterning needles.

On machines with *memory drums* you can use single motif cams to isolate your patterning, and you will have to guess at when to change your second yarn.

Adapting patterns to a 24 stitch repeat

You may often come across stitch patterns in hand knitting books, embroidery books, cross stitch books, etc. These may appeal to you, but they are not designed to fit into a 24 stitch repeat. It can be easy to enlarge them without changing the pattern.

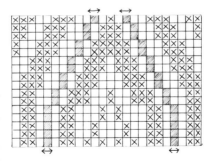

Adjusting a pattern to fit a 24 stitch repeat

(*1*) Copy the pattern onto graph paper.
(*2*) Cut the graph paper between the picture repeat.
(*3*) Spread the graph paper out or overlap it (depending on whether you wish to enlarge or contract the stitch pattern repeat) until your repeat is over 24 stitches.

Designing your own Fair Isle patterns for the punch card

One of the problems of designing your own stitch patterns is that knitted stitches are not square. The proportion varies but a stitch is usually one third again as wide as it is tall. Thus the true representation of a stitch would be three squares wide to two squares tall. Therefore, it is deceptive to draw your picture out onto squared graph paper because when you knit it up, it will be much shorter and fatter than when you have drawn it out. Here are three ways of getting round the problem.

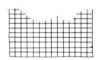

Fair Isle graph sheet compared with squared graph sheet

(*1*) You may use the elongation button on the machine to double the length of your pattern, thus compensating for the distortion in the punch card.
(*2*) You will find special pads of graph paper available that are designed to make allowances for the proportion of the stitches. These are provided for hand and machine knitters.
(*3*) Owners of electronic machines will find that the pattern cards for their machines represent the

Electronic graph sheet

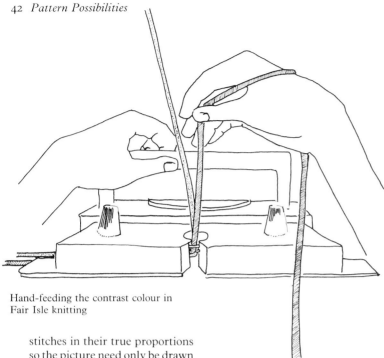

Hand-feeding the contrast colour in
Fair Isle knitting

stitches in their true proportions
so the picture need only be drawn
out and it will be reproduced
accurately in the knitting.

Using colour in Fair Isle patterning

Machine knitters can be very lazy
about using a variety of colour and
texture in their knitting. Because it is
so easy to be captured by the effort-
lessness of Fair Isle patterning, you
can fall into the trap of making as little
effort as possible.

A bit of additional planning, however, can result in an individuality
and a sparkle in a garment that a lazy
knitter would never achieve! If you
think ahead and spend a little more
time you will be repaid by results that
far outweigh the additional effort
expended.

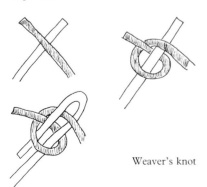

Weaver's knot

Here are some ideas for making
your knitting more exciting and creative. Have a go.

● Compile two balls of yarn by
tying together short lengths of different coloured yarns. This results in a
ball of 'space-dyed' yarn. This is a
way of using up your old oddments.
Knots are 'eaten' by the machine, and
you can have two balls of yarn that
match either in colour or tone. Use
them as you would two balls of yarn.
You will have made your own space-
dyed yarn.

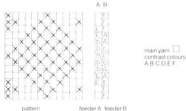

Colour changing with a Fair Isle punch
card

● Make it easier to change the yarn
frequently. Process one: feed it by
hand. Practise holding the yarn over
the feeder and allow it to slip over
your fingers as you push the carriage
across. In this way you can line up a
whole range of yarns at your feet and
change them quite easily. Remember
to pull up the slack at the end or
beginning of each row. Process two:
alternatively, if using the tension
mast, cut the yarn close to the tension
mast, tie the new yarn in and pull it
through. This saves re-threading.

● Make your own variegated yarns
by plying-up. Use several strands of
different colours at once and change
the strands one at a time to achieve
interesting effects.

● In regular Fair Isle patterns
change the colours at 'syncopated'
and frequent intervals, unrelated to
the pattern – thus giving unexpected
variations.

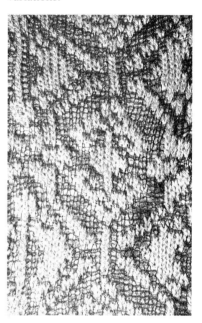

Thread and thick yarn effect

● Try using yarns of different
weights and textures at the same time
to give the fabric interest. For
example, put a thick yarn in one
feeder and sewing thread in the second feeder. Alternatively, put a
medium yarn in one feeder and fine
shirring elastic in the second feeder.

When using lots of different yarns
and changing them frequently you
may find you have lots of loose ends
that will need darning in at a later
date. You can minimize this by hooking any loose ends over working

Medium yarn and elastic effect

needles at the edge of your work, and they will be knit-in as you go, thus saving you work at the end.

> When adding new yarns you may find it useful to weigh down the ends by attaching bull-dog clips to them.

6 Punch Lace

How to make punch lace

This stitch pattern is closely related to the Fair Isle patterning technique, and the cards are interchangeable. They are also quite recognizable in that what you see is what you get. The

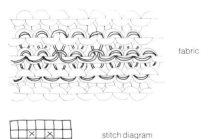

fabric

stitch diagram

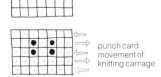

punch card
movement of
knitting carriage

Punch/thread lace diagram: fabric, stitch diagram, punch card with carriage movement

effect of punch lace relies upon the choice of yarn used. The standard procedure is to use a very fine, invisible nylon filament or fine but strong sewing thread in feeder B (the second feeder) and a thicker yarn or mohair in feeder A (the main feeder). As with Fair Isle patterning the main yarn is only knit by needles that correspond to the blanks on the pattern card. The difference lies in the second yarn. This yarn is *always* knit by *all needles*. Only the needles that correspond to the holes on the card will knit the second yarn, but *both* yarns will be knit simultaneously by needles corresponding to the blanks on the card. In this way you never get any floats with the second or finer yarn. You will only get floats with the thicker or main yarn.

This patterning possibility was introduced as an alternative to automatic true lace, which is accomplished by the transfer of stitches from one needle to the next, leaving the first needle empty. It is certainly very effective when done on a chunky or 9mm gauge machine where automatic transfer lace would be mechanically very difficult to achieve.

Although it would give a more lacy effect when an 'invisible' nylon filament was used as the second yarn, it

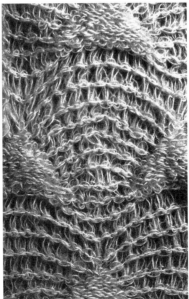

Punch lace with elastic

would probably produce a scratchy and unsympathetic fabric. A better alternative would be to use a strong sewing thread instead.

Creative possibilities with this kind of stitch patterning include the use of shirring elastic in either feeder A or feeder B, to achieve a gathered or smocked effect.

7 Plaiting

This technique is, properly speaking, not a stitch pattern. It is a special feeder for your yarn that produces a special effect in the knitting. This feeder can be used very effectively in conjunction with such stitch patterns as tuck stitch.

The plaiting feeder is attached to the sinker plate; in some cases you can insert it into your sinker plate instead of the standard two colour Fair Isle feeder and in some cases it is already built into your feeder.

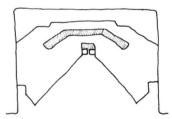

Bird's-eye view of the plaiting feeder

If you look at your plaiting feeder from above you will see two places for your yarn. There is the central hole that takes the main yarn and a crescent-shaped slot behind where you thread up your second yarn.

When you take the carriage across to knit the row you will find the yarn in the crescent-shaped feeder will trail behind the M.Y. and always be the second yarn to be gathered in by the needles. This second yarn will always appear on the purl surface of your fabric.

By putting scratchy yarn such as a metallic thread in the second feeder, you can produce a fabric with a sparkle effect that always appears on the purl side of the garment. The scratchy surface is worn away from the body, thus making it more comfortable – it isn't like wearing a brillo pad at all.

8 Weaving

This type of patterning is usually on the 'wrong' or purl side of the fabric. It is the most *inelastic* type of material you can produce on a domestic knitting machine. Perhaps this is why it is often used for 'cut and sew' projects.

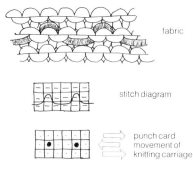

Weaving diagram: fabric, stitch diagram and punch card showing carriage movement

The technique introduces an additional yarn to the yarn used to produce the knitted (therefore stretchy) backing. This additional yarn is 'laid-in' across the surface of the fabric, preventing elasticity. The advantage of laying-in rather than knitting-in this contrast yarn is that, because the yarn is not being pulled through stitches by the needle hooks, you can use a yarn that is much thicker and more nobbly. Therefore you can produce a thicker and more heavily textured fabric, which is very stable and is often used for coats and bags, etc. where warmth, strength and durability are required.

Plain weaving

Manual weaving – This is the way to do weaving on all machines.
(1) Push selected needles to H.P. It is a good idea to push alternate

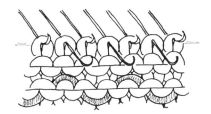

Needles selected manually

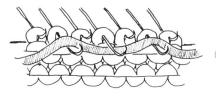

Manual weaving

needles to H.P., but you can vary the gap between needles pushed to H.P.
(2) Manually thread the weaving yarn up and down between the needles in H.P.
(3) Knit the row.

Automatic weaving – On a push-button machine or with a pattern punch card follow this procedure.

(1) On all machines with weaving brushes on the sinker plate you can achieve woven fabric by putting the weaving brushes into working position and threading the M.Y. into one side of the tension mast and the weaving yarn into the second side of the tension mast. On machines where the needles are selected to patterning positions before knitting the row, the weaving yarn needn't be threaded-up in the tension mast. You may lay the yarn across the needles, always remembering to start the yarn at the same edge where the carriage is, and travel away from the carriage with the yarn.
(2) Start the pattern by pushing the pattern buttons and pulling the set lever on *push-button machines*. On *punch card machines* insert your punch card and lock it on row 1. Set the machine to transfer the pattern card information to

the needles. On machines with a *pre-select row* you will have to move the change knob or pattern lever on the carriage and take the carriage across the needles to select them to patterning position or pull the set lever (C.O.R.). On machines with *memory drums* you will have to take the carriage past the card reading mechanism to transfer the information from the card onto the drums. Then you must push the side levers towards the back of the carriage (C.O.R.).
(3) You are then ready to weave. You must make sure the weaving yarn slips into the correct feeders at each side of the sinker plate. At the end of each row you must remove the weaving yarn manually from the side of the sinker plate and re-insert it into the weaving yarn feeder at the other edge of the sinker plate, between the carriage and the knitting. (The newer Knitmaster machines have an automatic feeding system for altering the feeding of weaving yarns. This is an additional attachment that speeds up the whole process.)

Wrapped weaving

This technique can be done on any machine providing needles are selected to W.P. and U.W.P. (or H.P.). It will be done automatically by any machine that has a pre-select patterning system (i.e. Jones/Brother and Toyota) but must be done manually by all simpler machines and machines with memory drums.
(1) Select the needles to H.P. (U.W.P.) and W.P. by the preferred method. (C.O.R.)
(2) With the weaving yarn, starting at the right hand edge of the knitting (the same side as the carriage), wind the yarn first under then over groups of needles, moving away from the carriage just as if you were doing an 'E' wrap cast-on. Always remember to work in the same direction the carriage will travel on the following row!

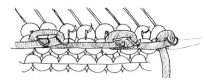

Manual weaving using the 'E' wrap technique

(*3*) Knit one row.
This procedure can be repeated at desired intervals.

Vertical weaving

You will be able to have several different strands of yarn woven into the fabric simultaneously. This technique can be done on any machine providing needles are selected to W.P. and U.W.P. (or H.P.). It will be done automatically by any machine that has a pre-select patterning system (i.e. Jones/Brother and Toyota) but must be done manually by all simpler machines and machines with memory drums. An attachment available for making the job much easier is the *garter bar*. The yarns are threaded up through the eyelets of the bar and thus held at fixed intervals so that they may be looped over the needles in H.P. at one fell swoop, instead of each strand being looped singly. You can make a yarn threader by making holes at fixed intervals along the edge of a stiff piece of card. This will serve the same purpose as the garter bar.

(*1*) Select the needles to H.P. (U.W.P.) and W.P. by the preferred method. (C.O.R.)

(*2*) Thread up your selection of

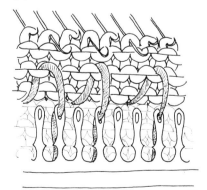

Weaving using the garter bar

weaving yarns in the garter bar or home-made threader or lay them over the needles manually.

(*3*) Knit one row. Repeat step (*2*) but carry the weaving yarns up the fabric from row to row rather than lay them across the fabric.

Very interesting effects can be achieved by your experimenting with this method, by looping, twining and twisting or braiding the yarns. You can also use fine ribbons or thin strips of fabric or leather.

Floats in weaving

Just as we have floats in Fair Isle knitting, we can have floats in weaving. Because the side where the floats appear is more commonly the 'right' side, more attention has been paid to this problem in this stitch technique. Floats can be a definite design feature in weaving.

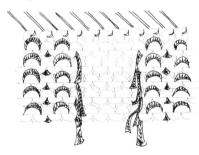

Cutting the floats = fringing

(*1*) *Cut floats* – This technique is used to give a three dimensional quality to the fabric produced. You can use ordinary punch cards, blocking off areas with self adhesive tape to create large floats as described in the Fair Isle section. The factor you must bear in mind when using this technique is that your second yarn, the yarn you are cutting, is not really permanently attached to your backing. It is only held in place by the stitches of the backing fabric. Therefore, the strands, once cut, can slip out and get lost. Remember this when you choose your yarn. Pick a yarn that is *not smooth*, but nobbly or hairy and that will attach itself to the back-

ing fabric. It also helps to use a smaller stitch size, thus making a firmer backing fabric to help hold the float strands in place.

(*2*) *Pick-up floats* – You can pick up floats onto needles from rows previously knitted, thus creating interesting undulating effects in the pattern. You will find this effective if you have rows of plain knitting between rows of weaving.

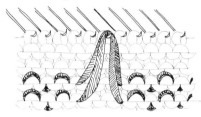

Picking up weaving floats onto another needle

(*3*) *Latch-up floats* – You can use floats in much the same way as you did when tying them in in Fair Isle knitting – that is, you can weave several rows and then latch the long loops up one by one, hooking only the last loop onto a needle.

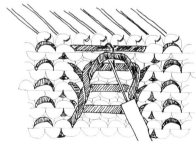

Latching up weaving floats

9   Lace

This will be the most difficult patterning process to understand. You can do lace manually by simply transferring single stitches or groups of stitches from needle to needle. When you leave the then empty needles in W.P. they will form stitches on following rows while other stitches, being doubled up onto single needles,

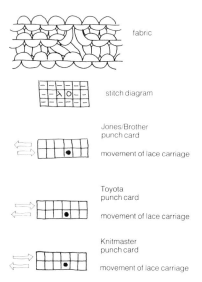

Lace diagram: fabric, stitch diagram and comparative punch cards and carriage movements for Japanese machines.

will knit together. You cannot have two adjacent empty needles! This will produce a lacy effect in your fabric with purpose-made holes.

The real advance in the modern domestic knitting machine, however, has been the facility to transfer stitches automatically, from one needle to the needle next door. Thus the hand-knitted effect of knitting two stitches together (decreasing one stitch) and putting yarn over the needle (increasing one stitch) is re-produced. The result is a hole, and you finish up with the same number of stitches you started with.

This type of complex patterning can be done with special carriages on the 4.5mm and 3.5mm gauge machines. The Passap and Pfaff machines have a similar technique, although not identical as the stitches are transferred from one needle bed across to the opposite bed. You are knitting two stitches together but one stitch is a purl stitch and one a plain stitch, whereas on the Japanese machines, all the transferring is done to adjacent needles on the same bed. The transfer device for the Passap and Pfaff machines is called the *U70* or *U80*.

Transfer lace is carried out by a separate carriage, specially made for

the job. It actually puts quite a strain on the needles, bending and twisting them to enable them to transfer the stitches. The selected needle is bent so that the adjacent needle, when it is brought forward by the lace carriage, will slip into the stitch and pull it off.

The stitch size is also quite critical in this type of knitting. If the stitch is

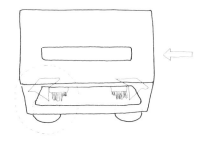

Lace carriage – bird's-eye view (Jones/Brother)

too small the loop won't transfer properly. If the stitch is too big, it will pop off the needles. You need a great deal of patience. It is also unwise to use difficult yarn for this type of patterning – for example, mohair, multi-stranded yarn, or very textured yarn. A fairly smooth, medium weight yarn is best.

There are two different types of lace carriage available: type 1 does only lace; type 2 is a knitting carriage

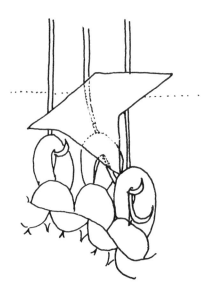

Enlargement of lace carriage transferring a stitch

incorporating lacing. These types are described below in detail.

Type 1: separate lace carriage

Jones/Brother and Toyota are Machines with a separate lace carriage designed exclusively to transfer stitches. The carriages are always used in conjunction with the standard knitting carriage, which is threaded with the yarn and executes the actual knitting. Because both carriages operate on the full needle bed it is necessary to have a resting place to put the carriage that is not in use. These machines are supplied with supplementary rails that can be inserted at the ends of the needle bed when they are required.

Although some people regard the addition of rails as a tiresome encumbrance, the ability to use the lace patterning possibilities in conjunction with the patterning possibilities of the main knitting carriage far outweighs any annoyance that the attached rails might incur. You can then do lace-tuck, lace-weaving, lace-slip and lace-Fair Isle if you wish.

Lace carriages with set lever machines

Machines that transfer the pattern to the needles using a *set lever* are the Jones/Brother push button and the Toyota punch card machines. (The lace carriage on the Jones/Brother transfers the stitches in the same direction as the movement of the lace carriage. The Toyota transfers the stitches in the opposite direction to the movement of the carriage.)

(1) Lace C.O.L., knitting C.O.R. Put the card in or push the pattern buttons to establish the pattern.
(2) Use the set lever to select the needles.
(3) Move the L. C. to transfer the stitches. Continue until the L. C. finishes at the left of the machine. Place it on the rails and this will leave you free to operate the K. C.
(4) It is only when the K. C. operates that the fabric is produced. The L. C. only moves the stitches from one needle to the next. As

the K. C. must always return to the rails at the opposite side to the L. C., there are always at least two rows of knitting in between each lace sequence.

Lace carriages with pre-select row machines

Machines with a *pre-select row* that is carried out by the lace carriage from a pattern card are: the Jones/Brother mechanical punch card patterning machines; the Jones/Brother electronic patterning machines; and the Toyota 901.

(*1*) Put the card into the machine. Lace C.O.L., knitting C.O.R. (card is locked on the mechanical machines to commence patterning).

(*2*) Move the L. C. from L. to R. Both carriages are on the right and the needles are selected (unlock the card on mechanical

Lace weave

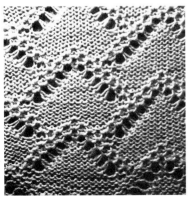

Lace tuck

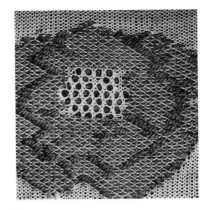

Lace weave

machines). The card has the direction of the L. C. indicated in a column of arrows on the left-hand edge. The L. C. is automatically 'locked' into the card-reading mechanism and every time it changes direction, the card is triggered to advance one row. The arrows on the left hand side of the card also indicate when the K. C. should move. In lace knitting the K. C. is not connected to the card so that when you knit two rows the pattern card does not advance.

(*3*) Continue to move the L. C., which will:

- transfer the stitches that have been selected to U.W.P. on the previous row in the same direction the carriage is moving *and*
- select the required needles that will be transferred on the following row. If no needles are selected it usually means that the K. C. will then operate for two rows.

(*4*) When required, operate the K. C.

It is only when the K. C. operates that actual knitting takes place. The movements of the lace C. serve only to move or transfer stitches across the surface of the fabric, creating stitch patterns. The K. C. is not connected to the card. The card does not move when the K. C. knits a row – thus the movement of the card bears no relation to the progress of the knitting. In fact it usually takes four passes or more of the L. C. for every two rows

of knitting completed. In multi-transfer lace you may have to operate the L. C. many times before you can continue with the knitting.

Lace carriages with knitting carriages

Combined patterning can be done on machines that use a lace carriage along with a knitting carriage that patterns. You can use both patterning facilities together on both machines with set levers, and lace carriages that set the needles to pattern.

On machines with **set levers** you merely operate the set lever before knitting a row with the K. C. in order to set the needles to patterning position. You must then set your K. C. to pattern by selecting the relevant patterning facility (e.g. tuck, weaving brushes, etc).

On machines where the lace carriage selects the needles according to a **mechanical punch card** both carriages are connected to the punch card, but the punch card will advance only when the belt at the back of the needle bed changes direction. This means that if both carriages move in the same direction consecutively (one following along behind the other as they will do when you change from using one carriage to the other one) *the card does not advance*. The same needles are re-selected to pattern on the following row. Every time you use *both* carriages the same line on the card will be transferred to the needles twice – once by one carriage and then again by the following carriage. This will be indicated by a U turn arrow on the left hand side of the card.

On **Jones/Brother electronic machines** the card is triggered by a magnet at the back of *each* carriage passing the centre of the machine. This means that each pass of each carriage will trigger the advance of the card. If you are transposing dual patterns (e.g. lace-tuck, lace-weaving, etc.) from a punch card pattern to the electronic machine you must *repeat* any row that corresponds to a U turn arrow on the left hand side of the punch card.

Type 2: Knitting carriage that incorporates lacing

Machines with a lace carriage that transfers the stitches and also carries out the knitting (that is a lace carriage that is also a knitting carriage) are the Knitmaster 4.5mm, 3.5mm new Toyota machine and the gauge punch card and electronic machines. These machines select, transfer and knit the row simultaneously with one carriage so you do not need the extension rails as you have no additional carriage to rest on them. You can also knit one row in between each transfer row. Every time the carriage moves across the needle bed the card advances and stitches are transferred in the same direction as the movement of the carriage. If you wish to execute multi-transfer lace you must remove the yarn and push the 'P' button to tell the carriage you are not knitting the next row, only transferring stitches. When you wish to recommence knitting (indicated by markings at the right hand edge of the punch card) you must re-thread the yarn and re-set the carriage.

A word of caution

(1) You cannot select needles to hold position and do partial knitting while you use the lace carriage. You must use the cast-on cord and knit needles manually back to N.W.P. to accomplish partial knitting in a lace pattern.

(2) You cannot interchange lace cards on any of the machines.

---

10   Comparison of lace

Because the lace cards are *not* interchangeable it might be useful to look more closely at the way various machines achieve a lace pattern. Then, if you wish to transfer a lace pattern from one machine to another, combine lace patterning with tuck or weaving, etc., or indeed invent your own lace patterns you will be able to do so.

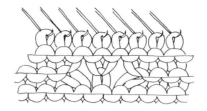

Lace produced by a machine with a separate lace carriage (Jones/Brother, Toyota) with stitch diagram below

Jones/Brother push button machines

ROW 1

(a) Push button 5

(b) Pull set lever. Needle 5 selected to U.W.P.

(c) L.C. moves L. to R. The stitch on needle 5 is transferred to needle 6.

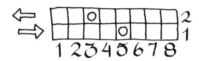

Needle selection and movement of lace carriage on Jones/Brother 710

ROW 2

(a) Push button 3.

(b) Pull set lever. Needle 3 selected to U.W.P.

(c) L.C. moves R. to L. The stitch on needle 3 is transferred to needle 2.

Knit two rows with the knitting carriage.

Toyota 858

This machine uses both push buttons and cards to select needles for patterning. The use of the set lever triggers the movement of the card.

ROW 1

(a) Push button 3.

(b) Pull set lever. Needle 3 selected to U.W.P.

(c) L.C. moves L. to R. The stitch on needle 3 is transferred to needle 2.

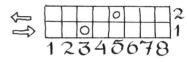

Needle selection and movement of lace carriage on Toyota 858

ROW 2

(a) Push button 5.

(b) Pull set lever. Needle 5 selected to U.W.P.

(c) L.C. moves R. to L. The stitch on needle 5 is transferred to needle 6.

Knit two rows with the knitting carriage. *Alternatively*, you can insert the card.

ROW 1

(a) Pull set lever. Needle 3 selected to U.W.P.

(b) L.C. moves L. to R. The stitch on needle 3 is transferred to needle 2.

ROW 2

(a) Pull set lever. Needle 5 selected to U.W.P.

(b) L.C. moves R. to L. The stitch on needle 5 is transferred to needle 6.

Knit two rows with the knitting carriage.

Jones/Brother pattern card machines

ROW 1

L.C. moves L. to R. Needle 3 selected to U.W.P.

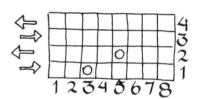

Punch card and movement of lace carriage on Jones/Brother machine

ROW 2

L.C. moves R. to L. The stitch on needle 3 is transferred to needle 2. Needle 5 is selected to U.W.P.

ROW 3

L.C. moves L. to R. The stitch on needle 5 is transferred to needle 6.

ROW 4

L.C. moves R. to L.

Knit two rows with the knitting carriage.

Toyota 901

ROW 1

L.C. moves L. to R. Needle 5 selected to U.W.P.

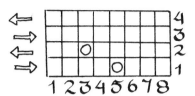

Punch card and movement of lace carriage on a Toyota 901 machine

ROW 2

L.C. moves R. to L. The stitch on needle 5 is transferred to needle 6. Needle 3 is selected to U.W.P.

ROW 3

L.C. moves L. to R. The stitch on needle 3 is transferred to needle 2.

ROW 4

L.C. moves R. to L.

Knit two rows with the knitting carriage.

Knitmaster

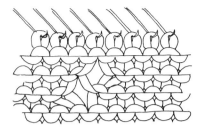

Lace and punch card of a machine that transfers stitches and knits simultaneously using one carriage only (stitch diagram below)

ROW 1

L.C. moves R. to L. The stitch on needle 3 is transferred to needle 2. The carriage knits one row.

ROW 2

L.C. moves L. to R. The stitch on needle 5 is transferred to needle 6. The carriage knits one row.

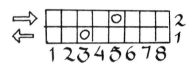

IV Manual Techniques

1 Why use manual techniques?

Manual techniques – otherwise called hand-work – include work done both on the machines while you knit and work carried out after the fabric has been removed from the machine. There are many exciting and unusual variations that can be incorporated into your knitting to transform it from the mundane to the exotic. Using hand-work can be an effective way of giving your garment that hand-knitted look and also help to improve the overall finish.

If you are knitting for profit you may find that time is money and that the effects achieved are not worth the effort involved. However, you may be surprised at how quick you become with practice at doing some fiddly task that seemed to be very difficult initially. Often, a small bit of hand-work (what a friend of mine calls 'furniture') can lift a garment out of the ordinary and justify a higher price! This decision is up to you.

Knitting a tube

One useful technique to know is how to knit a tube:

(1) Do an 'E' wrap cast-on over several needles. The number of needles you use will determine the width of your tube. The maximum number of needles for a neat tube is about six.
(2) Set your carriage to knit only in one direction:
- Jones/Brother – push one part button;
- Toyota – set pattern dial to empty in one direction;
- Knitmaster – set pattern dial to

slip and push one side lever forward and one side lever back.
(3) Hang a small claw weight onto the knitting and knit until the tube reaches the required length.

You can also knit a **strip** on six to eight needles and use it in much the same way you would use your tube. Alternatively, knit any number of tuck stitch or pull-up stitch variations on six to twelve needles, thus creating an effective strip of braid that can be used to edge or decorate garments.

2 Cables

Cables are one of the first basic manual techniques to learn.

In order to make cables you need *two* transfer tools with the same number of eyelets at the working end. (You can purchase a multi-transfer tool that is adjustable and will give you more than the three maximum eyelets found on the standard tools; if you are cabling more than 3 st × 3 st you will need two of these tools.) You can cross the stitches right-hand over left or vice versa, according to your pattern. The procedure is standard.

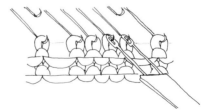

Removing stitches onto a double-eyed transfer tool

(1) Take one transfer tool and first remove the stitches you wish to cross behind.

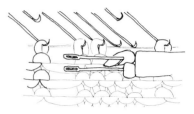

Holding the stitches out of the way

(2) Twist the tool so that you are holding it parallel to the needle bed.

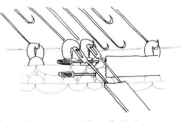

Removing a second lot of stitches onto a second double-eyed transfer tool

(3) Remove the second lot of stitches you require to transfer onto the second tool and replace them onto the appropriate needles (those that were emptied when you removed the *first* lot of stitches).
(4) Now, replace those first lot of stitches (that were held on the tool parallel to the machine) onto the remaining empty needles.

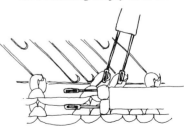

Replacing the second batch of stitches onto the first batch of needles

(5) Pull all needles to H.P., ensuring that you push the transferred

stitches back against the needle bed, well behind the needle latches. Set the carriage to knit all needles.

This is, in general, how cables are formed. Once you have mastered this technique you can then break the rules!

Cables may be done on a **single bed machine**, but they can be done more easily on a machine with a **ribber**. Cables are often found edged with purl stitches to mark them off from the rest of a stocking stitch fabric. If you don't have a row of purl stitches going up each side of a group of cable stitches, the cable tends to get lost. When you have a ribber this is no problem as you can alternate stitches on both beds. When you have only a single bed you are faced with two alternatives.

(*a*) You can leave one needle each side of the cable needles in N.W.P. This will result in a 'ladder' up each side of the cable. You may decide to make a decorative feature of this and leave two or three needles in N.W.P., thus making a wide gap between the cable and the rest of the fabric. Done with care this can be quite effective.

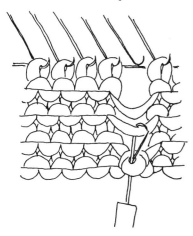

Latching up a stitch purl-wise

(*b*) You can 'drop' the neighbouring stitch either side of the cable after you have finished knitting the piece but before you have removed it from the machine. Run this stitch back to the point where you began the cable and latch it up from the purl side.

This will give you your purl stitch either side of the cable.

Another problem with cable knitting is that unlike hand-knitting where you can gather stitches together on a spare needle and push them up you can't push your needles closer on the machine. Therefore there is a maximum number of stitches you can cable when machine knitting (unless you take special measures). If, however, you are knitting cables on a machine with a ribbing attachment, you can add yarn available in the cable stitches by pushing needles to W.P. on the ribber, opposite the cable needles on the row before you will make your cable. When you have knit the row and are ready to cable, you can then drop the loops from these extra needles and return them to N.W.P. Having done this you will find that you will have the extra yarn needed to cross over the stitches.

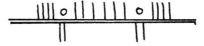

Needle selection on a double bed machine for cabling

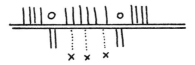

x marks extra needles selected manually on the ribber the row before cabling

To add extra yarn when cabling on a single bed you can do either of the following:

(*1*) With a needle in N.W.P. on either side to form a ladder push up to W.P. those two needles at the edge of your cable that were in N.W.P. on the row before you wish to cable. Knit one row. Drop the loop on the two extra needles and return them to N.W.P. until you require them again. Cable your stitches.

(*2*) With a stitch to be latched up either side of the cable, knit the row before you wish to cable as usual. Drop the stitches from the

needles that will be latched-up when the knitting is finished, thus giving you the extra yarn required to make the cable. Make the cable. (The dropped stitch won't matter as you will run them down and latch them up afterwards anyway.)

When doing any kind of cable it is always a good idea to push your needles to H.P. after transferring the stitches for one row. Set the carriage to knit all needles including those in H.P.

Some basic cables

The number of rows you will knit between each cable is optional.

Cable sample 1

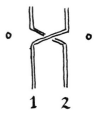

Sample 1. 1 over 1 cable

Needle arrangements: I = needle with a stitch in W.P.; O = empty needle in N.W.P.

Sample 1 – l l l l o l l o l l l l

Sample 2 – 1 1 1 1 o 1 1 1 1 o 1 1 1 1

Cable sample 2

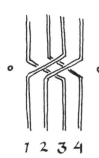

2 over 2 cable

Sample 2. 2

Sample 3 – 1 1 1 1 o o 1 1 1 1 1 1 o 1 1 1 1

Cable sample 3

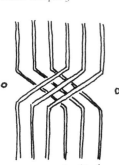

Sample 3. 3
over 3 cable

Sample 4 – 1 1 1 1 o 1 1 1 1 1 1 1 1 o 1 1 1 1

Cable sample 4

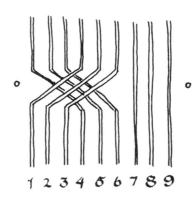

Sample 4. Step (*1*)

(*1*) cable and knit 4 rows.

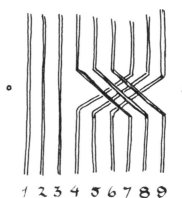

Sample 4. Step (*2*)

(*2*) cable and knit 4 rows.

Sample 5 – M.T. + 1 or 2 –
1 1 1 1 o 1 1 1 1 1 1 1 1 1 1 1 1 o 1 1 1 1

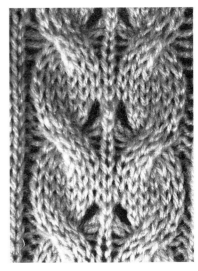

Cable sample 5

(*1*) cable and knit 1 row.

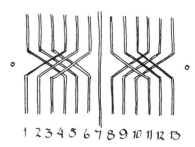

Sample 5. Step (*1*)

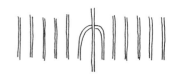

Sample 5. Step (*2*)

(*2*) transfer stitch 6 and stitch 8 to
needle 7. Leave empty needles in
W.P. Knit 7 rows.

Sample 6 – M.T. + 1 –
1111o1111111o1111

Cable sample 6

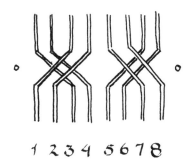

1 2 3 4 5 6 7 8

Sample 6. Step (*1*)

(*1*) cable and knit 4 rows. Repeat step 1 (8 rows). Knit 4 rows (12 rows).

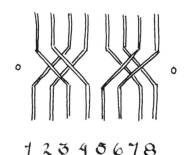

1 2 3 4 5 6 7 8

Sample 6. Step (*2*)

(*2*) cable and knit 4 rows (16 rows). Repeat step (*2*) (20 rows).

Sample 8

*Sample 7 –*1111o1111111o1111

Cable sample 7

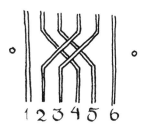

1 2 3 4 5 6

Sample 7

*Sample 8 –*1111o111o111o1111

Cable sample 8

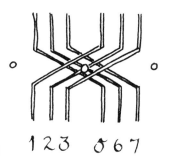

1 2 3   5 6 7

(*1*) push the needles in N.W.P. to W.P. for the row preceding the cable.

(*2*) drop the loops formed on these needles and return them to N.W.P.

(*3*) Cable.

Sample 9 Lobster claw –
1111oo111111oo1111

Cable sample 9

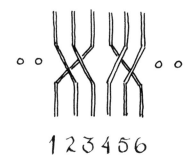

1 2 3 4 5 6

Sample 9

Cable sample 10

Sample 10 – M.T. + 1 or 2 –
1111oo1111111111111oo1111
If you are using a ribber: put the ribber to half pitch; on the row before the cable, push up spare needles on the ribber bed between cable needles 4 and 5, 8 and 9.

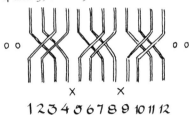

Sample 10. Step (*1*)

(*1*) cable and knit 8 rows. If you are using a ribber: put the ribber to half pitch and on the row before the cable push up spare needles on the ribber bed between cable needles 6 and 7.

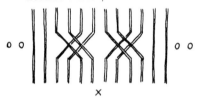

Sample 10. Step (*2*)

(*2*) knit 8 rows. (16 rows).

Sample 11 Basket weave –
1111o11111111111o1111

Cable sample 11

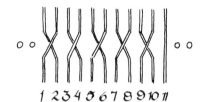

Sample 11. Step (*1*)

(*1*) cable and knit 2 rows.

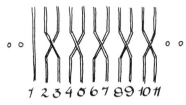

Sample 11. Step (*2*)

(*2*) cable and knit 2 rows.

Sample 12 Aran cable –
1111oo111111111oo11oo1111

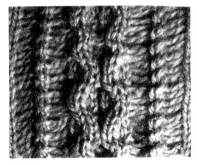

Cable sample 12

Sample 12. Step (*1*)

(*1*) cable and knit 2 rows.

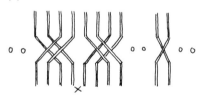

Sample 12. Step (*2*)

(*2*) cable and knit 2 rows.

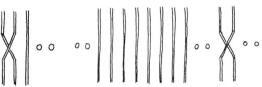

Sample 12. Step (*3*)

(*3*) cable and knit 2 rows.

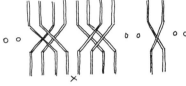

Sample 12. Step (*4*)

(*4*) cable and knit 2 rows.

Sample 13 – Cable with more than 3 × 3 stitches:

Sample 13

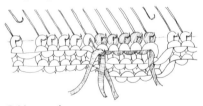

Cable sample 13

(*1*) Use an extra length of M.Y. to knit large cable stitches by hand before attempting to transfer the stitches.

(*2*) Use *two* extra separate lengths of M.Y. to knit each half of the stitches to be cabled by hand before attempting to transfer the stitches.

Sample 14 – Use partial or 'hold' knitting to knit each cable leg separately – then you can remove each leg from the machine separately onto W.Y. and tie the two legs before replacing the stitches back onto the machine.

Cable sample 14

1111o1111111111/1111111111o1111

(*1*) C.O.R. push all needles to the left of the cable needles *plus* the left half of the cable needles (10) to H.P. Set the carriage not to knit needles in H.P.
(*2*) Knit 1 row, C.O.L. Push all needles to the right of the cable needles to H.P.
(*3*) Knit 9 rows. Break the yarn.
(*4*) Thread up W.Y. and knit several rows. Break the W.Y. and drop the stitches off the needles. Push the needles to N.W.P.

Sample 14. Step (*1*)

Sample 14. Step (*2*)

Sample 14. Step (*5*)

(*5*) Put the C.O.L. Push the left 10 cable needles to U.W.P.
(*6*) Thread the carriage up with M.Y. and knit 10 rows on these needles.
(*7*) Break the M.Y. Thread up with W.Y. and knit several rows on these 10 needles. Break the W.Y. and drop these stitches off the needles.
(*8*) 'Tie' the two legs of the cables and replace the stitches onto the 20 needles. Pull out the W.Y. C.O.R.
(*9*) Thread up with M.Y. and continue to knit.

Sample 15 Use of 'hold' to knit a two colour cable – ...

1111o111/11o1111...

(*1*) C.O.R. Set carriage not to knit needles in H.P.
(*2*) Push all needles to the left of the cable and the three left-hand cable needles to H.P.

Sample 15. Step (*3*)

(*3*) Knit 4 rows in colour A. C.O.R.
(*4*) Push all needles to H.P.
(*5*) Remove colour A. and pass the carriage to the left. C.O.L.

4.15
Cable sample 15

Sample 15. Step (*6*)

(*6*) Push all needles to the left of centre plus the 3 left-hand cable needles to U.W.P.
(*7*) Thread up with colour B. Knit 4 rows. C.O.L.

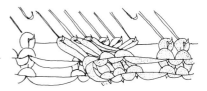

Sample 15. Step (*8*)

(*8*) *Cable* centre 6 needles.
(*9*) Remove colour B. Push all needles to H.P.
(*10*) Pass the carriage to the right.
(*11*) Push all needles to the right of centre plus the three right-hand cable needles to U.W.P.

Repeat from step (*3*) to step (*11*) for pattern.

Sample 16 Cable with decorative bobble –

1111o11o111111o11o1111

(*1*) Cable across the 6 centre stitches in the usual way.
(*2*) When the knitting is completed,

Cable sample 16

take two knitted strips and thread them through the ladder at either side of the cable. Make knots in the strips at intervals on the right side of the knitting.

Sample 17 Twisted cable –
1111o111o1111

Cable sample 17

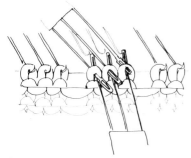

Sample 17. Transferring three stitches from one three-eyed transfer tool to another

This cable is done over three needles using two triple transfer tools but only by moving three stitches.

(1) Remove the stitches onto one of the transfer tools.
(2) Insert the second transfer tool into the stitches in the opposite direction to the first transfer tool.
(3) Remove the first transfer tool and twist the second transfer tool around so that it is facing the machine.
(4) Replace the stitches onto the empty cable needles.

Sample 18 – This is not a true cable as such but it certainly gives an interesting decorative effect.

Cable sample 18

Knit the fabric making lace holes manually across a chosen 7 stitch repeat. This can be anywhere in the fabric across the width of the needle bed. If you choose to have the cable in the centre you will be working on the second and fourth needles to the left of O and the first and third needles to the right of O on the needle bed.

(1) Choose which 7 needles you will use for the pattern. (They will be numbered from 1 to 7 L. to R. for patterning purposes.)
(2) Knit 7 rows.
(3) Transfer the stitch from needle 1 to needle 2. Transfer the stitch from needle 7 to needle 6.
(4) Knit one row.
(5) Transfer the stitch from needle 3

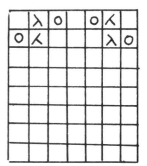

Sample 18. Stitch diagram for transferring stitches

to needle 2. Transfer the stitch from needle 5 to needle 6. Repeat steps (2) to (7) until the knitting is completed.

(6) Knit two strips three times the length of the knitted piece. Thread them up and attach the ends to the wrong side of the garment.

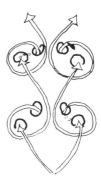

Sample 18. Threading diagram

Although most cables are done by transferring the stitches on the machine needles, some very interesting cable-like effects can also be achieved by manipulating strips of knitting and by pick-up and partial knitting techniques. The following samples are not 'true' cables but they will give an interesting cable-like effect.

Sample 19 Horizontal cable insert – There is no needle arrangement given as this is knitted across the whole width of the fabric.

(1) C.O.R. Set carriage not to knit needles in H.P.
(2) Leave 6 needles at the right of the knitting in W.P. Push the remaining needles to H.P.

Cable sample 19

Sample 19. Step (*2*)

(*3*) Knit 10 rows. C.O.R.

Sample 19. Step (*4*)

(*4*) Push 3 needles at the left of needles in W.P. to U.W.P.
(*5*) Knit 1 row. (9 needles in W.P.) C.O.L. Push three needles at the right of needles in W.P. to H.P. (6 needles in W.P.).

Sample 19. Step (*5*)

(*6*) Knit 9 rows. C.O.R.
(*8*) Set the carriage to knit all needles in H.P. Knit 2 rows.
(*9*) Repeat the procedure reversing the process from L. to R. until you have returned to the right hand edge of the knitting. If you don't repeat the 'cable' your work will have a built-in slant.

Sample 20 – This is a very complicated two colour horizontal cable that will require considerable concentration as it combines holding techniques with picking-up techniques. If you feel brave try it! It is most effec-

Cable sample 20

tive on chunky machines with contrasting strongly coloured yarns.

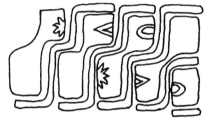

Sample 20. Fabric diagram

(*1*) Push all needles to H.P. except four at the right hand edge of the knitting. C.O.R.
(*2*) Colour B. Knit 1 row. C.O.L.
(*3*) Colour A. Knit 4 rows wrapping the edge needles every row. C.O.L.
(*4*) Colour B. Knit 1 row. C.O.R. Wrap edge needle.
(*5*) Push four needles at the left-hand edge of needles in W.P. to U.W.P.
(*6*) Colour B. Knit 1 row. C.O.L.
(*7*) Colour A. Knit 4 rows (8 needles in W.P.). C.O.L. Wrap edge needles every row.
(*8*) Colour B. Knit 1 row. C.O.R. Wrap edge needle.
(*9*) Push 4 needles at the left-hand edge of needles in W.P. to U.W.P.
(*10*) Colour B. Knit 1 row. C.O.L.
(*11*) *Pick-up* wrapped left hand edge stitch of the first band in colour A. and place onto the right-hand edge needle now in W.P.

Repeat from step (*7*) to step (*11*) for cable.

Cable sample 21

Sample 21 Single twisted strip cable
(*1*) 'E' wrap cast-on the required number of stitches for the strip (e.g. 11).
(*2*) Knit 12 rows.
(*3*) Make a hole in the centre of the strip by transferring the centre stitch to the adjacent needle. Leave the empty needle in W.P.

Sample 21. Step (*3*)
Sample 21. Step (*4*)

(*4*) Repeat steps (*2*) and (*3*) until you have knit a strip to the length required. Cast-off.

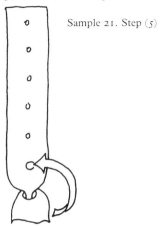

Sample 21. Step (5)

(5) Twist the strip pulling it through each hole in turn.

Sample 22 double twisted strip cable

(1) 'E' wrap cast-on the required number of stitches for the cable (e.g. 17).

Cable sample 22

(2) Knit 18 rows.
(3) Make a hole in the centre of the strip by transferring the centre stitch to the adjacent needle. Leave the empty needle in W.P.
(4) Repeat steps (2) and (3) until you have knit a strip the length required. Cast-off.
(5) Knit another strip identical to the first strip without holes.
(6) Thread the second strip through the holes in the first strip, always coming from the purl side through to the plain side and

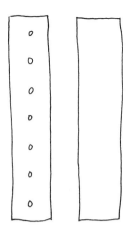

Sample 22. Step (5)

alternating, taking the plain strip behind the right, then the left side of the strip with holes. This will give you a plaited effect.

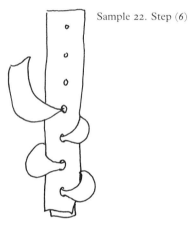

Sample 22. Step (6)

3 Bobbles and fringes

I have chosen to consider these two techniques together because they may overlap. Bobbles can be done with fringes to add interest to the fabric. There are three main ways of doing bobbles.

Manual bobbles

(1) To do bobbles manually choose the group of needles where you wish the bobble to be.
(2) You may transfer stitches to neighbouring needles that will not be included in the bobble at

Bobbles

this point. This will result in a 'bumpier' bobble. If you do this you will then have to cast-on extra stitches onto the needles you have emptied.

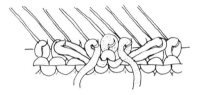

Manual bobble. Step (2)

(3) Push the selected needles to H.P. and place the yarn for the bobble into the needle hooks by hand.

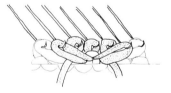

Manual bobble. Step (3)

(4) Pull the needles back (with your thumb on the needle butts) until the latches close over the yarn in the needle hooks.

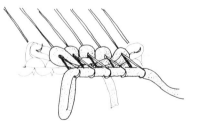

Manual bobble. Step (4)

(5) Pull the needles back to W.P. one by one until all the stitches have been knit through. It will help if you place a weight on the knitting just below the bobble needles.
(6) Repeat this procedure until you

have knit 4–8 rows (or as many rows as you require for the bobble).

(7) At this point you can: replace the stitches you moved before you began hand knitting the bobble; *or* pick up the edges of the bobble to prevent holes; *or* leave the bobble as it is.

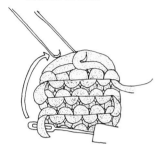

Manual bobble – replacing the stitches

(8) Continue to knit the garment.

Bobbles using holding position

When you are knitting a bobble you are knitting only selected needles. One of the ways of selecting needles that you require to knit is to push all unwanted needles to H.P. and to set the carriage not to knit needles in H.P. There are two ways to knit these bobbles depending on whether you wish to knit them in M.Y. or contrast yarn.

Main Yarn

(1) C.O.R. Thread the carriage up with the yarn you require for your bobble. Push all the needles to the left of where you require your first bobble to H.P. Set the carriage not to knit needles in H.P.

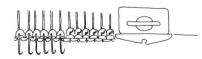

Bobble using holding position and main yarn. Step (*1*)

(2) Knit 1 row. C.O.L. Push all the needles to the right of the needles you require for your bobble to H.P.

Bobble using holding position and main yarn. Step (*2*)

(3) You may wrap the needles in H.P. at the edges of your bobble to prevent holes.

(4) Continue to knit several rows on the needles remaining in W.P. until you have completed the bobble. It will help if you place a weight on the knitting just below the bobble needles. C.O.R.

(5) Push all the needles to the *left* of the bobble to U.W.P. up to the needles you will select for your next bobble.

(6) Knit 1 row. C.O.L. Push all the needles to the right of the second bobble to H.P. and repeat step (*4*).

(7) You may continue to knit bobbles this way across the row. To avoid holes at the edge of your bobbles you may *either* wrap the edge needles; *or* pick up the edge bobble stitches after the bobble is completed. Then, *either* leave the stitches as they are for a fat, irregular sort of bobble; *or* pick up the first row of bobble stitches on the bobble needles after the bobble is completed.

Contrast Yarn

This technique is a bit trickier and requires careful threading-up of the contrast yarn.

(1) C.O.R. Push all needles to H.P., except those needles required for the first bobble on the right. Set the carriage not to knit needles in H.P.

(2) Thread up the carriage with contrast yarn and take the yarn over the top of the needles in H.P., then down below the knitting. It might be helpful to weight the end of the yarn with a bull-dog clip or tie the end of the yarn to one of the machine clamps.

(3) Knit 1 row, carefully making sure that the contrast yarn does not get tangled up in the brushes under

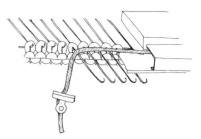

Bobble using holding position and contrast yarn. Step (*2*)

the sinker plate. C.O.L. It will help if you place a weight on the knitting just below the bobble needles.

(4) Continue to knit several rows on the needles remaining in W.P. until you have completed the bobble. C.O.L.

(5) Push all needles to H.P. You may break the yarn at this point or you may wish to carry it across to the next bobble.

(6) Push the next group of selected needles for the next bobble to U.W.P.

(7) Ensure that the required yarn comes from below the needle bed *up* at the right hand edge of the bobble and *over* the needles in H.P. and then into the carriage – otherwise, your stitches may not knit properly.

(8) Continue knitting bobbles in this way. You may choose to 'close-up' the bobble by picking up the first row of the bobble or close up the edges of the bobble by wrapping or picking up the edge stitches when the bobble is completed.

(9) When you have completed the required number of bobbles in the row, push all needles to H.P. and return the carriage to where it was when you started. (C.O.R.) Re-set the carriage to knit all needles. Continue to knit the garment.

Bobbles using part, slip or empty stitch patterning

As you may guess from the description of this method of making a bobble you must use the stitch patterning facility on your machine. You can use this stitch patterning whether you select the needles manually or automatically by punch card. We will deal with the technique that requires you to select the needles manually. Although this is slower, you will have more control, not only of the size of the bobble but also the distance between bobbles.

(1) Make sure your automatic patterning is not connected to the needles: on Jones/Brother and Toyota machines put the change knob/card lever on the carriage to N.L./O; on Knitmaster machines put your side levers forward to ◯ and on machines with a set lever, do not pull the set lever to select the needles.

(2) Set the carriage to knit all needles. Set the patterning on the carriage to slip, part or empty.

(3) Thread up the machine with yarn. It can be the same yarn as the garment or contrast yarn. C.O.R.

Fringes. Step (2)

(4) Push to H.P. or U.W.P. those needles where you require your bobble. Knit 1 row. C.O.L. It will help if you place a weight on the knitting just below the bobble needles.

(5) You can knit one bobble at a time with this method or you can knit several bobbles across the row. You must select the bobble needles *every row*.

If you knit one bobble at a time you can deal with the edges by wrapping the non-knitting needle at each edge of the bobble as you knit or you can pick up the edge stitches when the bobble is completed. If you knit several bobbles across the row simultaneously you will have 'floats' or strands of yarn between each bobble. This can be a decorative feature if you cut the floats and pull them through to the other side of the knitting and tie them into fringes – either separately or together. Alternatively, twist and

Cut floats

pick up the floats on the purl side of the fabric.

As you can imagine, this technique can also be used with a punch card. You can punch the card and lock it on one row to achieve the same effect. To do this you must connect the pattern facility on your carriage (change knob to K.C. Jones/Brother; card lever to C. Toyota; side levers back, Knitmaster; push buttons and pull set lever, etc.). If you wish wider gaps between your bobbles you may either reject the needles that have been selected by the machine (on those machines with a pre-select row, i.e. Jones/Brother or Toyota) or you may use your single motif facility. In this way you can combine bobbles with fringes.

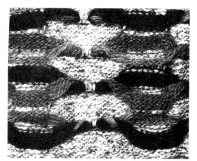

Pick-up floats

Fringes

We can see how fringes can be formed by cutting through yarn that floats between two sections of patterning. This can be done with automatic patterning on: Fair Isle, weaving, and slip, part or empty.

There is another useful way of

making lengths of unknitted yarn between two sections of knitted fabric. In some instructions for making a length of fringing the pattern will specify that you select two groups of needles to W.P. with a rather long section of needles in N.W.P. between them. This is rather tricky as you have to move the carriage across a greater distance without knitting the needles in between those in W.P. and in addition the unknitted yarn may become tangled.

The best solution, however, which avoids these problems is as follows:

(1) Arrange a group of needles in W.P. That is *all* the needles will be brought to W.P. without a gap between them in N.W.P.

(2) Do an 'E' wrap or closed edge cast-on on only a few needles at each end of the group in W.P. C.O.R.

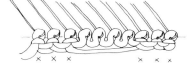

Fringes. Step (4)

(3) Knit 1 row. C.O.L. Place cast-on cord between the needles and the gate pegs. Knit four rows. Remove the cast-on cord.

(4) Knit the length of fringe required.

(5) Cast-off only the needles that were 'E' wrapped initially.

(6) *Unravel* those stitches that were knit on the needles between the cast-on/cast-off edges. This unravelled yarn will give you quite a deep fringe.

The basic principle that unravelled stitches give longer floats can also be used when you wish to make a fabric wider than you could knit on the machine. You can always knit your fabric as wide as possible on the needles available and then, for example, unravel every fourth needle stitch and produce a much wider fabric.

4 Hand weaving

Weaving can add a different dimen-
sion to your fabric as you create a
thick texture which can only be done
by hand. You can use fibres or materi-
als that are not flexible enough to be
woven in standard weaving on the
machine, such as strips of fabric or
leather, or tubes of knitting.

Weaving through holes

As you are knitting the garment you
can manually make sets of holes and
weave through the holes after completion of the garment. You can also
use these holes to tie in bows of fabric
or leather. Holes can also be left at the
edges of the garment pieces and the
pieces joined together by lacing-up
with strips of fabric.

Weaving through ladders

This technique is similar to that
above. You transfer selected stitches
and push the empty needles to
N.W.P. As you knit your fabric,
ladders form at the point of the
needles in N.W.P. When you have
finished the knitted piece you can
weave contrasting or matching tubes
of knitting or fabric, etc. through
these ladders.

Weaving through holes

Weaving for stocking stitch

The side of fabric most often used as
the right side with weaving is the purl
side. If you wish your weaving to
appear on the stocking stitch side you
must remove a group of stitches from
the needles with a multi-transfer tool
and pass the yarn to be woven *behind*
these stitches. You then replace the
stitches onto the needles. Thus the
weaving appears on the stocking
stitch side of the fabric.

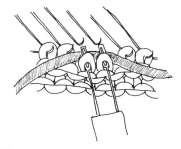

Weaving yarn to appear on the stocking
stitch side of the fabric

5 Stitch size

Varying of stitch size can also result in
interesting patterns. The size of the
stitch depends on the number on the
tension dial and the thickness of the
yarn. Yarn thickness may depend on
the number of strands you use – you
may have one strand on its own, two
fine strands or indeed ply up to four
fine strands knitted together as one.

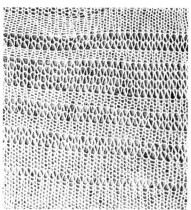

Varying stitch sizes

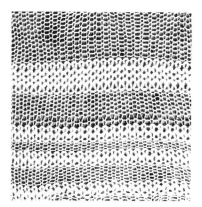

Varying yarn

Ladder effect

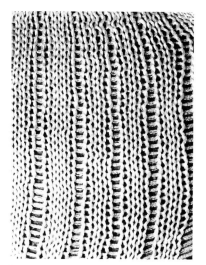

Ladder effect by unravelling

You can also arrange your needles
so that there are gaps caused by
needles in N.W.P. at intervals along
the needle bed. Also try knitting the
fabric on all needles and then unravelling the stitches on selected needles to
achieve a patterned effect (or to add
width to your knitting).

6 Add-ons

In addition to weaving in strips during or after your knitting, you can also add on material whilst knitting to create a three dimensional effect. The added material is usually knit first, then taken off the machine onto waste yarn. You can then pick up your add-ons onto selected needles when you wish. You can also 'draw' across the garment piece with previously knitted lengths of knitted tube or fringe or ruffles.

> It is very much easier to plan your garment out if you draw the positioning of your picked-up bits on your patterning attachment (knit leader, knit tracer, knit radar) before you begin to knit your garment piece. You can then judge the decorative effect before committing yourself.

Flaps

First knit your flaps. With straight strips follow this procedure.

Flaps and knots

(*1*) Cast-on in W.Y. over required number of needles (e.g. 10) and knit several rows.
(*2*) Change to M.Y. and knit the required number of rows.
(*3*) Knit several rows in W.Y. between each section knit in M.Y. These sections can then be cut through at the rows knit in W.Y.

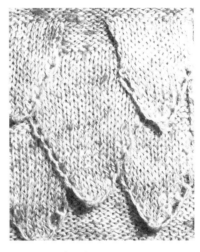

Flaps and triangles

For shaped bits such as triangles you must:
(*1*) 'E' wrap cast-on over two needles and C.O.R.;
(*2*) Knit one row. Push one additional needle to W.P. between the knitting and the carriage on every following row (increase 1 st.) until the desired size triangle is obtained;
(*3*) Thread up with W.Y. and knit several rows. Remove the triangle from the machine.

Other shapes can be achieved by 'E' wrapping several needles and using partial knitting to shape the bits of material. When putting these sections onto your knitting you can pick up one row of M.Y. loops next to the W.Y. and knit several rows. Then twist, knot, or loop or weave the bits before you pick up the last row of M.Y. loops next to the W.Y.

With shaped bits you can gather the picked-up edge or pick up the stitches onto every needle from the last row knit in M.Y. You can separate or interleave these bits.

Braiding

Braids, fringes, ruffles, etc.

You can knit strips of knitting or use lace and pick them up onto the surface of your fabric whilst you are knitting.

Pick-up lace

These strips can be patterned or plain.

You can also knit ruffles.
(*1*) Cast-on across all needles either 'E' wrap or make a small hem in M.Y.
(*2*) Knit the required number of rows to give you the depth you require for your ruffle.
(*3*) Thread up with W.Y. and knit several rows. Remove the ruffle from the machine.

When later you replace the last row of M.Y. loops next to the W.Y. onto your knitting, you put several loops onto one needle thus making your ruffle.

7 Pick-up techniques

With this method you achieve a similar effect as a tuck stitch pattern, but because you are manually selecting where and how much you are picking up you can do it on a much grander scale. You can also create less regular effects than you would be able to if you used the punch card for your pattern.

Smocked effects

This is most effectively obtained when you use a change of colour or texture of yarn. You can use the smocked effect selectively at one end of the needle bed to create shaping in a sideways knitted garment – for example, cuffs, shoulder shaping or waist gathering.

Smocking

To Knit a Sample –
(1) Cast-on 60 stitches and knit several rows in M.Y. C.O.R.
(2) Knit 2 rows Con. Col.
(3) Knit 10 rows M.Y.
(4) Pick up the last row of loops knit in Con. Col. with the triple transfer tool from below needles 30, 29, 28; 20, 19, 18; etc, across the row and place these loops onto the needles above them.

(5) Knit two rows Con. Col.
(6) Knit ten rows. M.Y. and repeat step 4 but pick up the stitches below needles 25, 24, 23; 15, 14, 13; etc.
Continue to knit this pattern.

Ruching

This sort of stitch pattern can be used in conjunction with Fair Isle knitting to create a dramatic three dimensional fabric. Essentially the Fair Isle pattern is used to help you to pick-up the appropriate stitches and to place them on the correct needles.

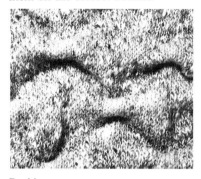

Ruching

To knit a sample
(1) Select a Fair Isle punch card (card 1 will do). Inset it into the machine and lock it on row 1.
(2) Cast-on over 60 st. and knit several rows. C.O.R.
(3) Thread up with Col. A and Col. B. in feeder A and B and commence Fair Isle knitting. C.O.R.
(4) Knit 20 rows.
(5) Pick up with your triple transfer tool the loops from the first row knit in Fair Isle below needles 60, 59, 58 and place these stitches onto needles 53, 52, 51. Repeat to loops below needles 50, 49, 48, onto needles 43, 42, 41, etc.
(6) Re-thread the machine with Col. C and Col. D. in feeders A. and B. Knit 20 rows. C.O.R.
(7) This time, pick up with your triple transfer tool, the loops from the first row knit in Fair Isle in Col. C. and D. below needles 53, 52, 51, and place them onto needles 58, 59, 60. Repeat across the row.

Continue to knit this pattern. As you can see, the pattern can be varied by:
• changing the card (or locking the card to get stripes);
• changing the colours; changing the number of rows knit between each 'picking up';
• changing the stitches picked up or where they are placed.

Ruched effect in a single colour

To adapt some hand knitted stitch patterns you can 'mark' the stitches you wish to pick up by pushing them to holding position for one row. Then they will be easier to see when you have continued to knit several rows and wish to go back to collect them.

Decorative braids

To knit a sample 'Punto a Onde'
(1) Cast-on 40 st. Knit several rows. C.O.R.
(2) Starting from the L. push needles 16,15,8,7,1,2,9,10,17,18 to H.P. Set the carriage not to knit needles in H.P.
(3) Knit one row. C.O.L. Re-set the carriage to knit all needles (or push needles in H.P. back to U.W.P.).
(4) Knit three rows. C.O.R. Starting from the L. push needles 12, 11; 4, 3; 5, 6; 13, 14 to H.P. Set the carriage not to knit needles in H.P.
(5) Knit one row. C.O.L. Re-set the carriage to knit all needles (or

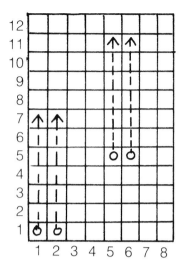

Pick-up diagrams for ruched effect

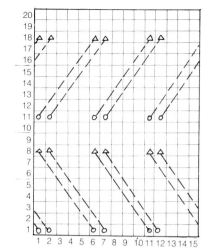

Pick-up diagrams for ruched effect

push needles in H.P. back to U.W.P.).

(6) Knit one row. C.O.R. Pick up the first tucked stitches onto the same needles you push forward to H.P. (i.e. needles 16,15; 8,7; etc.).

(7) Knit four rows. Pick up the second tucked stitches onto the same needles (i.e. needles 12, 11; 4, 3; etc.).

(8) Complete the stitch pattern by knitting two more rows. Then repeat the whole procedure again.

There are some additional diagrams for variations on the theme. With a little experimenting you can think up your own.

Decorative hems

By using contrast colours and picking up whole rows of stitches you can achieve many, varied decorative effects. Some of the variations can be achieved by:

• changing the colour of the hems;

• altering, or alternating the depth of the hems;

• altering the width of the hems and their position across the width of the knitting;

• making picot edges using the lace carriage;

• making scallops using tuck or pull-up stitch;

• altering the 'direction' of the hems by stitching them down afterwards.

To knit a sample

I

(1) Cast on 40 st. (20 × 20). K. 10 rows. C.O.R.

(2) Set carr. to H.P. Push 10 nds. at left of work (opposite end to carr.) to H.P.

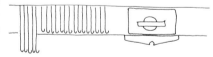

Sample 1. Step (2)

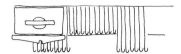

Sample 1. Step (3)

(3) K. one row. C.O.L. Push 10 nds. at right of work (opposite end to carr.) to H.P.

(4) Join contrast yarn. K. 10 rows on centre 20 nds. C.O.L.

(5) Pick up loops from first row of contrast yarn onto centre nds.

(6) Join M.Y. Push nds. at right side of work (opposite end to carr.) to U.W.P. K. one row.

(7) Set carr. to K. all nds. K. ten rows. Cast off.

II

(1) Cast on 40 st. (20 × 20). K. ten rows. C.O.R.

(2) Set carr. to H.P. Push 10 nds. at left of work (opposite end to carr.) to H.P.

(3) K. one row. C.O.L. Push 10 nds. at right of work (opposite end to carr.) to H.P.

(4) Join contrast yarn. *K. one row. C.O.R. Push one nd. at right hand end of centre group of working nds. to H.P. K. one row. C.O.L. Push one nd. at left hand end of centre group of working nds. to H.P. K. one row.*

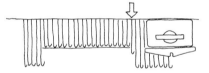

Sample 2. Step (4)

(5) Repeat from ★ to ★ ten times.

(6) Push centre 20 nds. carefully back to U.W.P. K. one row in con. yarn over these 20 nds.

Sample 2. Step (4)

(7) Pick up loops from 1st. row of contrast yarn onto centre nds.

(8) Join M.Y. Push nds. at right side

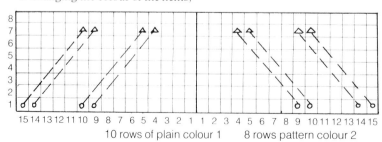

15 14 13 12 11 10 9 8 7 6 5 4 3 2 1 1 2 3 4 5 6 7 8 9 10 11 12 13 14 15

10 rows of plain colour 1   8 rows pattern colour 2

Pick-up diagrams for ruched effect

of work (opposite end to carr.) to U.W.P. K. one row.

(*9*) Set carr. to K. all nds. K. ten rows. Cast off.

III

(*1*) Cast on 40 st. (20 × 20). K. ten rows. C.O.R.

(*2*) Set carr. to H.P. Push ten nds. at left of work (opposite end to carr.) to H.P.

(*3*) K. one row. C.O.L. Push ten nds. at right of work (opposite end to carr.) to H.P.

(*4*) Join contrast yarn. *K. one row. C.O.R. Push one nd. at left hand end of centre group of working nds. (opposite end to carr.) to H.P. At the same time (taking the wool under) wrap the last nd. at the left of the right hand group of nds. in H.P. (The group at the same end as the carr.)

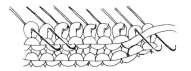

Sample 3. Step (*4*): wrapping the yarn under the last needle in H.P.

(*5*) K. one row. C.O.L. Push one nd. at opposite end of centre group of working nds. to H.P. At the same time wrap (take the wool under) the last nd. at the right of the left hand group of nds. in H.P. (The group at the same end as the carr.)*

(*6*) Repeat from * to * until five nds. left in W.P. in centre of work.

(*7*) **At opposite end of working group of nds. to carr. push one nd. back to U.W.P. K. one row.**

(*8*) Repeat from ** to ** until all centre 20 nds. are back in W.P.

(*9*) Pick up loops from first row of contrast yarn onto centre nds.

(*10*) Join M.Y. Push nds. at right side of work (opposite end to carr.) to U.W.P. K. one row.

(*11*) Set carr. to K. all nds. K. ten rows. Cast off.

Decorative braids

Pull-up stitches can be used to make decorative braids that simulate cables.

'Hearts'

To knit a sample –

Hearts

(*1*) Cast-on 'E' wrap over 12 needles, (six either side of O).

(*2*) Knit 10 rows.

(*3*) Pick up one edge stitch from either side of the strip ten rows below the needles and place these two stitches onto the centre two needles.

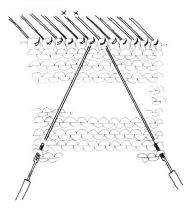

'Hearts'. Step (*3*)

(*4*) Repeat steps (*2*) and (*3*) until the desired length of braid is reached, picking up the edge stitches every ten rows.

A variation is to change the colour or texture of your yarn every ten rows as well. The advantage of this is that it then becomes easier to see which stitches to pick up.

'z'

(*1*) Cast-on 'E' wrap over 10 needles.

(*2*) Knit 12 rows.

(*3*) From the first row pick up the two stitches below needles 1 and 2. Lift these stitches up and place them onto needles 9 and 10 at the right edge of the work.

(*4*) Knit 10 rows. From 10 rows below, pick up the loops of the stitches under needles 9 and 10. Place them onto needles 1 and 2 at the edge of the work.

8 Knit-in beads

Beaded knitting is very fashionable, but if you have to sew the beads onto the finished garment this can be very time-consuming and the beads may not be totally secure. If you can thread the beads onto the knitting itself as you go along it has several advantages. It gives a more permanent finish and it is quicker and easier to do.

In the methods listed below, the first three embed the bead into the knitting in such a way that it can be clearly viewed from either side of the fabric. With the weaving method and attaching the bead to a slip stitch float, the bead will appear only on the purl side of the knitting.

The two major considerations when choosing beads which will determine the best method for inserting them into the knitting are the size of the hole and the size of the bead.

Crochet-hook method

The hole in the bead must be large enough to accommodate a 6mm or 7.5mm crochet hook. The bead must be small enough for the sinker plate of the carriage to pass over it when knitting the row without jamming or damaging the bead.

Crochet-hook method. Step (*1*)

(*1*) Put the bead onto the crochet hook.
(*2*) Put the crochet hook into the stitch where you wish the bead to go.

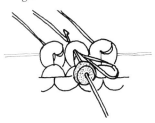

Crochet-hook method. Step (*2*)

(*3*) Push the needle of the stitch forward, then back by pushing the needle butt with your free hand. The stitch will fall onto the crochet hook.

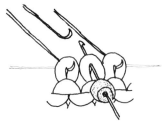

Crochet-hook method. Step (*3*)

(*4*) With the crochet hook, pull the stitch through the bead.

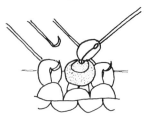

Crochet-hook method. Step (*4*)

(*5*) Lift the stitch back onto the needle. You may find it easier to push the transfer tool through the stitch, remove the crochet hook, then use the transfer tool to re-place the stitch onto the needle.

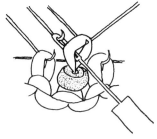

Crochet-hook method. Step (*5*)

Crochet-hook method with a large bead

If the bead is too big for the carriage to knit the row after the insertion of the bead try the following.

(*1*) On the row *before* you wish to insert the bead, transfer the stitch where the bead will go to the adjacent needle. Leave the needle in W.P. On the next row the needle will pick up a loop of yarn.
(*2*) Put the bead onto the crochet hook.
(*3*) Put the crochet hook into the loop of yarn on the needle.
(*4*) Push the needle of the loop forward, then back by pushing the needle butt with your free hand. The loop will fall onto the crochet hook.
(*5*) With the crochet hook, pull the yarn through the bead.

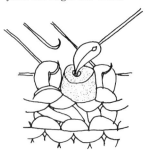

Crochet-hook method with a large bead. Step (*5*)

(*6*) Lift the loop back onto the needle. You may find it easier to push the transfer tool through the loop, remove the crochet hook, then use the transfer tool to re-place the yarn onto the needle. (You will find the hole from the row below will help to accommodate the larger bead.)

Beads applied with a needle and thread

Sometime you may find that the hole in the bead is too small for a crochet hook or that the smallest crochet hook will split the yarn when you pull it through the hole in the bead. Although this method seems to take a little longer, it is certainly just as effective.

(*1*) Thread up an ordinary needle with ordinary sewing cotton but do not break the cotton off the reel.
(*2*) Thread up all the beads you will require and leave them on the sewing cotton between the needle and the spool.

Beads applied using sewing cotton. Step (*2*)

(*3*) Put the sewing needle into the stitch where you wish the bead to go.
(*4*) Push the needle of the stitch forward, then back by pushing the needle butt with your free hand. The stitch will fall onto the sewing needle. Pull the needle and thread through the stitch.

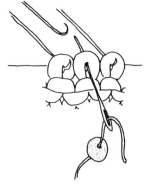

Beads applied using sewing cotton. Step (*4*)

(*5*) Thread the sewing needle *back* through the bead (*a*) and pull the stitch through behind it (*b*).
(*6*) Push the transfer tool into the stitch that you have pulled through the bead.

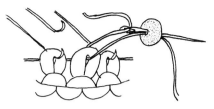

Beads applied using sewing cotton.
Step (*5a*)

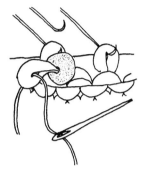

Beads applied using sewing cotton.
Step (*5b*)

(*7*) Remove the sewing needle and thread from the stitch.
(*8*) Lift the stitch back onto the needle.

Weaving in beads

This is a useful technique when dealing with larger or oddly-shaped beads.

(*1*) Thread all the beads onto a separate strong strand of cotton, silk or yarn.
(*2*) Select needles to H.P. or U.W.P. (set carriage to knit all needles). (You can use either manual selection or a punch card.)
(*3*) Lay the thread with the beads on it across the needles, spacing the beads out across your work. If necessary, weave the thread above and below the needles and pull the large beads down below the needles so that they will not

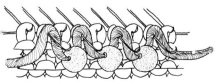

Weaving-in beads. Step (*3*)

interfere with the passage of the carriage.
(*4*) Knit 1 row. Then neaten up the work by gently pulling on the woven cord with the beads on it.

Using floats to insert beads

If you knit a row in slip, part or empty and have floats across a row of your knitting, you can pull these floats through the beads you wish to apply with either a crochet hook or a needle and thread and then lift the float onto a convenient needle.

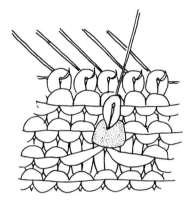

Using floats to insert beads

9 Intarsia

Intarsia is a manual technique that produces a very striking result. Remember that it is a time-consuming technique, requiring much patience. In return for your effort you can achieve:

- patterns that are larger than the standard 24 repeat;
- more than two colours in one row; and
- no floats (strands of yarn carried across the back of the work). To achieve this you must have a separate bobbin of yarn for every area of colour in your pattern.

When planning an intarsia pattern there are several golden rules to follow.

(*1*) Keep the different coloured areas as simple as possible in shape.
(*2*) Make the shapes as large as the

pattern will allow as they are easier to knit and more effective.
(*3*) Keep the colour changes in any one row to a minimum. The fewer the colour changes, the easier the pattern will be to knit and the fewer the ends will be to finish off afterwards.

Pattern drafting for picture knitting

With simple intarsia patterns you will not necessarily need to draft a pattern. If you are knitting simple shapes such as squares or triangles you will be able to knit these into your garment shape without having to follow a graphed pattern. For more complicated pictures such as animal motifs or large single motifs you can follow either option **I** or **II**.

I
Draw the picture on your pattern attachment (knit leader, knit radar, knit tracer, etc.) and use it as a guide when knitting the garment. You must make a tension square first using the main garment yarn so that you can set up your attachment properly. For a full shape and full scale attachment, i.e. the Jones/Brother K.L. 116, or K.L. 113, draw the pattern out as you wish it to appear on the knitting.

For a full shape and half scale attachment, i.e. the Knitmaster Knit Radar, draw the pattern of your garment out full size but half scale on your pattern sheet. Then you can draw your picture where and how you wish to knit it.

For a half shape and full scale attachment, i.e. the Jones/Brother KH 881, 891 with built-in Knitleader, Toyota Knit Tracer or the Knitmaster Knit Radar. This attachment only relates to half the needle bed (assuming that your knitting will be symmetrical) and you must either: (*i*) draw the picture out in full on tracing paper, then fold the paper in half. Transpose one half of the picture onto the patterning sheet in one colour ink, and the other half of the pattern in a contrast coloured ink. (*ii*) Draw the picture out in full on the pattern sheet and move your stitch

An intarsia drawing

Needles arranged for intarsia knitting.

gauge along so that the O on the gauge will correspond to the centre of your picture.

An intarsia drawing folded in half for a half size pattern attachment

For a half shape, and half scale attachment use a Knitmaster Knitleader or Passap Forma. You will have to repeat the procedure as described for the half shape and full scale attachment above but you will have to carry it out to half the scale – that is, draw the garment shape half scale and then draw the picture on it in half scale as well.

II
Draft your pattern onto graph paper and follow the pattern row by row as you would if you were hand knitting.

The important thing to remember when designing an intarsia or picture pattern is that squared graph paper does not give a true representation of your knitted fabric. Stitches are not square. They are short and fat, and you will require knitters' graph paper. Otherwise, you must remember to elongate your picture if you are using common squared paper.

Intarsia knitting

There are two ways of doing intarsia knitting. These depend on the type of machine you have and whether or not you have an intarsia carriage as an attachment.

Simple Intarsia
To do simple intarsia you merely bring all your needles forward and place the coloured yarn required into the needle hooks.

Bond machines – You must bring the needles to U.W.P. manually.

Jones/Brother push button machines 710 – You must turn the knob on the carriage to M.C. This will make the carriage leave the needles in the correct position after the row has been knitted. To knit the yarn that has been layed in you must push the part buttons.

Intarsia carriage – This is an attachment for automatic (punch card and electronic) machines and an alternative setting on the main carriage for the Jones/Brother KH 230. It will automatically leave the needles in the correct position for laying in the intarsia yarn when the row has been knitted. To lay the yarn onto the needles follow these steps.

(*1*) Always start laying your yarn from the carriage side of your work.

(*2*) Always bring the following yarn from behind the last yarn you laid in, thus twisting the two yarns where they meet. This will prevent holes forming in your work.

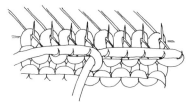

Yarn laid in needle hooks to prevent holes forming between two colours

(*3*) Leave all your yarns in front of your work so they are readily available.

You may find that lightly weighting the yarn or putting it under tension organizes your intarsia yarn by tensioning it. Use any of the following methods.

• Hanging bobbin weights on the

yarn or accessories that come with some intarsia carriages
- Using bull-dog clips on the yarn with small weights tied to them.
- Using an intarsia yarn break, which is an attachment that fits onto the front of your machine and automatically organizes and lightly tensions your intarsia yarn.

The yarn will twist when you are working in one direction and then untwist when you are coming back in the other direction.

Intarsia on Automatic Machines without an Intarsia Carriage
On these machines you cannot bring the needles forward and lay in the various yarns across the needle hooks. The carriage will not knit the yarns, and all your stitches will drop off. There is, however, a way to knit several colours in one row manually.
(*1*) Make sure the automatic needle selection system is not connected.
- Knitmaster: push side levers forward.
- Jones/Brother: carriage change knob to N.L.
- Toyota: card lever forward to O
(*2*) Set the carriage to slip/part/ empty.
(*3*) Push only the needles required to knit one colour to U.W.P. or H.P. (set carriage to knit all needles in H.P.).
(*4*) Thread-up the carriage and hand feed the yarn.
(*5*) Take the carriage across to knit only those needles selected.
(*6*) Bring the carriage back again, unthreading the yarn, and repeat the procedure for the next coloured yarn. Remember the next yarn must be brought behind the first yarn then up into the feeder, thus twisting the two yarns where they meet.

Jones/Brother intarsia feeder
This is a special feeder that can replace the feeder gate on the automatic machines. It combines a plaiting facility with a more open feeder which enables you to identify the

number of the needle as it pulls through the loop of yarn. If you concentrate very hard and watch very carefully through the feeder gap you can manually change the colour of your yarn as the carriage moves across the row. You may find it very difficult and opt to combine the easy-threading facility of this feeder with the part knitting technique described above.

10   The garter bar

The garter bar is designed to be used on a 4.5mm gauge machine. This means that the eyelets are 4.5mm apart. If you have a chunky machine where the needles are 9mm apart you will find for most things the garter bar will work equally well. The garter bar has several components as described below.
The Bar – You will find it in three sections. One of them has a clip at the end to enable you to clip it to the other short or long section depending on your requirements. It is wisest to use the smallest possible set-up as it can be rather unwieldy.

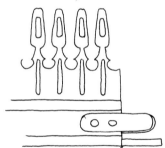

The clip for attaching two sections of the garter bar together

Needle stopper plates – There are two needle stopper plates, and their job is to keep the needles in H.P. when they have been selected there. They are adjustable. You push your needles to H.P. and place the stopper plates over the needle butts. The teeth of the plates should rest neatly over the gate pegs. If they do not, you must loosen the screws and adjust them so that they fit securely over the needle butts in H.P. and the gate pegs.

Sponge bar and clips – The Jones/ Brother garter bar has a sponge bar and clips to help with vertical weaving.

The garter bar has quite a few uses; it is easiest to use if you can remove the ribber, thus giving you easy access to the needle bed.

To reverse the work: garter stitch

(*1*) When you are ready to reverse your knitting, unthread the carriage and use the slip/part/empty setting to move the carriage to the opposite side of the needle bed without dropping your stitches or pushing the needles to H.P.
(*2*) Push all needles forward to H.P. and push the knitting back against the needle bed. You can put your needle stopper plates on at this point. Make sure all the latches are open by running your finger or a tool along the needle hooks.

Needle stopper plate in place on the needle bed

(*3*) Lower the garter bar onto the needle hooks with the grooves on the bar below the eyelets facing upward (facing you). Make sure

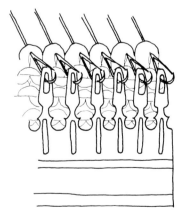

Garter bar on needles pulled out with stitches behind the needle latches

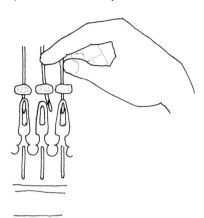

Manually adjusting the needle

all eyelets are engaged. If an eyelet has missed a needle, press down on the needle with your finger and move it sideways, under the eyelet until it is caught in the eyelet hole.

(4) Reach under the bar and pull the work towards you over the closed latches and onto the bar eyelets. Pull the stitches down past the hooks at the base of each eyelet.

(5) Lift the garter bar up, pushing the needle latches open and back with the teeth of the garter bar eyelets.

Reversing the work. Step (5)

(6) Rotate the bar so that the other side of the work is facing you. Make sure the knitting yarn is not caught up behind the bar.

(7) Make sure all needle latches are open again by running your finger or a tool along the needle hooks.

(8) Settle the grooves below the eyelets onto the open needle hooks. To ascertain whether or not the hooks are resting in the grooves, you may rock the bar gently from side to side. You will

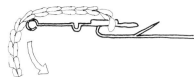

Reversing the work. Step (8)

notice the needles also moving from side to side.

(9) Pull the bar gently towards you. Although you cannot see it happening, the hooks of the needles will engage the loops of the stitches. It helps to have your knitting weighted.

(10) When you feel the stitches are caught on the needles, carefully swivel the bar around and down, still pulling the bar away from the needles and gently towards you. Slip the eyelets out of the stitch loops. Be extra careful not to slip the garter bar over the needles.

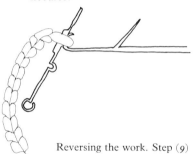

Reversing the work. Step (9)

(11) Re-thread your carriage and re-move the needle stopper plates before recommencing your knitting

Making a row of holes (lace work) or making cables

(1) Arrange your needles and stitches so that you can transfer selective-ly onto the garter bar.

Method A
Bring forward to hold position those needles from which you wish to trans-fer stitches. The stitches on these needles will slip behind the latches. Push these needles back gently. At the same time bring forward the remain-ing needles whose stitches are still in front of the latches (in the needle

hooks). Try to keep all latches for all needles *open*. Align the needles.

Method B
Push the needles forward so that the stitches push the needle latches open. Pull the needles of the stitches you wish to transfer slightly forward so that those stitches *only* fall behind the open latches. Align all needles care-fully (this is difficult) so *all* latches are still open, some needles with stitches behind the latches, some with stitches still in the needle hooks.

(2) With the grooves of the garter bar facing upwards, place the eyelets of the garter bar carefully into the hooks of the needles. Pull the work forward so that the stitches that are behind the open latches are pulled onto the garter bar. The stitches that were on the needle hooks in front of the latches will remain on the machine.

(3) Swivel the garter bar so that the eyelets point upward and the stitches that were transferred slip down towards the base of the bar.

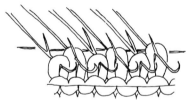

Making a row of holes. Method B. Some stitches are in front of the latches and some are behind the latches.

(4) Move the bar horizontally along the machine so that the eyelets of the bar with the stitches you wish to transfer are aligned with the

Pushing some stitches (selectively) from the bar back onto the needles.

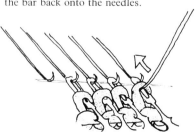

needles you wish to transfer the stitches onto.

(5) Hook the eyelets of the bar onto the needles and transfer stitches selectively using your finger or a transfer tool to push the stitches onto the needles.

Reducing stitches evenly across the row

There are two methods and you must practise both to find out which method suits you best.

Method A: Decrease stitches before using the garter bar –

(1) Decide how many stitches you need to lose. Transfer these stitches, spacing the transfers evenly across the needle bed. Push the empty needles back to N.W.P.

(2) Knit one row on all remaining needles in W.P. (You can knit this row using a cast-on cord if you wish, then unravel it after the decreasing has been completed.)

(3) Push all needles to H.P. Insure all latches are open. Place the garter bar eyelets onto the needle hooks and pull the work onto the bar. When you remove the bar from the needles try to lift it up in such a way as to push the needle latches open again.

(4) Leave in H.P. the number of needles you will require for the new number of stitches. (Push back to N.W.P. at the edge of the work the number of needles that correspond to the number of stitches you decreased.)

(5) Starting at one edge of your work,

Reducing stitches evenly across the row Step (5) some garter bar eyelets are empty.

engage the garter bar eyelets and transfer the stitches onto the needles in groups using a transfer tool as a pusher or your finger. When you come to an empty eyelet on the bar, lift it up and move it along so that when you have completed the transferring, there are no empty needles.

(6) You can then unravel the cast-on cord if you used it. If not just continue knitting.

Method B: decrease the stitches after transferring work to the garter bar –

(1) Push all needles to H.P. Ensure all latches are open. Place the garter bar eyelets onto the needle hooks and pull the work onto the bar. When you remove the bar from the needles try to lift the bar up in such a way as to push the needle latches open again.

(2) Leave in H.P. the number of needles you will require for the new number of stitches. (Push back to N.W.P. at the edge of the work the number of needles that correspond to the number of stitches you decreased.)

(3) Starting at one edge of your work, engage the garter bar eyelets so that the first eyelet with a stitch is engaged by the first needle in W.P. and transfer the stitches onto the needles in groups using a transfer tool as a pusher or your finger.

(4) You will have to place two stitches onto one needle at regular intervals across the row as you are returning the stitches to the needles. Plan to do this at regular intervals, moving the bar horizontally along the needle bed so that you will have two stitches on one needle and no stitches left on the bar when you come to the end of the needles in W.P.

Increasing evenly across the row

This is done in much the same way as you decreased in method B above – that is, you will remove the work onto the bar and then have to replace the

stitches in groups, leaving enough extra needles in W.P. across the row to widen your knitting.

(1) Push all needles to H.P. Ensure all latches are open. Place the garter bar eyelets onto the needle hooks and pull the work onto the bar. When you remove the bar from the needles try to lift the bar up in such a way as to push the needle latches open again.

(2) Push up to W.P. the number of needles corresponding to the number of stitches you wish to add.

(3) Starting at one edge of your work, engage the garter bar eyelets and transfer the stitches onto the needles in groups using a transfer tool as a pusher or your finger. You will have to move the bar along so that some needles are *empty*. Try to space out the *extra* empty needles evenly across the row.

(4) To avoid holes pick up the heel of the stitch next door to the empty needle and place it onto the empty needle.

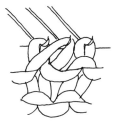

Picking-up the heel of the stitch next door

The use of the garter bar to 'hold' stitches

The garter bar can be an invaluable aid for taking stitches off the machine and, because it hangs perfectly on the gate pegs of the 4.5mm standard gauge machine it will prevent the marking of your work. It is a real boon and it is especially useful when you are knitting light coloured yarns.

(1) Push the needles for the stitches you wish to remove forward to H.P. so that the stitches fall behind the latches. Hang a transfer tool onto the hook of the last

needle in W.P. (next to the needles you have pushed forward).

(2) Place the eyelets of the garter bar onto the needles in H.P. and pull the work gently forward onto the bar. Be careful not to lose the remaining stitches.

(3) Swivel the bar so that the eyelets are pointing upwards. Slip the eyelets between the gate pegs of the needle bed. The garter bar will remain there and not interfere with the movement of the carriage.

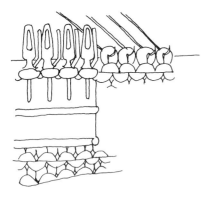

Hanging the garter bar on the gate pegs

The garter bar as an aid to vertical weaving

To use the garter bar as an aid to vertical weaving you will need:

- one bobbin or ball of yarn for every vertical woven thread;
- a section (or sections) of the garter bar which will be long enough to cover the width of the fabric you wish to weave;
- The sponge bar and clips.

To thread up the garter bar –

(1) Hold the bar with the eyelets pointing upwards and the grooves below the eyelets on the side of the bar *away* from you.

(2) Take your latch tool and pull one strand of yarn through each eyelet according to the diagram for your chosen weaving pattern.

(3) When you have finished threading up the required eyelets, tie the ends together securely into a knot. Pull the knot so that you have approximately 40–60cm

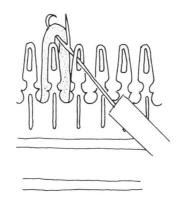

Threading up the eyelets

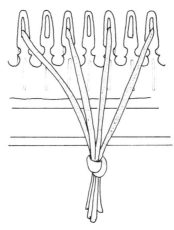

Several different yarns threaded up at the same time

(16–24in.) of weaving yarn between the knot and the eyelets.

(4) Turn the bar over so that hollows of the grooves below the garter bar eyelets are now facing you.

(5) Place the sponge bar on top of the garter bar so that it catches and firmly holds the weaving yarn down beneath it. Attach the clips to hold the bar (and yarn) firmly in place.

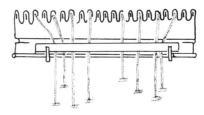

Weaving yarns held by the sponge bar and clips

(6) You are now ready to begin weaving. You can attach a weight to the weaving yarn knot to hold it down for the first row of weaving, but after you have knit-in the first row of weaving the weighting is unnecessary.

To weave –

(1) Push all needles to H.P. (or 'E' position).

(2) Bring the garter bar up from below the needle bed and up over the needles so that the yarn threaded through the eyelets passes between the needles.

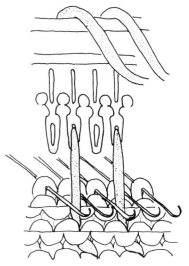

Garter bar lifting weaving yarns over selected needles

(3) Hold the bar up so that the weaving yarn passes over the stems of the needles and then down again between the needles again so that the yarn lies looped over the needle stems.

(4) Drop the bar below the needle bed so that it hangs there, held by the weaving yarns, while you proceed to knit the row.

Weaving patterns –

The weaving patterns are determined by:

- the sequence used when threading up the bar;
- the colours of yarn used when threading up the bar;
- the direction you move the bar when looping the weaving yarn over the needles.

Weaving patterns

These instructions are for the weaving patterns illustrated. To follow the threading and weaving directions please read the diagrams from left to right. All number sequences start at the left hand edge.

SAMPLE ONE

(1) *Main yarn*: Col. A. Weaving yarns: Col. B, Col. C.

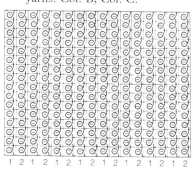

m.y. = white

1 = turquoise
2 = black

Sample 1

(2) *Threading up*:
   (a) Col. B. Eyelets 1, 3, 5, 7, 9, etc.
   (b) Col. C. Eyelets 2, 4, 6, 8, etc.
   All eyelets are threaded.
(3) *Method*:
   (a) Push all needles to 'E'.
   (b) Bring the bar up so that one strand of yarn passes between each needle.
   (c) Pass the bar over the top of the needles in a counter-clockwise direction and drop it down so that the yarn lies over the top wrapped around each needle in a counter-clockwise direction.
   (d) Knit one row.
   Repeat for pattern.

SAMPLE TWO

(1) *Main yarn*: Col. A. Weaving yarn: Col. B., Col. C., Col. D.
(2) *Threading-up*:
   (a) Col. B.; eyelets 3, 4, 12, 13, etc.
   (b) Col. C.; eyelets 5, 6, 14, 15, etc.
   (c) Col. D.; eyelets 7, 8, 16, 17, etc.
For the threading sequence 6 eyelets

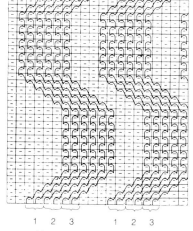

m.y. = white

1. turquoise
2. black
3. pink

Sample 2

are threaded and the following three eyelets are left empty.
(3) *Method*:
   (a) Loop the weaving yarn in a clockwise direction, starting with the first weaving yarn over needle 3. Knit 1 row.
   (b) Loop the weaving yarn in a clockwise direction but move the garter bar one needle to the right so that the first needle at the left with a loop of weaving yarn is needle 4. Knit 1 row.
   (c) Continue to loop the weaving yarn in a clockwise direction, moving the bar 1 needle to the right each time until you have knit 5 rows.
   (d) Loop the weaving yarn over the same needles in a counter clockwise direction. Knit 1 row.

(e) Loop the weaving yarn in a clockwise direction over the same needles. Knit 1 row.
(f) Repeat steps (d) and (e) until you have knit nine rows.
(g) Loop the weaving yarn in an anti-clockwise direction over the needles, moving the garter bar one needle to the left. Knit 1 row. Repeat until you have knit 5 rows.
(h) Repeat the straight weaving (i.e. steps (d) and (e)) The pattern repeat is over 30 rows.

SAMPLE THREE

(1) *Main Yarn*: Col. A. Weaving yarns; Col. B., Col. C., Col. D.
(2) *Threading up*:
   (a) Col. B.: eyelets 15, 16, 17, 18 23, 24, 25, 26.
   (b) Col. C.: eyelets 5, 6 19, 20, 21, 22.
   (c) Col. D.: eyelets 3,4 7,8.
For the threading sequence 6 eyelets are threaded up, 6 eyelets are empty, and the next 12 eyelets are threaded up.
(3) *Method*:
   (a) Loop the weaving yarn in an anti-clockwise direction starting with the first weaving yarn at the left over the third needle from the left. Knit 2 rows.
   (b) Take the garter bar under the needles and bring it up so that the yarn passes up between two needles further to the right of the first woven loops. Take the weaving yarns over the needles in an anti-clockwise direction and bring them down between the needles again. The first loop at the left is over the fifth

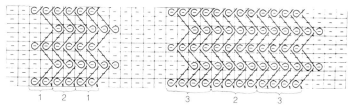

Sample 3. M.Y. = white; *1* = lime green; *2* = mid-purple; *3* = dark purple

needle from the left. Knit two rows.

(c) Repeat steps (a) and (b) to knit the pattern. This pattern is a four row repeat.

SAMPLE FOUR

(1) *Main yarn:* Col. A. Weaving yarn: Col. B.

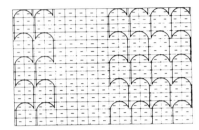

Sample 4. M.Y. = red weaving yarn, white bouclé

(2) *Threading-up:*

(a) Col B.: eyelets 1,3 7,9,11,13. For the threading up sequence alternate eyelets are threaded, first a group of two followed by six empty eyelets, then a group of four alternate eyelets are threaded up.

(3) *Method:*

(a) Knit 4 rows.

(b) Take the weaving yarns up and over the needles in a clockwise direction so that the first weaving loop at the left falls over the first *two* needles at the left edge of the knitting. All weaving loops lie over the stems of *two* needles at once.

(c) Knit 4 rows.

(d) Take the weaving yarns up and over the needles in an anti-clockwise direction so that the first weaving loop at the left passes up between needles 2 and 3 at the left and then down past the left hand edge of the knitting. The first loop at the left lies over needles 2, then 1.

(e) Knit four rows.

Repeat this weaving sequence to knit the pattern. This pattern is an 8 row repeat.

SAMPLE FIVE

(1) *Main yarn:* Col. A. Weaving yarn; Col. B., Col. C., Col. D.

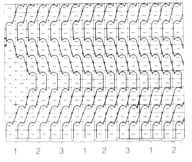

Sample 5. M.Y. = white; *1* = turquoise; *2* = gold; *3* = black

(2) *Threading up:*

(a) Col. B.: eyelets 1, 2, 7, 8, 13, 14, etc.

(b) Col. C.: eyelets 3, 4, 9, 10, 15, 16, etc.

(c) Col. D.: eyelets 5, 6, 11, 12, 17, 18, etc.

All eyelets are threaded up two by two by two in colour sequence.

(3) *Method:*

(a) Knit 2 rows.

(b) Loop the weaving yarn over the needles in a clockwise direction so that the first weaving yarn at the left lies over the first needle at the left-hand edge of the knitting. Knit 2 rows.

(c) Loop the weaving yarn over the needles in a clockwise direction so that the first weaving yarn at the left lies over the *second* needle from the left-hand edge of the knitting. You are moving the garter bar *one* needle to the *right* every time you loop the yarn. Knit 2 rows.

(d) Repeat this looping of the weaving yarns with the first loop lying over the *third* needle from the left. Knit 2 rows.

(e) Loop the weaving yarn over the same needles as you did in step (d) this time in an anti-clockwise direction. Knit 2 rows.

(f) Continue to weave after two rows of knitting, looping the yarn over the needles in an anti-clockwise direction and always moving one needle to the *left* three times.

Repeat this sequence to knit the pattern. The pattern repeats every 14 rows.

SAMPLE SIX

(1) *Main yarn:* ten rows Col. A. and ten rows Col. B. Weaving yarn: Col. C. and Col. D.

(2) *Threading up:*

(a) Col. C.: eyelets 1–8, 17–24, etc.

(b) Col. D.: eyelets 9–16 25–32, etc.

All eyelets are threaded up in groups of eight to a colour.

(3) *Method:*

(a) Knit 2 rows.

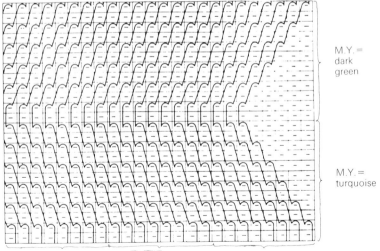

M.Y. = dark green

M.Y. = turquoise

white   green   white   Sample 6

(b) Loop the weaving yarn up and over the needles in an anti-clockwise direction so that the first weaving loop at the left lies over the first needle at the left-hand edge. Knit 2 rows.

(c) Continue to weave, looping the yarns over the needles in an anti-clockwise motion, always starting one needle further to the left. Loop the yarns after two rows knitting.

(d) Repeat this five times. (Knit 10 rows.) Change the main yarn. Knit 2 rows.

(e) Loop the weaving yarns over the same needles this time in a clockwise direction.

(f) Now continue to loop the weaving yarn over the needles in a clockwise direction, always moving the yarns one needle to the right.

Repeat to knit the pattern. The pattern repeat is 20 rows.

SAMPLE SEVEN

This sample will require a length of dowling to produce the 'loops'.

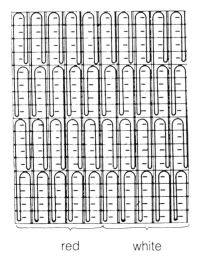

red   white

Sample 7. M.Y. = white

Alternatively, you could try holding your cast-on comb underneath the needles to catch the weaving yarn and hold it looped down.

(1) *Main yarn:* Col. A. Weaving yarn: Col. B., Col. C.

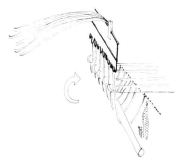

Using a dowel to get looped weaving

(2) *Threading up:*
   (a) Col. B.: eyelets 1–5, 11–15, etc.
   (b) Col. C.: eyelets 6–10, 16–20, etc.

All eyelets are threaded up in groups of five needles in colour sequence.

(3) *Method:*
   (a) Knit 4 rows.
   (b) Loop the weaving yarns up and over the needles in an anti-clockwise direction, then bring them down and either hang a piece of dowelling onto the weaving yarns or hang the hooks of the cast-on comb onto weaving yarns to hold them down.
   (c) Knit 4 rows. Loop the weaving yarns (down under the dowelling/comb) then up and over the needles in a clockwise direction.

Repeat to knit pattern. The pattern repeat is eight rows. The distance you bring the weaving yarn loops down under the needles before you take them over the needles again should be constant to achieve a neat tidy fabric.

SAMPLE EIGHT

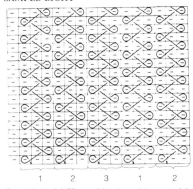

          1   2   3   1   2

Sample 8. M.Y. = white bouclé; *1* = gold; *2* = brown; *3* = orange

(1) *Main yarn:* Col. A. Weaving yarn: Col. B., Col. C., Col. D.

(2) *Threading up:*
   (a) Col. B.: eyelets 1, 10, etc.
   (b) Col. C.: eyelets 4, 13, etc.
   (c) Col. D.: eyelets 7, 16, etc.

Every third eyelet is threaded up. Two eyelets are empty between every threaded up eyelet.

(3) *Method:*
   (a) Loop the weaving yarns up and over the needles in an anti-clockwise direction. The first loop of yarn at the left lies over the second needle from the left edge of the knitting. Knit one row.
   (b) Loop the yarn under the needles then bring the yarn up and over two needles to the right in a clockwise direction (thus completing a 'figure of eight' movement). The first loop of yarn at the left lies over the fourth needle from the left edge of the knitting. Knit one row.

Repeat this sequence to knit the pattern. The pattern repeat is over two rows.

Stitch patterns using the garter bar to turn the work

These are manually manipulated patterns combining other manual techniques such as pick-up stitches with garter stitch.

Pull-up top loop: fabric and stitch diagram
Pull-up bottom loop; fabric and stitch diagram

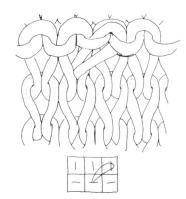

Pull-up stocking stitch loop; fabric and stitch diagram

(*1*) *One colour pull-up pattern* – 2st., 4rw. Repeat

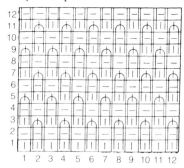

Sample 1

One colour pull-up pattern. Sample 1, front

K.1 rw. Turn
K.1 rw. Turn
Pick up the top loop
Sts. 2,4,6, etc. onto nds. 2,4,6, etc.

K.1 rw. Turn
K.1 rw. Turn
Pick up the top loop
Sts. 1,2,5, etc. onto nds. 1,3,5.

One colour pull-up pattern. Sample 1, back

(*2*) *Two colour pull-up pattern* – 6st., 8rw. repeat

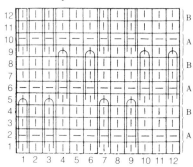

Sample 2

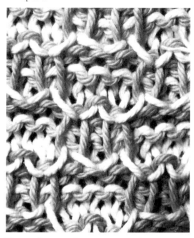

Two colour pull-up pattern. Sample 2

Col. A.
    K.1 rw. Turn
    K.1 rw. Turn
Col. B.
    K.2 rws.
    Pick up top loop of last row knit in Col. B. before
Col. A.
    Sts. 1&3, 7&9, etc. onto nds. 1&3, 7&9.
Col. A.
    K.1 rw. Turn
    K.1 rw. Turn
Col. B.
    K.2 rws.
    Pick up top loop of last row knit in Col. B. before Col. A. Sts. 4&6, 10&12, etc. onto nds. 4&6, 10&12

(*3*) *Two colour pull-up stitch pattern* – 2st., 8rw. repeat

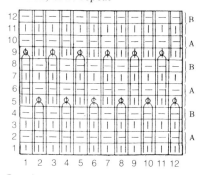

Sample 3

Two colour pull-up stitch pattern. Sample 3

Col. A.

  K.1 rw. Turn

  K.1 rw. Turn

Col. B.

  K.1 rw. Turn

  K.1 rw. Turn

  Pick up top loop and twist of last row knit in Col. B. before Col. A. Sts. 2,4,6, etc. onto nds. 2,4,6, etc.

Col. A.

  K.1 rw. Turn

  K.1 rw. Turn

Col. B.

  K.1 rw. Turn

  K.1 rw. Turn

  Pick up top loop and twist of last row knit in Col. B. before Col. A. Sts. 1,3,5, etc. onto nds. 1,3,5, etc.

(4) *Two colour pull-up stitch*

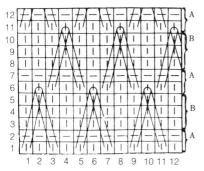

Sample 4

Col. A.

  K.1 rw. Turn

  K.1 rw. Turn

Col. B.

  K.3 rws.

  Pick up the top loop of the last row knit in Col. B. before Col. A. 1&3 onto nd. 2,5&7 onto nd. 6 etc.

Col. A.

  K.1 rw. Turn

  K.1 rw. Turn

Col. B.

  K.3 rws.

  Pick up the top loop of the last row knit in Col. B. before Col. A. Sts. 3&5 onto nd. 4;7&9 onto nd. 8 etc.

(5) *One colour pull-up stitch* – 6 sts., 8rw. repeat

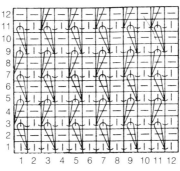

Sample 5

K.1 rw. Turn

K.1 rw. Turn

K.1 rw. Turn

K.1 rw. Turn

Pick-up bottom loop from row 1 as follows:

Bottom loop between 1 and 2 (1/2) onto nd. 1; bottom loop between 3/4 onto nd. 3; bottom loop between 5/6 onto nd. 5, etc.

K.1 rw. Turn

K.1 rw. Turn

K.1 rw. Turn

K.1 rw. Turn

Pick-up bottom loops from row 4 (3 rows below) as follows: Bottom loop 2/3 onto nd. 3, 4/5 onto nd. 5, 6/7 onto nd. 7, etc.

(6) *Two colour pull-up stitch* – 6st., 8rw. repeat

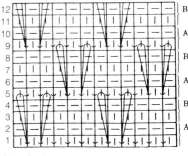

Sample 6

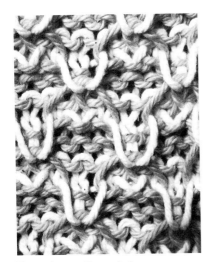

Two colour pull-up stitch pattern. Sample 4

One colour pull-up pattern. Sample 5

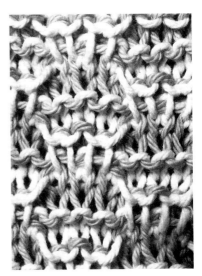

Two colour pull-up stitch pattern. Sample 6

Col. A.
  K.1 rw. Turn
  K.1 rw. Turn
Col. B.
  K.1 rw. Turn
  K.1 rw. Turn
  Pick up the bottom loops of the
  1st. row knit in Col. A. before
  the last group of rows knit in
  Col. B. as follows:
  Bottom loops 1/2 onto nd. 1,
  Bottom loops 3/4 onto nd. 3
  Bottom loops 7/8 onto nd. 7
  Bottom loops 8/9 onto nd. 9
  etc.
Col. A.
  K.1 rw. Turn
  K.1 rw. Turn
Col. B.
  K.1 rw. Turn
  K.1 rw. Turn
  Pick up the bottom loop of the
  first row knit in Col. A. before
  the last group of rows knit in
  Col. B. as follows:
  Loops 4/5 onto nd. 4,
  Loops 5/6 onto nd. 6,
  Loops 10/11 onto nd. 10,
  Loops 11/12 onto nd. 12 etc.

(7) *One colour pull-up stitch* – 6 st.,
  8rw. repeat

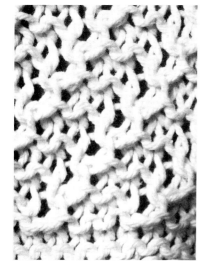

One colour pull-up stitch pattern.
Sample 7

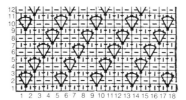

Sample 7

K.1 rw Turn
K.1 rw Turn
Pick up the bottom loops from
two rows below and share each
loop between two needles as
follows:
Loop 1/2 onto nds. 1/2
Loop 5/6 onto nds. 5/6 etc.
K.1 rw. Turn
K.1 rw. Turn
Pick up the bottom loops from
2 rows below and share each
between two needles as
follows:
Loop 2/3 onto nds. 2/3
Loop 6/7 onto nds. 6/7 etc.
K.1 rw. Turn
K.1 rw. Turn
Pick-up the bottom loops from
two rows below and share each
loop between two needles as
follows:
Loop 3/4 onto nds. 3/4
Loop 7/8 onto nds. 7/8
K.1 rw. Turn
K.1 rw. Turn
Pick up the bottom loops from
two rows below and share the
loop between two needles.
Loop 4/5 onto nds. 4/5
Loop 9/10 onto nds. 9/10 etc.

(8) *Two colour tuck stitch* – 4st., 8rw.
  repeat

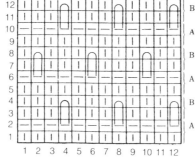

Sample 8

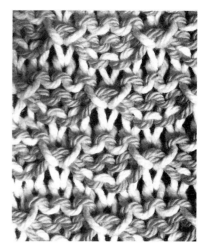

Two colour tuck stitch. Sample 8, front

Two colour tuck stitch. Sample 8, back

Col. A.
  K.1 rw. Turn
  K.1 rw. Turn
Col. B.
  Push needles 4,8,12, etc. to
  H.P. Set carriage not to knit
  needles in H.P.
  K.2 rws.
    Set carriage to knit all
  needles.
Col. A.
  K.1 rw. Turn
  K.1 rw. Turn
Col. B.
  Push needles 2,6,10, etc. to
  H.P. Set carriage not to knit
  needles in H.P.
  K.2 rws.
  Set carriage to knit all needles.

(9) *Two colour slip stitch pull-up pattern* – 2st., 4rw. repeat

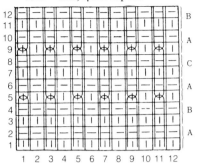

Sample 9

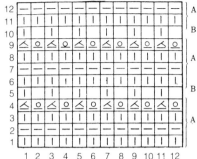

Sample 10

Two colour slip stitch pull-up pattern. Sample 9

Col. A.
K.1 rw. Turn
K.1 rw. Turn
Col. B.
K.1 rw. Turn
K.1 rw. Turn
Pick up the top loop of the last row knit in Col. B. before the rows knit in Col. A. as follows:
St. 1 onto nd. 1
St. 3 onto nd. 3
St. 5 onto nd. 5 etc.

(10) *Two colour lace pattern* – 2st., 5rw. repeat
Col. A.
K.1 rw. Turn
K.1 rw. Turn
K.1 rw. Turn
K.1 rw. Turn
Make a row of holes by transferring alternate stitches to ad-

Two colour lace pattern. Sample 10, front

Two colour lace pattern. Sample 10, back

jacent needles. Push empty needles to N.W.P.

Col. B.
K.1 rw.
Push all needles to W.P.

(11) *'E' wrap weaving stitch* – 2st, 4rw. repeat

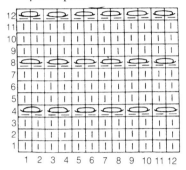

Sample 11

'E' wrap weaving stitch. Sample 11

Col. A.
K.3 rws. Turn
Push all needles to H.P.
'E' wrap a separate piece of yarn around two needles at a time across the row.
K.1 rw. Turn

(12) *Two colour pull-up stitch* – 6st., 8rw. repeat
Col. A.
K.1 rw. Turn
Col. B.
K.2 rws.
Pick up the top loop (stocking-stitch loop) from the last row knit in Col. B. before the row knit in Col. A.
St. 1,5,9 onto nds. 1,5,9, etc.
K.1 rw. Turn

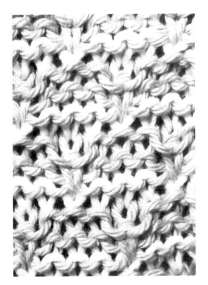

Two colour pull-up stitch. Sample 12

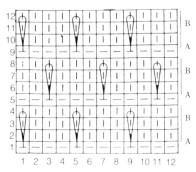

Sample 12

Col. A.
   K.1 rw. Turn
Col. B.
   K.2 rws.
   Pick up the top loop (stocking-stitch loop) from the last row knit in Col. B. before the row knit in Col. A.
   Sts. 3,7,11, onto nds. 3,7,11, etc.

11 Adding colour

There are two main ways of adding colour to the fabric after the garment has been knitted, which are explained below.

Swiss darning

In this technique you thread-up a wool darning needle with a *blunt* end with the coloured yarn you wish to add. You then sew the yarn into the knitting following the yarn of the stitch you wish to cover over with the new yarn. You can follow a chart for small areas but once you master the knack you will find it very easy. The disadvantage is that where you have swiss-darned, your fabric will be twice as thick because of the double stitches at this point.

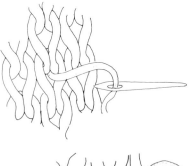

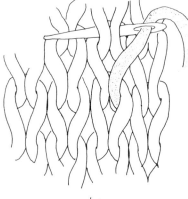

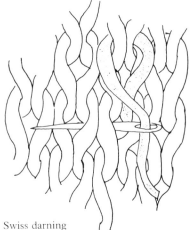

Swiss darning

Fabric dye

Nowadays there are many fabric dyes available, and you can use them to colour selected areas of your knitting. You can use the additional colour to liven up your fabric or to accentuate and highlight your stitch design. You can also use paints or crayons. You must be careful to find out the following information.

- Are the dyes you want to use effective on your yarn. Some acrylic yarns will not accept dye. Some dyes are only suitable for natural fibres.
- Does the particular dye require heat to 'fix' it (that is, stop it from bleeding or running). If heat is required, will it have a detrimental effect on your knitting?
- Will the colour of the dye take on the colour of your yarn. You will not be able to dye a very dark yarn to a lighter colour!

Dyes can be purchased from your local art or hobby shop. You will also find them in the haberdashery department of larger stores.

Using a sewing machine

A sewing machine can be used with manual techniques to create interesting effects on your knitted fabric, such as pleats or gathers, just as it would be used on woven fabric for dressmaking. You can also use the sewing machine to *add* to your knitted fabric.

Quilting

You can use the sewing machine to quilt knitted fabric. Use the stitch pattern to guide you when planning your quilting. If you have knitted a Fair Isle fabric, you can stitch around the Fair Isle shapes. You can also superimpose a quilting pattern onto plain knitting to achieve a quilted fabric.
(1) First wash and block your knitting. Carry out all quilting before assembling the garment.

Quilting

Appliqué

(2) Pin or tack the padding onto the back of your knitted fabric. You can use thin quilting wadding purchased from your local fabric shop. Make sure that the cleaning properties are the same as your yarn, e.g. if the yarn is washable, the wadding must be too.

(3) If you are not using the stitch pattern as a stitching guide for your quilting you will have to tack your machine stitching design in place.

(4) For the backing of your quilting you should use a stretchy fabric such as a fine jersey or knit a lining.

Appliqué

The sewing machine can be used to put appliqué onto your knitted fabric. You can apply any type of fabric to knitting – for example, woven fabric, leather or pieces of knitted fabric.

(1) You must wash and block your knitting first. Carry out all appliqué before assembling the garment.

(2) Prepare your appliqué. You can iron Vilene onto the wrong side of your appliqué and mark out the shape you require onto the Vilene before cutting it out and placing it onto your knitting. Alternatively, you may just mark out the shape you require and cut it out, leaving a small allowance around the edge of your shape. If you wish to pad your appliqué you may sew the padding onto the wrong side of your appliqué then trim the padding back to the edge of your appliqué shape.

(3) Position the appliqué carefully onto your knitting. Fix it to the knitting by sewing it or tacking it around the edge with a straight stitch. If you have backed your appliqué shape with padding and trimmed the padding back past the edge of your shape, sew down only the fabric shape. Be careful not to sew the padding or flatten it out when attaching the shape. You may do this on the sewing machine.

Cross-section view of padded appliqué

(4) Trim the appliqué shape back to the straight-stitch line.

(5) Carefully over-sew the edge of the shape with a wide, short zig-zag stitch on the sewing machine. You can place a thin piece of paper between the feed-dog (teeth) in the sole plate of the sewing machine and the knitting.

V Problems and Solutions

1 Preventing problems with patience

A knitting machine is rather like an animal. It seems to sense if you are nervous or frightened of it and, in a contrary way, it seems to take advantage of you. It is never a good idea to work on the machine when you are tired, anxious or fraught. Especially if you are a beginner you must never go at the machine like a bull in a china shop. You must learn to adopt a relaxed attitude. Never rush it; take your time. The machine will do the knitting quickly enough. If you find things are not going well, close your eyes, take a deep breath and then have another go. If you still find the work difficult, leave the machine and take a break. Go and have a cup of tea, or, if it's late, go to bed. Things that were difficult in the middle of the night will be crystal clear the morning after.

After a while you will find the carriage will 'speak' to you – that is, when you push the carriage across the needle bed you can feel through the handle if there are any difficult stitches. In other words the operation of the carriage will not be as smooth as you expect and will warn you when some problem has occurred.

The basic operation of forming knitted fabric on the machine is really quite simple but an ounce of prevention is worth a pound of cure. You must watch what you are doing when you are knitting – this is the most important ounce of prevention. Knowing how stitches are formed is essential too, so you know what to watch out for. The other important thing to remember is not to be in a hurry. The machine knits quite fast enough without you trying to hurry it along. Relax! Take your time and it will save you time in the long run.

When learning, always use medium weight, light coloured yarn. Never use fancy textured, dark coloured, stranded or cheap yarns. They are a false economy. Instead, buy yourself a wool winder. It will save you a fortune in the long run. You can save and reuse your practice yarn and you can often salvage a disastrous garment by unravelling it and reknitting it much quicker than you think.

Some golden rules for working at your knitting machine

(1) Never work late at night.
(2) Never work when you are overtired or anxious. It's much more efficient to go away and have another cup of tea first!
(3) Never work too long at the machine. You get stale and careless and cause more errors than you cure.
(4) Never work in poor light, on an unsuitable chair, or put your machine on an unstable stand or table. I heard of one woman who attached her machine to a trolley with wheels and then wondered why, every time she took the carriage across to knit a row, the whole machine went shooting off across the room!

2 Solving problems with know-how

As the machine forms stitches these are some of the important points to watch out for.

I

When the carriage pushes the needle forward the stitch may not go behind the latch because of one of the following:

A large stitch jumps off the needle

(a) The stitch (loop of yarn) is too big and jumps up off the needle.
(b) The stitch is not pulled down (the work is not weighted) and it jumps up off the needle.

A stitch not properly weighted jumps off the needle

(c) The brush wheels on the sinker plate (brush assembly/presser plate) are not working properly and are not pushing the stitches down and back behind the latches as the needles come forward. This may be because they are dirty and

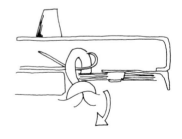

Brush wheels on the sinker/presser plate pushing the stitches behind the latches on the needles

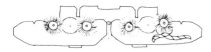

Yarn caught in the brushes underneath the sinker/presser plate

clogged up with yarn; they are broken; or the sinker plate is bent or out of alignment. The stitches then jump up off the needles. Alternatively, if there isn't enough knitting available for the brushes to push the stitches behind the latches, the stitches will jump off the needles. This fault commonly occurs when you cast on, and it can be avoided by your hanging a cast-on comb on the cast-on edge or by placing some waste knitting on the needles first and knitting one row with the cast-on cord before casting-on.

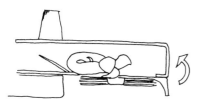

Stitches jumping up off the needles before the brushes can work properly

After casting on with the 'E' wrap or latch tool method the needle butts of the working needles may be carefully pushed forward with one hand while you hold the stitches below the needles back against the machine with the other hand.

II

The yarn must flow freely when the carriage places the working yarn into the hook of the needle. If the yarn is not in the right place in the yarn feeder of the carriage, the needle hook cannot catch the yarn to pull it back through the stitch that is now behind the latch. Thus when the needle is pulled by the carriage back to 'B' position, the stitch slips over the closed latch and drops. If the yarn is not in the right place to be pulled back by the working needle this may occur

because of one of the following problems.

(a) The yarn is not flowing freely *onto* the tension mast because the yarn is caught around the base of the cone; the ball is not wound correctly and the yarn is pulling; or the yarn is tangled or there is a knot which has become caught in the yarn brake (this often happens near the end of a ball of yarn).

(b) The tension mast has not been correctly threaded up, and the yarn is not flowing freely into the carriage. This happens if the yarn brake is too loose and the yarn flows too freely; or if the yarn brake is too tight and the yarn is pulled taut. If the yarn is pulled taut the stitches become too small and will not slip over the closed latches on the working needles. This may occur particularly at the edges of the knitting.

(c) The wires of the tension mast are entangled and are not tensioning the yarn properly; thus the slack yarn is pulled up at the end of the row. Alternatively, the carriage has been taken too far beyond the edge of the knitting, and there is too much slack yarn for the tension wires to really do their job properly. If the yarn is not pulled up taut at the edge of the knitting and it falls below the sinker plate before the carriage passes over the working needles, it may get caught in the sinker plate brushes.

(d) The yarn is lumpy and gets caught in the tension unit or on the sinker plate brushes.

(e) The yarn is too fluffy and gets caught on the gate pegs, sinkerplate brushes or in the tension unit. To minimize this problem the yarn can be waxed (winding it round an ordinary household candle). Shetland wool and wool mixtures are often sold 'ready waxed', or a small wax disc can be placed on the tension mast which waxes the yarn as it is used. A wax spray in an aerosol can is also available. Mohair can be put in the refrigerator to reduce the static electricity.

(f) The yarn must be fed correctly into the carriage. It must move freely in the yarn feeder unit.

(g) If the carriage is set incorrectly, stitches may be dropped. If it is set to knit Fair Isle or punch lace and there is only one yarn in the feeder the stitches will drop. The yarn may not be in the correct feeder.

III

The carriage pulls the needle back. The latch closes over the new loop of yarn and pulls it through the old stitch, which then slips over the closed latch and falls off the needle.

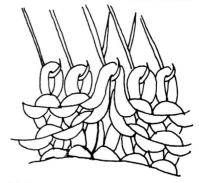

Stitches are pulled too tight to be able to pass over the closed latches

This problem may arise if the old stitch is too tight and won't pass over the closed latch. This may be because:

● the stitch size is too small;
● the yarn has been pulled tight either by the tension mast or because of faulty yarn feeding on the previous row when the stitch was formed;
● the hook of the needle or the latch is damaged and catches the yarn.

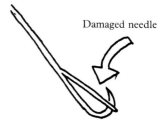

Damaged needle

IV

The machine will not knit patterns. This is because you have not pushed all the correct buttons or pulled all the correct levers. In this case *consult your manual*. It is surprising how one break in the chain will result in spaghetti! If you have forgotten even one small button you could have a disaster on your hands. You must try to understand the purpose or effect of each thing you do. Study your controls carefully and find out how each one works and what each one does.

There are basically *two* steps in pattern knitting. You must get the pattern to the needles. Then you must use your carriage so that it will knit the selected needles in the correct pattern.

(*1*) You must transfer the pattern information to the needles.

● Manually select the needles to patterning position.

● Pull the set lever after pushing the pattern buttons or inserting the punch card.

● Automatic machines (Jones/Brother, Toyota): connect the card to the needles by moving a button or lever on the carriage and then taking the carriage across the needle bed. This will set up the needles for patterning.

● Automatic machines (Knitmaster, Passap/Pfaff): take the carriage or the deco unit past the card reading mechanism so that the pattern drum in the carriage or in the deco unit registers the pattern information. Then connect the drums to the needles (or pushers) by moving the side levers on the carriage or the dial on the deco. This will mean that the next row knit will be knit in the pattern.

(*2*) Having registered the pattern information (whether it is on the needles, which you can easily see, or in the drums, which you can't), you must now tell the carriage what to do with the needles or pushers in the two selected (working and upper working) positions. You must push your patterning buttons or turn your pattern lever to make the carriage knit the needles in the selected pattern. If you have failed to register or transfer the pattern

information to the needles or failed to set the carriage properly you will not get the pattern knitting properly. You must also remember to *unlock* your pattern card if knitting on an automatic machine.

It is well worth while going over all the buttons, levers and knobs before you actually begin to knit. It is also a good idea to check carefully that the yarn is threaded-up properly, especially if you are knitting a pattern which requires you to add a new yarn (e.g. Fair Isle or weaving) or to change yarn frequently. If you are still having trouble with pattern knitting on automatic machines check carefully that you have passed:

● the card reading mechanism;

● the centre of the machine;

● far enough past the last needle in working position.

3 Unravelling, retrieving and resetting

The knitting of a garment is often no problem at all – it is quick, easy and effortless. It takes far less time to knit on the machine than it would if knit by hand, but solving a problem that arises often takes longer than knitting the garment itself (or at least one of the component pieces). It can sometime be quicker just stripping the knitting in question off and re-knitting the whole section rather than trying to correct the mistake! *Don't lose heart!* If you allow the machine to intimidate or frighten you, you will not master it. Take your time. Stop and *look carefully* at what has happened. Most important of all, be patient and don't lose your temper.

If you get stuck in the middle of a row –

(*1*) Lock the card or note the pattern row.

(*2*) Remove the sinker plate (presser plate, brush assembly, front of the carriage, or the strippers).

(*3*) Remove the carriage from the knitting. Consult your manual.

(*4*) Return all needles to W.P. If the

needles have been pushed forward far enough so that the stitches are now behind the open latches, you can return them to the needle hooks in front of the latches using the transfer tool. *Do not just push the needles back to W.P. If the stitches are behind the open latches they will drop off!*

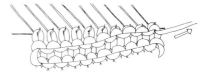

Yarn pulling tight at the end of a row of knitting

(*5*) Unravel the yarn(s) to the end of the row.

To unravel yarn –

(*1*) One row or part of a row. Pull the yarn sideways and parallel to the needle bed. 'Rock' the yarn until it jumps out of the needle hooks. Return the needles to W.P.

(*2*) Several rows: repeat (*1*) above, remembering to push needles firmly back to W.P. in between each row if the yarn pulls them forward. Alternatively, push all needles to H.P. but keep the work in the *hooks of the needles*. Don't let the stitches pass behind the open latches. Then pull the yarn firmly sideways, parallel to the needle bed, lifting it slightly. You will find that the stitches will unravel quite easily. NB This is easier to do without a ribber attached as it might interfere with the work when it is pulled forward.

To knit half a row –

If you become stuck mid-way across a row in plain knitting and you wish to continue without unravelling the half a row that has knit successfully, follow these precautions.

(*1*) Push all unknit needles to H.P. Push all the needles that have knit to W.P.

(*2*) Place the carriage on the same side as the needles which have been knit. Thread up the carriage carefully.

(*3*) (On the Knitmaster push side

levers forward – disconnecting the pattern drums) Set the carriage to part/slip/empty and set it to knit needles in H.P.

(*4*) Take the carriage across and only the needles in H.P. will knit.

To return all needles to W.P. if they are completely out of order –

(*1*) Knit one row with the cast-on cord and unravel the cast-on cord row *or*

(*2*) return all needles manually with the transfer tool.

To return to pattern knitting – you must have your work on the machine and all needles in W.P. Firstly, return the card to the locked row. If you have made a note of the row where the pattern went wrong there will be no problem. If you wish to check the card against your work you may look at the holes in the card and compare them with your pattern. On mechanical machines the pattern repeats at fixed intervals and a hole will correspond to an ordinary knit stitch, a hole (in lace) or the contrast yarn (in Fair Isle), and a blank corresponds to a pattern stitch in slip and tuck and the main yarn in Fair Isle knitting. Alternatively, insert the card into the machine and move it up five to seven rows (depending on the type of machine) past the row you decided was the correct row. Lock the card.

Secondly, you must get the pattern back to the needles. On *manual machines* you must arrange the needles according to your pattern. On *push button machines* push the buttons and pull the set lever. Have the carriage on the same side as the yarn. Thread up the carriage and set it for pattern knitting. Knit.

On *automatic machines with a preset row* (Jones/Brother and Toyota) place the carriage on the needle bed on the opposite side of the work to the end of yarn. Set the machine to part/empty. Turn the change knob/card lever on the carriage to K.C. or C. Take the carriage across the needle bed (if it is difficult turn the tension dial (stitch size) down to a small number for this row only). This will set the needles.

Re-set the machine by pushing the correct pattern buttons or turning the pattern lever to the correct setting on the carriage. Turn the tension dial to the correct number if you have altered it. Unlock the pattern card.

On machines with a memory drum (Knitmaster) place the carriage on the needle bed on the opposite side of the work to the end of yarn. Set the carriage to slip and the lace carriage to 'P'. Push the side levers forward to disconnect the drums from the needles. Take the carriage across the needle bed (if it is difficult, turn the tension dial down to a small number for this row only). This will register the pattern on the drums without knitting the row. Re-set the machine by pushing the side levers *back* on the carriage to reconnect the pattern drums to the needles. Turn the pattern lever to the correct setting. Turn the tension dial to the correct number if you have altered it. Unlock the pattern card. *You can now continue to knit your garment.*

VI Compendium of Techniques and Tips

1 The importance of design

If we were all professional designers we could sit at the machine just creating beautiful fabrics, then hand the samples to our knitters, along with a few brief sketches, and leave them to knit the garments. But unfortunately we are not. We not only have to create the fabric and design the garment shape, but we also have to manufacture the finished article. We must concern ourselves with producing the component parts and then assembling them and presenting them all together as a work of 'high fashion art'.

You may need imagination and courage for your designing to try out new colours, stitches and yarns. When you can visualize the finished article you are faced with the next problem of how to go about the mechanics of actually achieving it. This is where you doff your artist's beret and don your engineer's helmet.

You must now consider your project in a different way. It is very important to decide carefully how you will approach each component part of your garment before you begin to knit. By this I mean not just the front, back, sleeves, etc. but what sort of finishing the garment will require – i.e. the hems, necklines, fastening, making-up, etc. You must think the whole project through *before* you begin and most importantly you must do all your samples and testing before you start the actual knitting.

The following section on techniques is intended to offer you the alternative approaches to various 'engineering' problems that will arise when you begin to knit your own designs. It is not only important to try out these techniques until you find the one that will solve your particular problem, but, in trying them out, you must follow the instructions *step by step*, in the order in which they are presented. If you don't, they won't work. Never assume there are unwritten instructions between the lines. To help yourself you might keep a blank piece of paper next to the book as you try the samples and make a note of each step as you carry it out. Write down the number of the last step you completed. This will ensure you don't miss a crucial step and save you a great deal of heartache in the long run.

2 The transfer tool and the latch tool

Before you begin on this section you must be sure you have mastered the use of the transfer tool. Understanding how to use the transfer tool is essential in machine knitting because you need to use it to move the stitches from one needle to another. Without it you cannot increase, decrease or cast-off.

Hold the transfer tool firmly but lightly in your hand. Make the tool and the needles work for you. Even

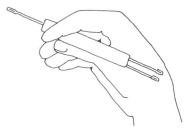

Holding the transfer tool to slip stitches back onto the needles

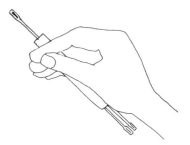

Holding the transfer tool to remove stitches from the needles

though you are only using one hand to hold the tool, always use both hands when working at the machine. If one hand is holding the tool, the other hand may help by controlling the tension on the knitted fabric or by moving the needles to and fro by pushing the needle butts.

Transferring a stitch from one needle to another

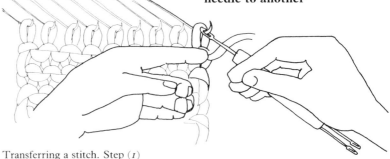

Transferring a stitch. Step (1)

(*1*) Place the eye of the tool onto the hook of the needle. Hold the work down and back against the needle bed with your free hand. Keep the tool in a continuous straight line with the needle.

Transferring a stitch. Step (*1*)

Transferring a stitch. Step (*2*)

(*2*) Gently pull the needle towards you, allowing the stitch in the needle hook to pass behind the latch. Do not press down with the tool – you will only catch the stitch in the hook of the needle.

Transferring a stitch. Step (*3*)

(*3*) When the stitch has passed behind the latch, push gently on the needle. As you push the needle back towards the machine, the stitch will be pushed forward over the closed latch and off the needle, onto the tool. You now have the stitch on the transfer tool.

Transferring a stitch. Step (*3*)

(*4*) Tip the tool so that the eye of the tool is up and the handle is down.

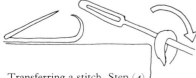

Transferring a stitch. Step (*4*)

The stitch will slip down the shank of the tool towards the handle, and you will not lose it.

(*5*) You can now move the tool freely and you will be able to hook the eye of the tool into the hook of another needle.

(*6*) When you have hooked the eye of the tool into the hook of a needle you can swivel the tool so that the handle is up and the eye is down. You can pull down on your knitted fabric with your free hand, and the stitch will slide down the shank of the tool and transfer onto the hook of the new needle.

Transferring a stitch. Step (*6*)

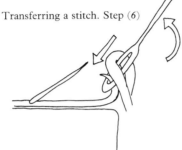

The latch tool

The other tool in your battery which will be invaluable is the latch tool. It can be used for both casting off and picking up dropped stitches. The tool resembles a rug hook. If you look closely you will see that it is just one of the needles similar to those found in the machine except that it doesn't have a butt and is set into a handle.

To pick up a dropped stitch you will use the latch tool in conjunction with your transfer tool.

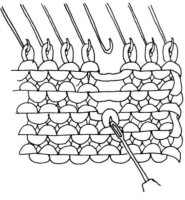

Picking up a dropped stitch. Step (*1*)

(*1*) Put your transfer tool into the dropped stitch. If you find this difficult, push the tool through the loop below the stitch.

(*2*) Push the tool through the stitch and up towards the needle bed until it emerges from behind the top of your knitting.

(*3*) Put the hook of the latch tool into the eye of the transfer tool then pull the latch tool back through the stitch.

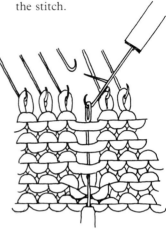

Picking up a dropped stitch. Step (*3*)

(*4*) Use the latch tool to latch-up the dropped stitch.

(*5*) Using a push-pull motion push the tool down until the stitch on the stem of the tool goes behind the latch.

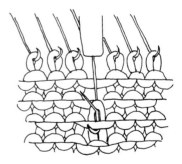

Picking up a dropped stitch. Step (*5*)

(*6*) Swivel the tool until one 'bar' of the knitted yarn is in the hook, in front of the latch.

(*7*) Swivel the tool and pull the bar of yarn through the stitch on the stem of the latch tool.

(*8*) Repeat until you have the last stitch on the tool. Drop this stitch

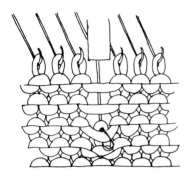

Picking up a dropped stitch. Step (6)

onto the empty needle, or slip the transfer tool into the stitch and then drop it onto the empty needle.

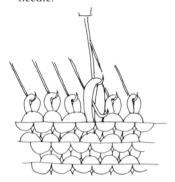

Picking up a dropped stitch. Step (8)

3 Casting-on

Casting-on is really just getting the knitting onto the machine. There are some techniques that are suitable for all machines. However, some machines have tools that can make the whole procedure much easier. Remember that the basic principle of forming stitches on a knitting machine involves the carriage pushing the needle forward and at the same time pushing the yarn (already in the hook of the needle) back behind the latch. When the yarn is put into the hook of the needle, the needle draws this new loop of yarn back through the stitch already behind the latch, thus forming a new stitch.

In casting-on or adding a group of new stitches to your work you can help the machine by following these two rules.

- Make sure the loops of yarn already on the needles are firmly pushed back against the needle bed and behind the latches when the needles come forward. This is done by pushing the needle butts forward manually with one hand while pushing the work already on the needles back with the other hand before you bring the carriage across the needle bed to knit the next row.
- Make sure the old loops are then pulled down over the closed latches when the needles pull the new loop of yarn back through to form the new stitch. This is usually done by careful weighting of the work to pull it down. Normally casting-on is done by symmetrically selecting the same number of needles either side of O in the middle of the needle bed. This will help to ensure that your work is evenly balanced. This is not done when you knit the front of a cardigan or when you are knitting a garment which is not symmetrical such as a batwing sweater which would be knit sideways.

Please make sure when you follow any of the techniques listed below that you firstly, read through the instructions carefully and secondly follow each set of instructions step by step. Don't miss any of the steps or skip over them. Take your time. Don't be in a hurry. Once you get your knitting on the machine you'll knit your garment quickly enough and if you are careless in casting on you'll only waste time in the long run getting into a muddle at the beginning. Thirdly, refer back to your manual from time to time. These techniques are intended to supplement your manual, not replace it.

The basic open edge cast-on using a cast-on cord

With most Japanese single bed machines the cast-on or ravel cord is a cord which is very smooth and strong. Special care should be taken to keep this cord free of knots. Your machine manual will tell you if you can use this technique to get your knitting started.

The advantage of this method is that it is very quick. The disadvantage is that it is not a finished edge so it will ravel back. However, you can use a variation that will give you a locked edge.

Basic Open Edge Cast-on
(1) C.O.R. Thread up the machine and put your yarn in the yarn clip.

Threading up the machine

(2) Select the required number of needles to working position.
(3) Set the tension dial (which dictates the stitch size) on the carriage to a large number – e.g. 7–9.
(4) Remove the yarn from the yarn clip and thread the carriage carefully, making sure that the yarn is correctly placed in the yarn feeder. On some machines this can be rather fiddly. Hold the yarn firmly in two hands, one above and one below the sinker plate.

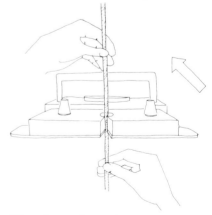

Threading up the carriage

(5) Knit one row from R. to L. All needles have loops.
(6) Look carefully at your needle

butts and make sure they are all aligned properly. Sometimes the tension of the yarn break can make the yarn pull the edge needles nearest the carriage forward slightly, thus making the loops on these needles smaller. If necessary, push these needle butts back into working position.

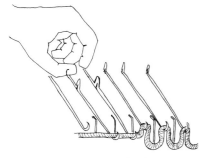

Realigning any edge needles that may have been pulled forward

(7) Place your cast-on cord between the hooks of the needles and the gate pegs. If you have a number of stitches you wish to cast on, loop the cast-on cord down between the gate pegs at several intervals across the row and hold it down firmly.

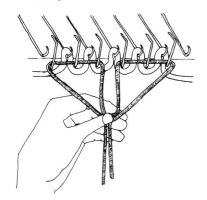

Holding down the cast-on cord

(8) Pull down very firmly on the cast-on cord.
(9) Pull down the yarn behind the yarn brake taking up any slack. Do not allow the yarn to loop down below the sinker plate between the edge of your knitting and the carriage as you bring the carriage back. If necessary, stop before the carriage reaches the

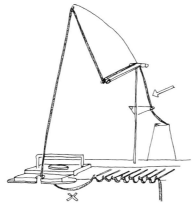

Watch carefully for 'drooping' yarn

working needles and pull the yarn down behind the yarn brake again to avoid 'drooping' yarn.
(10) Knit one row L. to R.
(11) Push the first row of stitches down below the needles by hand before knitting the next row.
(12) Knit three to four rows. Pull out the cast-on cord.
(13) Hang claw weights.

Cast on by altering the needle selection
A variation of the cast-on cord method can be done by altering the needle selection. This method has the advantage of resulting in a locked edge. However, it is not sufficiently attractive to serve as the edge of a garment but could be used if it was folded over and sewn down.
(1) C.O.R. Thread up the machine, and put your yarn in the yarn clip.
(2) Select the required number of needles to working position. Push every alternate needle back to non-working position.
(3) Set the tension dial on the carriage to a large number – e.g. 7–9.
(4) Remove the yarn from the yarn clip and thread the carriage carefully, making sure the yarn is correctly placed in the yarn feeder.
(5) Knit one row from R. to L. All needles in working position have loops. Now push the needles which are in non-working position between the needles which are in working position (and have

loops on them) to working position. All needles are now lined up in working position, and alternate needles have loops in their hooks.
(6) Look carefully at your needle butts and make sure they are all aligned properly. Sometimes the edge needles nearest the carriage are pulled forward a bit. If necessary, push these needle butts back into working position.
(7) Place your cast-on cord between the hooks of the needles and the gate pegs. If you have a number of stitches you wish to cast on, loop the cast-on cord down between the gate pegs at several intervals across the row and hold it down firmly.

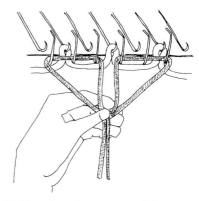

Holding down the cast-on cord for an alternate needle cast-on

(8) Pull down very firmly on the cast-on cord.
(9) Pull down the yarn behind the yarn brake taking up any slack. Do not allow the yarn to loop down below the sinker plate between the edge of your knitting and the carriage as you bring the carriage back. If necessary, stop before the carriage reaches the working needles and pull the yarn down behind the yarn brake again to avoid 'drooping' yarn.
(10) Knit one row L. to R.
(11) Push the first row of stitches down below the needles by hand before knitting the next row.
(12) Knit three to four rows. Pull out the cast-on cord.
(13) Hang claw weights.

The basic open edge cast-on using a cast-on comb that hangs from the gate pegs

In addition to a cord, some Japanese knitting machines supply a comb with the machine that can be suspended in front of the needle bed by little clips that hook onto the gate pegs. This comb does the job of a cast-on cord, among other chores. These combs are normally provided with Jones/Brother standard gauge and fine gauge machines. They can be purchased separately to be used on other machines with gate pegs, but you must check to find out if they will fit your machine. By altering your needle selection you can also achieve a locked-edge cast-on as with the previous cord method.

Basic Method

(*1*) C.O.R. Thread up the machine and put your yarn in the yarn clip.

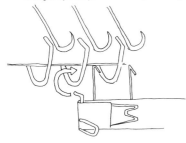

Turning the hook at the end of the cast-on comb

(*2*) Carefully hang your cast-on comb, ensuring that the centre of the comb will line up with the centre of the group of needles you select to working position. Make sure that the little hooks at each end of your comb are resting securely in the bottom of the gate pegs and not perched on top of the needle bed.

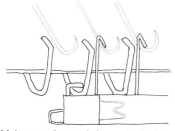

Make sure the comb hangs in the *bottom* of the gate pegs

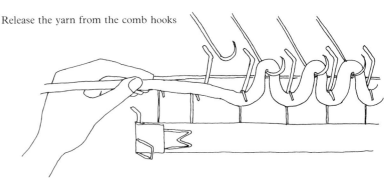

Release the yarn from the comb hooks

(*3*) Select your required needles to working position.

(*4*) Set the tension dial to a fairly large number.

(*5*) Remove the yarn from the yarn clip and thread up your carriage carefully. Hold the yarn straight down through the carriage feeder, making sure to keep it well away from the bottom of the sinker plate and its brushes.

(*6*) Knit one row from R. to L. All needles have loops.

(*7*) Turn the little clips at either end of your cast-on comb and allow the comb to drop down with the hooks resting on the loops of yarn between the needles.

(*8*) Remember to align your needle butts and release your yarn from under the hooks of the cast-on comb between the last working needle and the carriage. You may have to move your carriage quite far down the needle bed and away from your work to do this. Ensure that the yarn passes straight from the last needle in working position over the top of the sinker plate and into the carriage feeder.

(*9*) Pull the yarn down behind the yarn brake, taking up any slack. This is very important.

(*10*) Move your carriage slowly from L. to R. and keep checking that the yarn is taut and does not droop between the needles in working position and the carriage.

(*11*) Hang claw weights on your comb and continue to knit.

Variation for closed edge cast-on

(*1*) C.O.R. Thread up the machine and put your yarn in the yarn clip.

(*2*) Carefully hang your cast-on comb, making sure that the centre of the comb will line up with the centre of the group of needles you select to working position. Make sure that the little hooks at each end of your comb are resting securely in the bottom of the gate pegs and not perched on top of the needle bed.

(*3*) Select your required needles to working position.

(*4*) Push alternate needles back to non-working position.

(*5*) Set the tension dial to a fairly large number.

(*6*) Remove the yarn from the yarn clip and thread up your carriage carefully. Hold the yarn straight down through the carriage feeder, ensuring that you keep it well away from the bottom of the sinker plate and its brushes.

(*7*) Knit one row from R. to L. Alternate needles have loops.

(*8*) Align all your needles, pushing back to working position the needles you pushed to non-working position on the previous row.

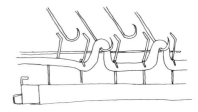

Cast-on comb hangs more easily from a cast-on using alternate needle selection

(*9*) Turn the little clips at either end of your cast-on comb and allow the comb to drop down with the hooks resting on the loops of yarn between the needles.

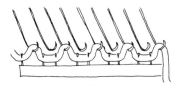

Comb hangs on the first row

(*10*) Remember to align your needle butts and release your yarn from under the hooks of the cast-on comb between the last working needle and the carriage. You may have to move your carriage quite far down the needle bed and away from your work to do this. Ensure that the yarn passes straight from the last needle in working position over the top of the sinker plate and into the carriage feeder.

(*11*) Pull the yarn down behind the yarn brake, taking up any slack. This is very important.

(*12*) Move your carriage slowly from L. to R. and keep checking that

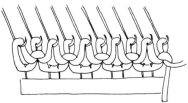

Second row knit on *all* needles

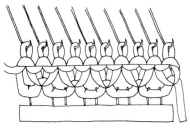

Third row

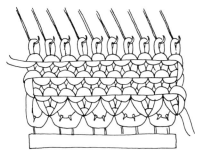

Fourth row

the yarn is taut and does not droop between the needles in working position and the carriage.

(*13*) Hang claw weights on your comb and continue to knit.

Cast-on for machines with a cast-on comb that does not hang from the gate pegs

Some single bed Japanese knitting machines provide a cast-on comb which does not hang from the gate pegs but is designed to hang onto the knitting itself. The *Toyota* machine has a cast-on comb that is quite heavy and is useful for weighting the fabric while you are knitting. However, the hooks on this comb are twice as far apart as those on a Jones/Brother comb. The Jones/Brother chunky machines also provide a cast-on comb similar to those found with their standard gauge machine, except they do not have hooks at the ends, thus preventing them from hanging on the gate pegs. They also come apart and each section can be used separately to provide combs of differing lengths. They have twice as many hooks as the Toyota combs but are not as heavy. The best way to use them is as follows:

Basic method
(*1*) C.O.R. Thread up the machine and put the yarn in the yarn clip.
(*2*) Select the required number of needles to working position. Push

alternate needles back to non-working position.
(*3*) Set the tension dial to a large number.
(*4*) Remove the yarn from the yarn clip and thread up the carriage. Remember to hold the yarn straight down through the yarn feeder.
(*5*) Knit one row from R. to L. Alternate needles have loops. Return all required needles to working position, making sure that all needle butts are aligned properly.
(*6*) Hang the cast-on comb onto the loops of yarn that occur between the needles. Make sure that the centre of the comb is in the centre of the group of working needles. The comb can be hung from front to back or can be brought up from underneath the needle bed and hooked onto the loops of yarn from behind.
(*7*) When you hang your comb make sure you don't catch yarn between the last needle in working position and the carriage under the hooks on the comb.
(*8*) Pull down the yarn behind the yarn brake taking up any slack. Make sure before you begin to knit the next row that you have not caught the yarn either under the comb hooks or in the brushes on the underside of the sinker plate.
(*9*) Knit one row carefully from L. to R.

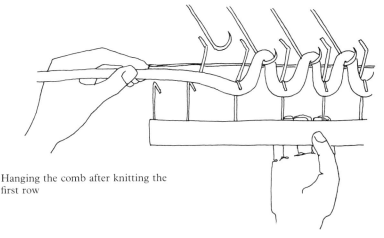

Hanging the comb after knitting the first row

Types of cast-on suitable for all machines

These two techniques will give you a neat finished – i.e. closed edge – cast-on and are suitable for machines without gate pegs, such as the Bond. They are both easier to achieve if you have something to pull your stitches down. A cast-on comb or claw weights will do or stitches that have already been mounted on the selected needles. These are mounted by using a basic open-edge cast-on in waste yarn or by picking up the edge of a spare swatch of knitting with a transfer tool onto your needles and knitting one row with a ravel or cast-on cord. This can then can be removed when the piece of knitting is finished, allowing the spare swatch to drop off.

I

The 'E' Wrap Cast-On
The basic method – needles in H.P.

(*1*) C.O.R. Select required needles to H.P.

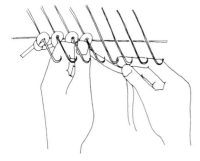

An E wrap cast-on

(*2*) Make a slip knot and attach the yarn to the first selected needle at the left.

(*3*) Using both hands wrap the yarn *loosely* and evenly in an anti-clockwise direction around each needle. Using the right hand to wrap the yarn, use the left thumb to push the loops you make back behind the needle latches. If your carriage is on the left hand side you must wind the yarn in the opposite direction – i.e. clockwise. The yarn always goes first under, then up and over the needle.

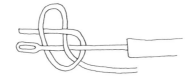

A slip knot

(*4*) Thread the carriage up and knit one row. C.O.L. To ensure that the first few rows knit successfully either *carefully* push the (needle butts) needles forward to hold position with one hand while pushing the stitches which are already in the needle hooks back behind the latches. Knit one row

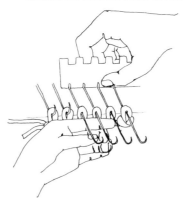

Pushing the needles forward with the pusher while holding the stitches back against the machine with the other hand

C.O.R. Continue to help the machine knit these new stitches in this way until you have enough knitting on your needles to hang weights (approximately four rows). Alternatively, place the cast-on cord between the hooks of the needles and the gate pegs as you did when doing a simple open edge cast-on. Knit several rows with the cast-on cord in place. This cord will hold the stitches down and ensure successful knitting for the first few rows. Then the cord may be pulled out.

Needles wrapped in working position

(*1*) C.O.R. Select required needles to working position.

(*2*) Make a slip knot and attach the yarn to the first selected needle at the left.

(*3*) *Using both hands*, wrap the yarn *loosely* and evenly in an anti-clockwise direction around each needle. Using the right hand to wrap the yarn, use the left hand to push the needles forward to receive the yarn loops and back to pull the loops back against the machine and make them an adequate size. This second method of wrapping the needles can really be used best in conjunction with a cast-on cord, waste knitting or cast-on combs to pull the first wrapped row down.

The waste yarn method

(*1*) Select needles and cast-on with waste yarn. Knit approximately ten rows. C.O.L.

(*2*) Knit one row with the cast-on cord. C.O.R.

(*3*) Push all needles to hold position, pushing waste yarn carefully behind the latches. Set carriage to knit needles back to working position.

(*4*) Attach main yarn to the left edge needle with a slip knot and loosely wrap the yarn around each needle as in the basic 'E' wrap method. The loops you form around the needle stems must be even and loose.

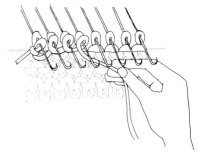

An E wrap with waste knitting on the machine

(*5*) Thread the carriage up and proceed with your knitting. You may hang weights on your waste knitting so you needn't push your needles forward while pushing your work back behind the latches for the first few rows.

Jones/Brother cast-on comb for standard gauge machines

(*1*) Hang the cast-on comb carefully on the gate pegs.

(*2*) Select the required needles to hold position. C.O.R. Set carriage to knit needles back to working position.

(*3*) Attach the main yarn to the left edge needle with a slip knot and proceed to 'E' wrap the yarn loosely around the stem of each needle in an anti-clockwise direction.

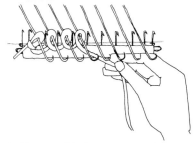

An E wrap with the cast-on comb hanging on the machine

(*4*) Thread up the carriage.

(*5*) *Drop* the cast-on comb so the hooks of the comb rest on the loops of yarn between the needles.

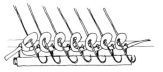

The cast-on comb dropped onto the E wrap

(*6*) Make sure the yarn does not pass under the hooks of the comb between the last needle in working position and the carriage.

(*7*) Hang weights on the comb and knit the first row carefully.

Toyota and Jones/Brother chunky machine cast-on comb

This cast-on comb is one which you cannot hang on the gate pegs but must be hung on the yarn after it is looped on the needles.

(*1*) C.O.R. Select required needles to hold position. Set carriage to knit needles back to working position.

(*2*) Attach main yarn to left edge needle with a slip knot and proceed to 'E' wrap the yarn from left

to right. Using both hands, keep the loops loose, even and back against the machine.

(*3*) Thread up the carriage. Take the cast-on comb and hang it on the loops of yarn between the needle stems. The comb can be hung from the front of the work or brought up and hung through the loops between the needles from behind the work. Leave the comb resting on the yarn. You can hang weights on the comb. Make sure you do not hook the comb on the yarn between the last needle wrapped on the right hand edge and the carriage.

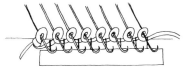

The cast-on comb hung onto a completed E wrap cast-on

(*4*) Proceed with the knitting.

This method of casting on can be used to start a garment or it can be used to add more than one stitch to the edge of work already on the machine.

'E' wrapping alternate needles

Another variation can be to 'E' wrap alternate needles instead of every needle.

(*1*) Using any of the above methods, select all needles to hold position. Set carriage to knit needles back to working position. C.O.R.

(*2*) Attach the end of the main yarn to the left edge needle with a slip knot.

An E wrap cast-on over alternate needles

(*3*) Wrap the yarn as above, wrapping it around the stem of every *alternate* needle.

(*4*) Hang the comb on the loops of yarn between the needles and proceed to knit.

II

Latch tool or crochet edge cast-on

This type of cast-on results in an extremely attractive and useful finished edge. It is worthwhile mastering the tricky technique of using the latch tool. As with the 'E' wrap cast-on you can start your cast-on with one of these methods.

(*a*) The basic method – mount your cast-on directly onto the empty needles. In this case you must take great care knitting the first few rows. If necessary you must push the needles to hold position before knitting each row.

(*b*) The waste yarn method – knit several rows with waste yarn and one row with the cast-on cord; then, mount your cast-on onto the needles in front of the waste yarn knitting.

(*c*) The method for the cast-on comb that hangs from the gate pegs – the comb is first hung onto the gate pegs, the cast-on is mounted on the needles, and then the comb is dropped onto the loops of yarn between the needles before you knit the first row with the carriage.

(*d*) The method for the cast-on comb that is hung directly onto the knitting – the cast-on is mounted on the needles and the comb is then hung on the loops of yarn between the needles before you knit the first row with the carriage.

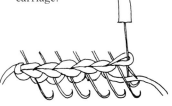

Latch-tool cast-on from above the needles

You can mount your latch-tool cast-on in two ways: you can use the latch-tool from above the needles or you can use the latch-tool from below the needles. Both ways produce an equally attractive edge, and your decision will depend on which you find easier.

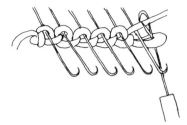

Latch-tool cast-on from below the needles

The basic technique

(*1*) Thread up the machine. C.O.R. (If using method (*b*) first knit several rows with waste yarn, one row with the cast-on cord then thread up machine with M.Y.)

(*2*) (If using method (*c*) hang your cast-on comb on the gate pegs.) Select the required needles to hold position.

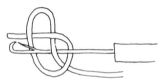

A slip knot on a latch-tool

(*3*) Make a slip knot in the main yarn and slip it onto your latch tool so that the loop of yarn falls behind the open latch.

(*4*) Pass the latch tool between the first two needles at the left edge of the group of selected needles.

(*5*) Place the yarn around the left end needle and into the hook of the latch tool and pull this loop through the stitch on the stem of the tool.

(*6*) Push the latch tool so that the new stitch now passes behind the latch and rests on the stem of the tool.

(*7*) Move the tool between the next two needles and passing the yarn by on the other side of the needles pull it through with the tool again forming another stitch.

(*8*) Repeat this procedure until you reach the last needle, making sure you keep the cast-on quite close to the needle bed.

(*9*) At the last needle put the hook of the tool into the hook of the needle and swivel the handle of the tool upwards so that the

stitch on the tool slips over the closed latch and onto the last needle. (If you are using method (*c*) drop your cast-on comb onto the chain you have formed on the needle butts. If you are using the method whereby the cast-on comb is hung directly onto the knitting hook your cast-on comb onto the chain you have mounted on your needles.)

(*10*) Thread yarn through the carriage and pull the yarn down firmly behind the yarn brake to take up any slack. Begin knitting. (If you are using the basic method (*a*) it is advisable to push your needles carefully to hold position and your stitches back behind the open latches each time before you knit the first few rows.

The weaving cast-on

This method of casting on is very quick and easy, but your machine must have weaving brushes. Before you attempt this technique you must either push your weaving brushes to working position (consult your manual) or attach them to the sinker plate, brush assembly or presser plate if they are supplied separately.

(*1*) C.O.R. Select the required needles to working position. Push alternate needles to hold position. Set carriage to knit all needles. (On Knitmaster machines make sure that the side levers which connect the needles to the pattern selection system are not pushed back.)

(*2*) Attach or push the weaving brushes to working position.

(*3*) Thread up the machine and carriage and pass the yarn across from R. to L. over the needles.

(*4*) Slowly move the carriage across to knit the row at the same time pulling the yarn down and away over the needles.

(*5*) C.O.L. Push the stitches down over the needles and pull the yarn down behind the yarn brake to pull up any slack. Continue to knit.

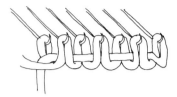

After knitting the first row of a weaving cast-on

Cast-on using Part/Slip/Empty knitting

With this method your machine must be able to do simple pattern knitting. You must be able to set the machine to knit alternate needles that are selected to upper working position while 'ignoring' or 'passing by' needles that remain at working position. The needles can be selected either manually, by push button or by punch card.

To use this method you may, as in the 'E' wrap and latch tool cast-on, use the basic method, the waste yarn method, the method whereby the cast-on comb hangs from the gate pegs or is hung directly on the knitting (*see* p. 90ff). If attempting this cast-on it is much easier if you have a good understanding of the patterning system of your machine. If you push the wrong button you can very easily wind up with a mass of spaghetti and not really know where you have gone wrong.

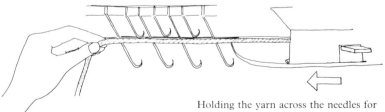

Holding the yarn across the needles for a weaving cast-on

The basic technique

(1) C.O.R. (If using the waste yarn method (b) knit several rows with W.Y. C.O.L. Knit one row with cast-on cord. If using method (c), hang the cast-on comb on the gate pegs. Select required needles to working position. Set carriage to part/slip/empty (that is the carriage will only knit needles selected to upper working position).

(2) The machine must be set to pattern. *Machines with manual selection*: push alternate needles to upper working position with the pusher. *Push button machines*: push buttons 1, 3, 5, 7. Slide lever on A. Pull the set lever to select the needles. *Punch card machines where the carriage pre-selects the needles*: put card number 1 from the basic set into the machine and lock it on row 1. C.O.L. Needles in working position. Connect the card to the needles by moving the change knob or pattern selector levers on the carriage and passing the carriage from L. to R. with the part/empty buttons pushed in. Unlock the card. *Punch card machines where the pattern information is stored on drums in the carriage*: put card number 1 from the basic set into the machine and lock it on row 1. Take the carriage across the machine with the side levers forward and the pattern lever to slip. As the pattern drums in the carriage pass the card reading feelers they register the pattern. C.O.R. Unlock the card. Push the side levers on the carriage back.

Cast-on using part/slip knitting. First row

(3) Thread up the carriage and knit one row. If you are using method (a) a cast-on cord can be placed between the hooks of the needles and the gate pegs and pulled down firmly. If you use method (c) drop the cast-on comb onto the row of loops between the needles. With method (d), hang the cast-on comb onto the row of loops between the needles.

(4) C.O.L. prepare to knit the next row. *Manual machines*: push empty needles forward to upper working position. *Push button machines*: put slide lever to B and pull set lever. *Punch card machines*: continue to knit in pattern.

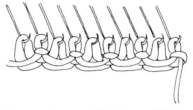

Cast-on using part/slip knitting. Second row

(5) Knit one row. C.O.R.
(6) Repeat steps (2)–(4) knitting four rows in all. These four rows complete the cast-on, and you can proceed to knit as usual. Remember to cancel your pattern buttons.

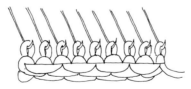

Cast-on using part/slip knitting. Third row

Cast-on using part/slip knitting. Fourth row

This edge is very elastic and can be used when introducing a pattern on the cast-on edge of a garment, e.g. a scallop made with a manually selected pull-up tuck stitch. It can also be used if you wish to pick up the stitches to add an edge later.

4 Casting-on with a ribber

When casting on with your ribber you don't have the same opportunities for variation that you do with the single bed machine. No matter what sort of double bed needle arrangement you wish to use ultimately, you must remember two important points when casting-on. Firstly, before you knit your first row you must select your needles so that the yarn will form a zig-zag from bed to bed on the first row. *The yarn must never pass from one needle to the adjacent needle on the same bed on the first row.* Secondly, the needle beds must be arranged so that the working needles on each bed will bypass the working needles on the opposite bed. Once you have completed your cast-on you can then arrange the stitches on the needles with your transfer tool and your double-eyed bodkin to continue your knitting.

The basic ribber cast-on

(1) Remove the single bed sinker plate. Push the ribber up to working position. Connect the carriages with the connecting arm.
(2) Arrange the needles so that the yarn will form a zig-zag on the first row knitted. Take the empty carriage across to align the needles and finish with the C.O.R.
(3) Thread up the machine, the yarn break or tension mast, and the carriage. It will be easier to drop the yarn between the needle beds if you thread it through one eye on your double-eyed bodkin and drop this down between. Alternatively, you can lie the yarn down between the beds and 'blow' it

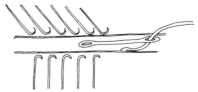

Using the double-eyed bodkin to drop the yarn between the beds

Hanging the ribber comb

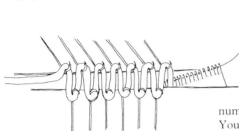

through, catching it below. Secure it below the beds.

(4) With the smallest possible number on the tension dial of *both* carriages, knit one row. A zig-zag of yarn is formed between the beds.

(5) Hang your cast-on comb. You may have to remove the wire entirely from the teeth of the comb. However, if you have room, you may be able to poke one end of your cast-on comb up between the needle beds and pull the wire out of the teeth far enough to clear enough teeth. This will enable you to push the comb up through the yarn zig-zag and push the wire back into place without taking it out of the comb altogether.

(6) Now you must set your carriages to knit circular knitting. The manual will explain how to set your carriages after the first row. What you are doing is telling the carriages to knit only in one direction and to pass the needles by in the other direction. Each carriage is set to do this on alternate rows. Thus you may be only knitting from left to right on the main bed; at the same time you will be knitting only from right to left on the ribber.

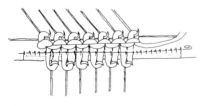

Second row of the cast-on for the ribber

(7) At this point you will gradually increase your stitch size (the number on your tension dial). You need only do this to the carriage (main bed or ribber) that is set to knit the next row.

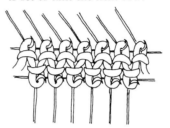

Knitting on both beds. Ribbed knitting

(8) Knit two to three circular rows. This will complete your cast-on. You can now rearrange your stitches and needles.

(9) Hang your weights. They must be distributed *evenly* across the cast-on comb. Continue to knit.

(10) After a few rows remember to hang edge weights.

When you remove your work from the machine you may not be happy with the look of the first row. Remember when you put the garment on, the rib is likely to stretch out anyway and the first row will be less noticeable. However, there are several ways you can avoid a loopy or pulled-out cast-on edge. To neaten a cast-on edge:

● Thread a fine elastic through the second feeder of your yarn brake. Then run it through the main feeder of your carriage alongside your main yarn. Knit it into the first zig-zag row. You can also leave it in while doing the first few circular rows as well. You can remove it before continuing with your rib.

● After completing your first zig-zag row and before going on to knit your circular rows, lay the cast-on cord on the zig-zag after you have completed hanging your comb. It will be enclosed in

the cast-on, and when you have removed your work from the machine, and the comb from your work, you can grasp both ends of the cord and pull firmly, thus neatening the cast-on edge before you pull the cord out of your work. **NB** Don't hang the ribber weights on your cast-on comb until you have completed the cast-on including the circular rows.

● Before the zig-zag row, push the ribber needles to H.P. and set the ribber carriage to hold. After completion of the zig-zag row and after the comb has been hung, reset the ribber carriage to N and continue as in the basic cast-on.

Basic cast-on pulled thread methods

Method 1

(1) Follow steps (1)–(4) as in the basic method.

(2) When you hang your cast-on comb make sure that the teeth of the comb come up between the needles in working position on the main bed and opposite the needles in working position on the ribber bed.

(3) Unhook the ribber carriage and take it across by itself, thus dropping all the stitches on the ribber bed. The comb is now hanging on loops from the main bed stitches only.

(4) Now do a standard cast-on – that is, knit one row on both beds (another zig-zag row) and two or three rows circular (steps (6), (7) and (8) of the basic cast-on).

(5) When you finish your piece of knitting and remove it from the machine, you can pull the bottom thread, and all the loops will disappear.

Method 2

(1) Follow steps (1)–(5) as in the basic method. You have now knit a zig-zag row and hung your cast-on comb. C.O.L.

(2) Set the main bed carriage to knit.

ck Cable used to edge a simple cardigan

Buttons made from Fimo to echo the colour and pattern of
the knitting

Cable inset dividing the front also used on the sleeves sideways

Bottom edge and cuffs added after the main knitting is
completed. Contrast piping is used in the armhole seams

A garment inspired by an accessory — the belt

The body of the garment is knit in two sections. The centre
seams (front and back) are joined on the machine by knitting
the first half in at the same time as the second half

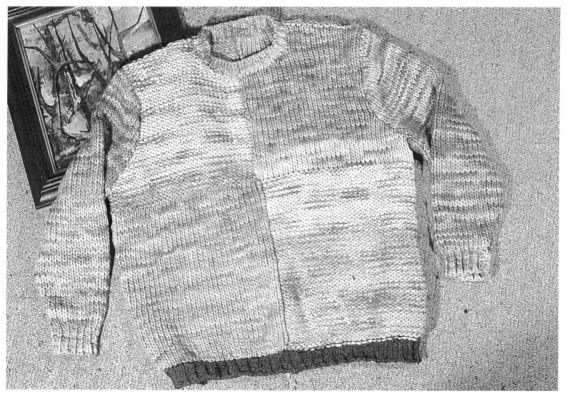

A tension square using a wider range of coloured yarns.
The yarns are hand-fed

Broiderie Anglaise gathered and sewn onto the front edge of
a cardigan

Garment knit in three sections only; left (tuck stitch), right
(stocking stitch), and cable (middle). The neck is 'cut and sewn'

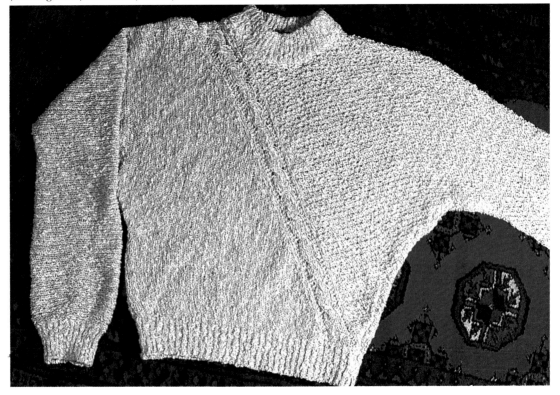

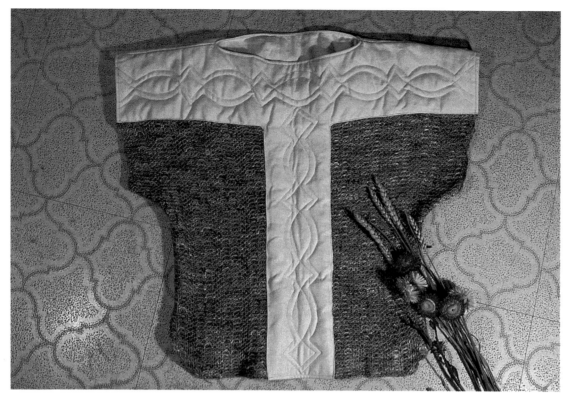

Knitting combined with quilted fabric in one garment

A sewing pattern with woven fabric and knitting combined.
The pattern shape is drawn out on the pattern attachment

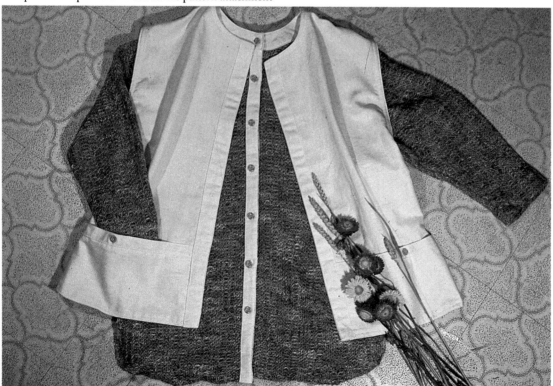

A sewing pattern drawn out on the patterning attachment
makes even the most complicated shaping easy!

Set the ribber carriage to tuck. Knit one row. C.O.R.

(3) Set the main bed carriage to slip/part/empty. Set the ribber carriage to knit. Knit one row. C.O.L.

(4) The next two rows must be knit circular. See step (8) of the basic method.

(5) When you finish your piece of knitting and remove it from the machine, you can pull the bottom thread and all the loops will disappear.

Cast-on using waste yarn

(1) Make a basic cast-on using waste yarn. Knit several rows in rib. Remove the waste yarn from the feeder. C.O.R.

(2) Disconnect the two carriages and take the empty main bed carriage across and back. All your main bed stitches will drop off and run back to the comb, but the comb will stay on your work. C.O.R.

(3) Thread up the carriage with the main yarn. Repeat all the steps for the basic cast-on except for hanging the comb as it is already on the waste knitting.

(4) When you have finished your garment you can remove the waste knitting. You will have a neater edge.

Cast-on with 'E' wrap using waste yarn

(1) Make a basic cast-on using waste yarn. Remove the waste yarn from the feeder. C.O.L.

(2) Thread the feeder up with the cast-on cord and knit one row with the cord. C.O.R.

(3) Remove the cord from the feeder. Transfer all stitches to the main bed. Drop the ribber.

(4) Push all needles to hold position. Set carriages to knit needles in hold position. Secure the main yarn to the working needle at the left edge with a slip knot. Proceed to do an 'E' wrap cast-on as for the single bed.

(5) When you have completed the 'E'

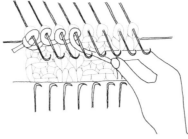

'E' wrap cast-on for ribbed knitting

wrap, push the ribber back up to working position. Select your needles and transfer your stitches to produce the required rib pattern.

(6) Thread up the main yarn and continue to knit the garment.

Racking cast-on

(1) Arrange your needles as if you were to start an ordinary cast-on. C.O.R. (Pitch lever to H.P.)

(2) Thread the machine up with your main yarn.

(3) Before you knit the first zig-zag row, rack the ribber one whole number to the right.

(4) Set the carriages to knit at the main tension for your rib. The tension dial must not be set at too small a number because you will not then be able to rack the ribber after knitting the cast-on or zig-zag row. Knit one row forming a zig-zag between the beds with your yarn. C.O.L.

(5) Hang the cast-on comb and the weights.

(6) Rack the ribber one whole number to the left.

(7) Continue to knit in rib.

This is a very loose but rapid method of casting on for ribbing.

Decorative cast-on

(1) Follow steps (1) through to (5) as for the basic ribber cast-on. *See* method (a).

(2) Once you have aligned your needles, threaded up and knit the first zig-zag row, completed hanging the cast-on comb and the ribber weights, you do not have to knit circular rows. You may just knit your rib but your cast-on edge will have a decorative, looped edge.

If you wish to knit only on one bed with your ribber carriage ensure the row will knit by pushing all the needles on that bed to holding position and setting the carriage to knit needles in hold position before you knit the row. This is a safety measure which will work on either bed.

5   Transfer of stitches

As it is a vital skill to be able to transfer the stitches from one needle to another when using a single bed knitting machine, so it is equally important to be able to move the stitches from one bed to the other when using a double bed knitting machine. The technique used is slightly different. You can move the stitches manually to help you carry out basic tasks like increasing, decreasing and casting off. Also, you can transfer stitches to produce different patterns and textured effects in the knitted fabric you are making.

There are various devices on the market to speed up the process of transferring stitches. The U 70 and the U 80 for the Passap and the transfer carriages for the Brother/

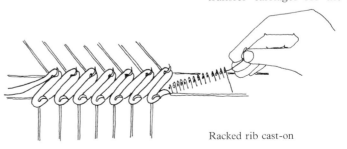

Racked rib cast-on

Jones and Knitmaster machines transfer stitches automatically across the whole needle bed. However, you may not always wish to transfer all the stitches but only a selected few, in which case it is easier and quicker to do it by hand.

Here are four different approaches to the task. Stitches can be transferred in either direction with any of the following methods. The whole process is made easier if the row before the transfer can be knit in a larger stitch size. However, if you only wish to transfer a few stitches this may not be desirable.

I Transfer of stitches using the double-eyed bodkin

This small tool is invaluable and, unfortunately, easily lost. It is a good idea to secure it somewhere convenient – for example, affix it with a piece of Blu-Tack or a small magnet to the corner of your machine.

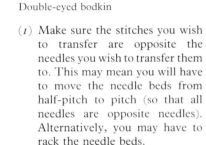

Double-eyed bodkin

(1) Make sure the stitches you wish to transfer are opposite the needles you wish to transfer them to. This may mean you will have to move the needle beds from half-pitch to pitch (so that all needles are opposite needles). Alternatively, you may have to rack the needle beds.

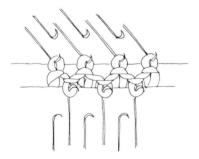

1 × 1 Rib knitting

(2) Place the eye of the bodkin onto the hook of the needle which has the stitch you wish to transfer.
(3) Using the bodkin, pull the needle

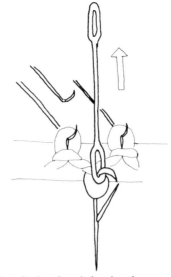

Transferring the stitch using the double-eyed bodkin. Step (2)

straight away from the bed until the stitch falls behind the needle latch.

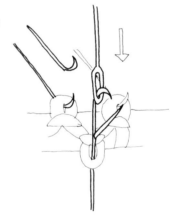

Transferring the stitch using the double-eyed bodkin. Step (3)

Transferring the stitch using the double-eyed bodkin. Step (6)

(4) Still using the bodkin in the same way you use the transfer tool, push the needle straight back until the stitch passes over the closed latch of the needle and onto the bodkin. You now have the stitch on the bodkin and can put it where you like.
(5) Rock the bodkin and hook the opposite eye onto the hook of the needle on the opposite bed where you wish to transfer the stitch.
(6) Swivel the bodkin until the stitch slips off onto the needle.

II Transfer stitches using a single bed transfer tool

(1) Move the front bed slightly to the right relative to the back bed. If your machine is on pitch (needles opposite each other) you may move it to half-pitch. If your machine is on half-pitch you will have to rack the front bed one movement to the right. (One number lower on Japanese machines.)

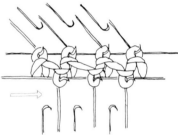

Move the ribber bed slightly to the right in relation to the main bed to make the transfer of stitches easier

(2) Push the needles for the stitches you wish to transfer to H.P.
(3) Slip the transfer tool into the

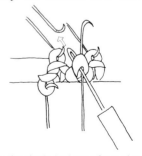

Using the single bed transfer tool to pull out the ribber stitch

stitch from behind the stitch –
that is, slip the tool into the stitch,
moving the tool along the shank
of the needle towards the needle
hook on the side of the needle
nearest to the needle where you
wish to transfer the stitch.

(4) Push the tool across to the needle
on the opposite bed and place the
eye of the tool into the hook of the
needle.

(5) Pull the needle through the
stitch. (The stitch is now shared
between two needles, one on each
bed.)

(6) Pull the unwanted needles out of
the stitches by pushing back the
butts.

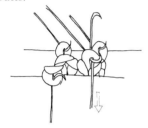

Push the main bed needle into the
ribber stitch.

III Transfer of stitches by using a sharp pointed tool

With some machines you will find one
of the transfer tools has a sharp,
slightly bent, pointed 'finger' at the
opposite end. Alternatively, you may
find this 'finger' at the other end of a
crochet hook, which is supplied with
the machine.

Crochet hook/pointed tool

(1) Set up your needle bed as described for method **II**, that is, the
stitches between the beds under
tension, racking the front bed to
the right.

(2) Push the needles for the stitches
you required to transfer to H.P.

(3) With the tool in one hand, place
the point of the tool into the stitch
from behind, pulling the stitch
loop sideways away from the
needle and towards the needle

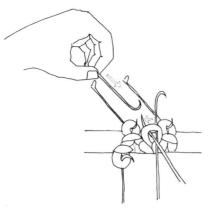

Pushing the main bed needle into the
ribber stitch

where you wish to transfer the
stitch to.

(4) With your other hand on the
butts of the needles on the opposite bed, push the needle where
you require the stitch to be transferred through the stitch loop.

(5) When you have finished transferring your stitches, you may then
push the unwanted needles by the
butts back out of the stitch loops.

IV Transfer of stitches with a single bed transfer tool backwards

For this method you will find it easier
if the needles you wish to transfer
your stitches to are opposite the
needles from which you are transferring stitches.

(1) Put the eye of the tool onto the
hook of the needle and pull the

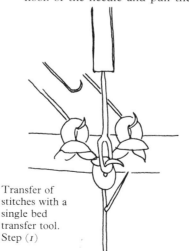

Transfer of
stitches with a
single bed
transfer tool.
Step (1)

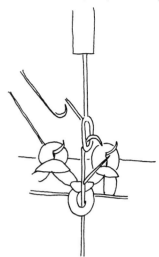

Transfer of stitches with a single bed
transfer tool. Step (2)

needle away from the machine
until the stitch falls behind the
latch.

(2) Using the tool, push the needle
back until the stitch passes over
the closed latch and onto the stem
of the tool.

(3) Pull the stitch up away from the
machine, thus pulling the stitch
into a bigger loop.

(4) With your other hand on the butt
of the needle on the opposite bed,
push this needle through into the
enlarged loop of the stitch.

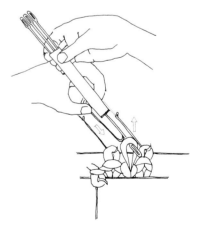

Transfer of stitches with a single bed
transfer tool. Step (4)

(5) Drop the stitch into the 'new'
needle and slide the transfer tool
backwards out of the stitch.

6 Casting off

Once you have finished knitting your work you will want to remove it from the machine and fix the edge so that the work does not unravel and disappear. Although this seems self-evident, there are in fact various ways of doing this with various different results. Casting-off has always been the bugbear of machine knitting. It is tedious and can be very time-consuming. In some cases it may take as long to cast-off as it did to knit the piece of work, if not longer. The most important thing to consider when finishing off your piece of knitting is the final effect you desire. While the fabric you are creating has an inbuilt mobility factor, casting-off frequently does not. It can limit the amount of stretchability your work will have. Neckbands and waistbands will need to have quite a bit of elasticity, and shoulder seams will be required to hold the garment shape – otherwise the shoulders will droop to the elbows, whether you have designed the garment that way or not. The type of fabric you are knitting can also determine your approach to casting-off. Woven fabric is very firm, with no horizontal give at all; tuck stitch fabric, when removed from the machine, often expands in width, thus requiring a much looser cast-off if it is not to be distorted. Ribbed fabric, of course, is a totally different ball-game altogether and must be considered separately.

Basic transfer tool method

This method can be used either for finishing off a piece of work or casting-off a few stitches when shaping the garment. It may be done either with the main yarn from the knitting itself or a spare length of main yarn.

(*1*) Using the single transfer tool and starting from the same side as the carriage (if using the yarn the garment is being knit with), transfer the end stitch onto the adjacent needle with a stitch. You now have two stitches on one needle.

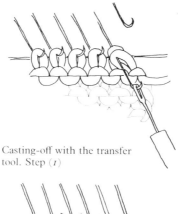

Casting-off with the transfer tool. Step (*1*)

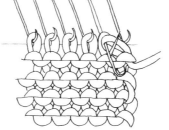

Casting-off with the transfer tool. Step (*2*)

(*2*) Pull this needle forward with the transfer tool only far enough so that the loops of both stitches fall behind the open latch. (Don't pull the needle any further forward than necessary.)

(*3*) Place the yarn into the hook of the needle in front of the open latch.

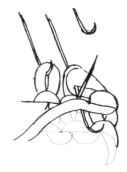

Casting-off with the transfer tool. Step (*3*)

(*4*) With your thumb on the needle butt, pull the needle back so that the yarn is knit through both stitch loops. Pull down on the knitted fabric, pulling the stitch you have just made down into the needle hook.

(*5*) Repeat this procedure until all

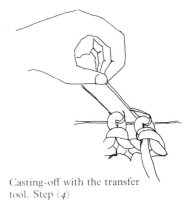

Casting-off with the transfer tool. Step (*4*)

required stitches have been cast-off.

When casting off with this method, you may use various techniques to ensure a cast-off with an even tension. You can also control the amount of elasticity in the cast-off row as follows.

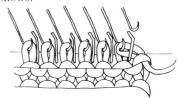

Stitch transferred behind the gate peg

• When transferring the stitch from one needle to the adjacent needle, take the stitch *behind* the gate peg.

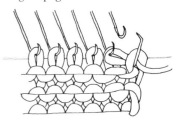

End stitch hooked up on the gate peg

• Hook the edge of the knitting where you intend to begin your cast-off onto an adjacent gate peg before you begin. This will help to stop your casting-off from pulling up too tight.

• Hang a claw weight onto the first stitch cast-off. This will help to keep your cast-off loose.

• For an extremely loose cast-off, the yarn may be wrapped around an adjacent or nearby needle,

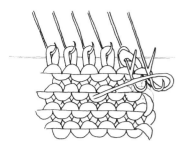

Casting-off wrapping yarn over adjacent empty needle before knitting the stitch through

before being placed into the hook and pulled through the two stitches behind the latch. This method will give you a very loose cast off suitable for stitches needing expanding edges – e.g. tuck or rib stitches – and for edges which require a considerable degree of elasticity, such as waistbands or some neckbands.

Figure-of-eight cast-off

This method is really a slight variation on the basic transfer tool method.

(*1*) Starting from the same side of the work as the carriage, approach the end stitch with the transfer tool pointing towards you and the handle of the tool above the needle bed – not in front of the machine.

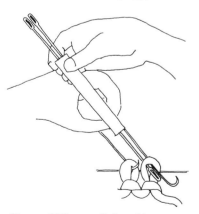

Figure of '8' cast-off. Step (*2*)

(*2*) Slip the tool into the stitch from behind.
(*3*) Swivel the handle of the tool up, around and down until the tool

is now pointing away from you and is headed in the direction of the second needle with a stitch. The handle of the tool is in front of the gate pegs and needle bed. The stitch from the first needle is on the tool and is now twisted around the shank of the tool in a figure of eight. It is also still in the hook of the first needle so it is *shared* between the needle and the tool.

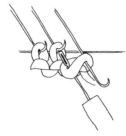

Figure of '8' cast-off. Step (*3*)

(*4*) Place the eye of the tool into the hook of the second needle with a stitch and swivel the handle of the tool upwards. The half-stitch on the tool will slip onto the second needle and be shared between the first and second needles.
(*4a*) A variation on this step is to knit the half-stitch on the second needle through the stitch already on the needle by pushing the needle forward far enough so that the first stitch falls behind the latch; the transferred stitch remains in the needle hook and can then be pulled through.

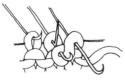

Figure of '8' cast-off. Step (*4*)

Now you can proceed with step.
(*5*) Knit the yarn through the loop that remains on the needle. Pull this needle forward with the transfer tool only so far that the loops of both stitches fall behind the open latch. (Don't pull the needle any further forward than necessary.)

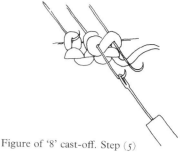

Figure of '8' cast-off. Step (*5*)

(*6*) Place the yarn into the hook of the needle in front of the open latch.

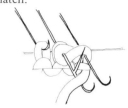

Figure of '8' cast-off. Step (*6*)

(*7*) With your thumb on the needle butt, pull the needle back so the yarn is knit through both stitch loops. Pull down on the knitted fabric, pulling the stitch you have just made down into the needle hook.
(*8*) Continue to cast off in this manner, always transferring half a stitch to the next needle by twisting it with your transfer tool. You will leave the other half of your stitch on the first needle after you have knit it off the second needle. The advantage of this method is that it ensures an even, loose cast-off. However, it is rather tedious to execute and results in a ridge at the cast-off edge.

Finished edge transfer tool method

This method is very similar to the basic transfer tool method, the difference being that the sequence of steps is slightly altered, thus giving a different final appearance to the work.

(*1*) Using the single transfer tool and starting from the same side as the carriage (if using the yarn the garment is being knit with), transfer the stitch from the sec-

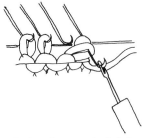

Transferring the second stitch from the edge to the edge needle

ond needle from the end onto the end needle with a stitch. You now have two stitches on the end needle, and the second needle from the end is now empty.

(2) Pull the end needle (with two loops on it) forward with the transfer tool, but only so far that the loops of both stitches fall behind the open latch. (Don't pull the needle any further forward than necessary.)

(3) Place the yarn into the hook of the needle in front of the open latch.

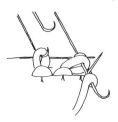

Casting off the two stitches on the edge needle

(4) With your thumb on the needle butt, pull the needle back so the yarn is knit through both stitch loops. Pull down on the knitted fabric, pulling the stitch you have just made down into the needle hook.

(5) With the transfer tool move this new end stitch onto the adjacent empty needle towards the rest of your work.

(6) Repeat this procedure until all required stitches have been cast-off.

As with the basic transfer tool method, you can still control the tension of this cast-off technique by using variations of the techniques on page 100.

Latch tool cast-off

The advantage of using the latch-tool method is that when it is practised it can prove to be very quick indeed. The disadvantage can be that it requires special techniques to result in a loose enough edge for some purposes. The fabric's elasticity depends on your ability to make the last row of knitted stitches large enough to prevent the edge from tightening up.

There are several ways of ensuring that the last row is large enough to prevent a tight cast-off. However, if the main tension of your garment is 6 or less, the garment is knit in stocking stitch, Fair Isle or slip stitch (in other words a stitch which is not wide or a fabric which does not expand in width when removed from the machine) and you knit the last row before your cast-off on tension 10, you may not find it necessary to take any additional precautions against a tight cast-off.

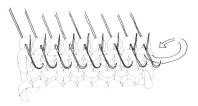

Knitting a loose row manually (*a*)

There are several precautions you can take for a loose cast off.

Alternative one: to get a row of big loops knit the last row by hand as follows. Push all needles forward to H.P. and push all stitches back, be-

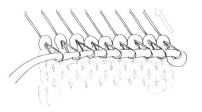

Knitting a loose row manually (*b*)

hind the latches (*a*). Check that all the latches are open. Carefully lay the yarn across the needle hooks in front of the open latches. Gently pull the needles back by the needle butts until the latches just close over the yarn in the hooks (*b*). One by one, starting at

the end opposite the free end of yarn, pull each needle butt right back to N.W.P., thus knitting the yarn through each stitch and making very big loops on the needles (*c*). Before attempting to cast-off with the latch tool, pull the work down firmly and hang weights on it to prevent the stitches from jumping up off the needles.

Alternative two: knit the last row on the loosest possible tension but using a finer yarn.

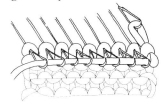

Knitting a loose row manually (*c*)

Alternative three: use the ribber to make the last row very loose as follows. C.O.R. (*a*) Remove the single bed sinker plate. (*b*) Push up the ribber and connect the main bed carriage to the ribber carriage. Set the ribber so that the needles will not collide when pushed to W.P. (On Japanese machines use the half-pitch setting.) (*c*) Select alternate needles on the ribber to W.P. opposite the needles in W.P. on the main bed. (*d*) Knit one row: tension 10 of the main bed, tension 2 on the ribber. Weights are not necessary to knit one row; however, you may push all needles to H.P. to ensure they will knit properly. When the row is complete, disconnect the ribber carriage and slide it across the ribber, thus dropping all the stitches off the ribber needles. Pull the work down firmly and weight it evenly to prevent the loops from jumping up off the needles.

There are several different ways to accomplish a latch tool cast-off. Which one you choose depends largely on your ability to wield the tool itself.

Method 1
(1) Knit the last loose row from R. to L. Finish with C.O.L.
(2) Push all needles to H.P. carefully pushing the stitches of your work

back behind the latches when you push the needles forward.

(3) Hold the work firmly in the left hand and use your index finger to control the stitches on the needles as you latch them off with your tool. Begin at the right hand edge of the knitting.

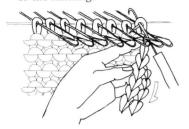

Latch-tool cast-off method 1. Step (4)

(4) Hold the latch tool in your right hand as if you were shaking hands with it. Push the tool up through the first stitch. Catch the stitch in the hook of the tool and pull it off the needle. Stop the adjacent stitches from being pulled off by holding them back with the index finger of the left hand.

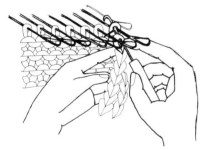

Latch-tool cast-off method 1. Step (5)

(5) Push the tool up until the first stitch falls behind the latch of the tool. Hold that stitch behind the latch with the index finger of your right hand.

(6) Push the tool up through the next stitch on the next needle and catch this stitch in the hook of the tool. Pull this stitch off the needle.

(7) You now have two stitches on your latch tool: one in front of the latch and one behind the latch. Swivel your hand so the stitch on the tool behind the latch drops down over the stitch in the hook.

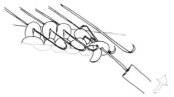

Latch-tool cast-off method 1. Step (7)

(8) Repeat steps (6) and (7) until you have latched off all your stitches and are left with one on the tool. Break your yarn and pull the end through the last stitch.

Method 2

(1) Knit the last loose row from R. to L. Finish with C.O.L.

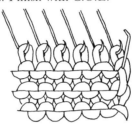

Latch-tool cast-off method 2. Hang the heel of the first stitch onto the gate peg.

(2) Begin at the right hand edge of the knitting. Hang a claw weight on the edge of your knitting or hook the edge stitch onto the gate peg. Hold your latch tool in your right hand as if you were shaking hands with it.

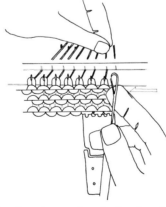

Latch-tool cast-off method 2. Step (1) hang claw weight.

(3) Place your left hand on the needle butts. Push the right hand edge needle forward with your left hand on the butt and keep the

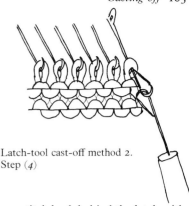

Latch-tool cast-off method 2. Step (4)

stitch back behind the latch with your right index finger.

(4) Place the hook of the latch tool into the hook of the needle as you pull the needle back again.

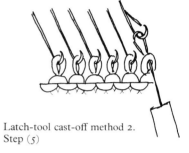

Latch-tool cast-off method 2. Step (5)

(5) When you pull the needle back the stitch will slip over the closed latch of the needle into the hook of the tool.

(6) Lift the tool with the stitch in hook up off the needle. You have now transferred the stitch from the needle onto the latch tool.

(7) Push the latch tool up so that the stitch falls behind the open latch of the tool. Hold it there with your right index finger.

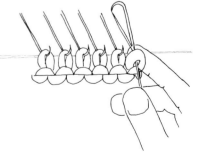

Latch-tool cast-off method 2. Step (7)

(8) Push the next needle forward with your left hand on the needle

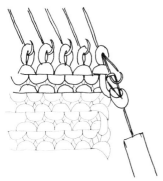

Latch-tool cast-off method 2. Step (8)

butt until the stitch falls behind the open latch of the needle.

(9) Begin to pull the needle back, hooking the hook of the tool into the hook of the needle as you pull it back. The stitch on the needle will slip over the closed needle latch and fall into the hook of the tool. Be very careful that you don't miss putting the hook into the hook otherwise you may lose your stitch altogther!

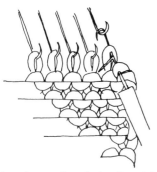

Latch-tool cast-off method 2. Step (9)

(10) Lift your tool off the needle hook. You have two stitches on your tool; one in front of the latch and one behind the latch. Swivel the tool and pull the

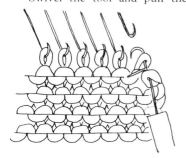

Latch-tool cast-off method 3. Step (10)

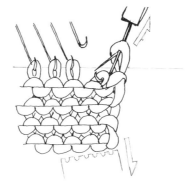

Latch-tool cast-off method 3. Step (10)

second stitch up through the first.

(11) Repeat steps (7) to (10) until all stitches have been latched off. Break yarn and pass the end through the last stitch and pull up tight.

Method 3

This method is rather different from the two preceeding methods in that it does not rely on a loose last knit row. Because you are using the yarn to latch off your last row you can control the amount of elasticity in your cast-off.

(1) Knit the last row and finish with C.O.R. Remove the yarn from the yarn feeder on the carriage and the yarn brake. Hold the yarn in your left hand wound around your little finger, with three fingers against your palm, leaving your thumb and index finger free. Hold the transfer tool in your right hand as if you were shaking hands with it.

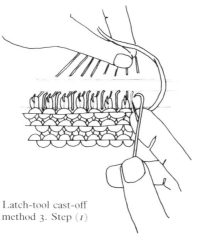

Latch-tool cast-off method 3. Step (1)

(2) Push the right hand edge needle forward with your left hand on the butt, holding the stitch back against the machine with the index finger of your right hand until the stitch falls behind the needle latch.

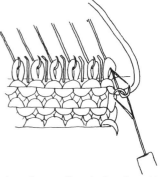

Latch-tool cast-off method 3. Step (2)

(3) Pull the needle back again hooking the hook of the tool into the hook of the needle so that the stitch on the needle is transferred onto the tool.

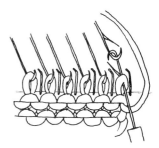

Latch-tool cast-off method 3. Step (3)

(4) Lift the tool off the needle and push it up so that the stitch falls behind the latch on the tool.

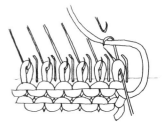

Latch-tool cast-off method 3. Step (4)

(5) Place the end of yarn behind the gate peg and into the hook of the tool. Pull the yarn through forming a new stitch.

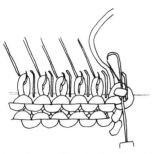

Latch-tool cast-off method 3. Step (5)

(6) Push the right hand edge needle forward again until the stitch passes behind the open latch and pull the needle back hooking the hook of the tool into the hook of the needle until the stitch is transferred onto the latch tool.

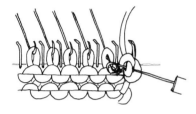

Latch-tool cast-off method 3. Step (6)

(7) Push the tool up so that the two stitches fall behind the latch on the tool.

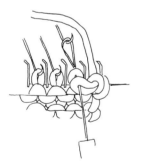

Latch-tool cast-off method 3. Step (7)

(8) Place the loose end of yarn into the hook of the tool, first passing it behind the gate peg (this will ensure a loose cast-off) before pulling it through the two stitches.

(9) Repeat steps (6) to (8) until the latch tool cast-off is complete. At the last stitch break the yarn and pull it through to finish off.

Bind off with needle

This method can be done while the work is still on the machine. Because you are using a needle you can adjust the tension of the binding-off to suit your needs. This method is easier to do if you do not have a ribber on the machine.

Method 1
Binding-off from left to right

(1) Knit the last row from right to left. Finish with the carriage on the left.

(2) Pull all needles to holding position, being very careful to keep the stitches in the hooks of the needles in front of the latches.

(3) Break the main yarn leaving a tail three times as long as the width of the needles with stitches on them.

(4) Thread up a wool darning needle with the main yarn tail. Insert the needle into the last stitch knit on the left edge of the knitting. Pull the yarn through this stitch.

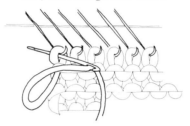

Needle bind-off (L. to R.). Step (4)

(5) Pass the needle from front to back, through the next stitch on the right, and then from back to front through the left edge stitch. Pull the yarn through loosely.

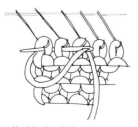

Needle bind-off (L. to R.). Step (5)

(6) Repeat step (5) back-stitching through each loop in turn until you have completed binding-off for all the stitches on the machine.

Method 2
Binding-off from right to left

(1) Knit the last row from left to right. Finish with the carriage on the right.

(2)–(3) As in method 1 above.

(4) Thread up a wool darning needle with the main yarn tail. Insert the needle into the second-to-last stitch at the right edge of the knitting from back to front. Pull the yarn through.

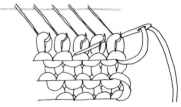

Needle bind-off (R. to L.). Step (4)

(5) Insert the needle from front to back into the last stitch at the right edge of the knitting, then pass it behind the next stitch at the left and bring it through, (from back to front) the next stitch at the left.

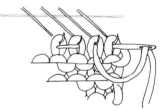

Needle bind-off (R. to L.). Step (5)

(6) Continue from right to left in this manner inserting the needle into the first stitch from front to back, skipping the second stitch, and bringing the needle out again from back to front through the third stitch until the binding off is complete.

Waste yarn method of casting off

When using the waste yarn method of casting-off you can remove your work from the machine and cast-off at your leisure. Just because you are using a knitting machine, there is no rule that says you have to carry out all tasks while your work is on the machine. The advantages of casting-off with a needle or crochet hook from work on waste yarn are:

- you can more easily control the amount of elasticity in your cast-off edge;
- you can do the work anywhere once you have released it from the machine;
- you can achieve a decorative edge more easily.

You may find it easier to accomplish this hand-finishing away from the machine as it is easier to hold and manipulate the work and the needle or crochet hook.

After completing the knitting, break the main yarn leaving a spare piece of yarn at least three times as long as the width of the working needles. It is much easier to complete the finishing of your garment if you use a W.Y. which is smooth and a complete contrast in colour to your M.Y. If you knit one row with your cast-on cord before you start the waste knitting it will be easier to pull out and remove the waste knitting when the finishing is complete. Thread up the machine with waste yarn, and knit several rows (at least ten). Then strip the work off the machine by removing the yarn from the carriage and taking it across the needle bed without any yarn. You may press the waste yarn *only* at this stage. This will 'lock' the waste knitting and prevent it unravelling while you are working on it.

After pressing the waste knitting, you must fold it down at the point where it joins your main knitting. You can turn the work so that the stocking stitch side of your garment is facing you. You will then fold the waste knitting down towards you so that the purl side is facing you.

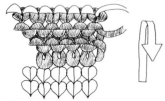

Stocking stitch facing, fold W.Y. down towards you

Alternatively, you can have the purl side of your garment facing you in which case you will fold the waste knitting down away from you, leaving the last row of M.Y. loops sitting up at the top of your work at the fold line.

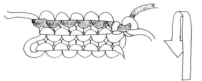

Purl side facing, fold W.Y. down away from you

Method 1 Binding-off with needle
  (A) Back stitching from left to right
(1) After knitting the last row of M.Y. C.O.R.
(2) Remove the work from the machine onto waste yarn and press the waste yarn.
(3) Thread the needle with the tail end of main yarn.
(4) Fold the waste knitting down over the work so that the last row of M.Y. loops is at the top of your work.
(5) Beginning at the last stitch knitted in main yarn at the left insert the needle into this loop from back to front and pass it through.

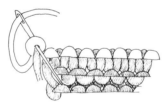

Needle bind-off with W.Y. method A. Step (5)

(6) Insert the needle from front to back into the next main yarn loop. Bring the needle out from back to front through the first loop at the left.

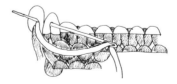

Needle bind-off with W.Y. method A. Step (6)

(7) Insert the needle from front to back through the third M.Y. loop and bring it back out from back to front through the second M.Y. loop.
(8) This movement will give you a back stitched finished edge. Continue back stitching across the width of the edge to be cast-off. Be careful not to pull the stitches too tight.
  (B) Back stitching from right to left
(1) After knitting the last row of M.Y. C.O.L.
(2)–(4) As in method (A) above.
(5) Insert the needle from back to front into the second main yarn loop.

Needle bind-off with W.Y. method B. Step (5)

(6) Put the needle from front to back into the first M.Y. loop and then bring it (skipping the next stitch) through the third main yarn loop from back to front.

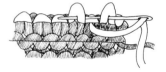

Needle bind-off with W.Y. method B. Step (6)

(7) Continue back stitching in this way across the width of the edge to be cast-off. Be careful not to pull the stitches too tight.

Method 2 Latch tool method
  (A) Crochet edge with extra M.Y.
(1)–(4) As in method 1 (B) above. With this method it is not necessary to break the main yarn off when the knitting is finished. When the work is turned so that the stocking stitch side is facing you, the tail of M.Y. is at the right hand side of the work.
(5) Using the latch tool and the main yarn, crochet loosely through the last row of main yarn loops.

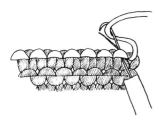

Latch-tool bind-off with W.Y.

(6) When you have finished, break the main yarn and pull it through the last loop.

(B) *Crochet edge without extra M.Y.*

(1)–(4) As in method 1 (A) above. With this method you must knit the last row of M.Y. knitting on a much looser tension.

(5) Using the latch tool crochet the last row of M.Y. loops through. When you reach the tail of M.Y. at the left hand side of your work, break the M.Y. and pull it through the last loop.

Part, slip or empty cast-off

This method uses the carriage to knit together the stitches transferred with the tool. It is best done with a fairly smooth standard yarn and should not be attempted with a furry, bouclé or knobbly yarn.

(1) Knit the last row on main tension and finish with the carriage on the right.

(2) Set the carriage to knit needles pushed to H.P.

(3) Make sure the punch-card patterning information is disconnected from the needles. On the Knitmaster machine the side levers are forward, on the Jones/Brother and Toyota machines the needles will not be selected to U.W.P.

(4) Hang a claw weight at the right-hand edge of the knitting.

Cast-off using carriage pattern setting

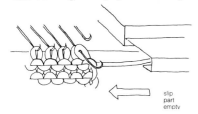

slip
part
empty

(5) Transfer the first stitch at the right onto the second needle and pull this needle to H.P. – two stitches on this needle.

(6) Set the carriage to slip, part or empty. Take the carriage from right to left and back again. The one needle in H.P. will knit.

(7) Repeat steps (5) to (6) until one stitch remains. Break the yarn and pull it through this last stitch.

Special note

When casting-off only a few stitches in shaping a garment – e.g. armholes, centre necklines, shoulders, etc. – but not the whole row at once, you may have to use special techniques. The following are some suggestions you might try depending on the circumstances.

(1) Cast-off your stitches on the side of work opposite to the carriage using a spare piece of M.Y., using the transfer tool technique. This can be particularly useful when doing Fair Isle work and you are knitting each row in two colours simultaneously.

(2) On machines with a pre-select row patterning system: when knitting Fair Isle patterning, ensure that all needles to be cast off knit the same colour yarn by manually selecting all needles to be cast off to W.P. or U.W.P. at the opposite end of work from the carriage before knitting the row. When knitting other stitch patterns select all needles to U.W.P. to ensure they all *knit*.

(3) On machines without the pre-select row, you may achieve a similar effect by manually selecting all needles to be cast off at the opposite side of the work to the carriage to H.P. and setting the carriage to knit before knitting the cast-off row. Alternatively, move your pattern isolating cams on the needle bed in from the edge needles, thus leaving the edge needles to knit plain and not pattern.

(4) When you use the Swiss machines for single bed work (Passap or Pfaff) you may push up needles to W.P. opposite the needles to be cast-off on the needle bed which is not in use. Alternatively, knit one row. Loops will form on the empty needles on the second bed. Drop these loops off the needles on the second bed manually. This will leave you with larger loops on your main knitting just where you need to execute a latch tool cast-off. Return the now unwanted needles to N.W.P. and latch off the required number of stitches on the main bed.

7 Casting off with a ribber

Ribbed fabric is far more elastic than single bed fabric so special care must be taken to ensure that the casting-off is not too tight and inelastic. Some of the methods explained below are suitable only if you wish to cast-off all your work rather than just a few stitches for shaping purposes.

I Transfer method

With this method you transfer all your stitches onto one bed and then use one of the single bed techniques to cast-off. The advantage of this method is that you may be more adept at working on the single bed and thus find this method easier. The disadvantage is that you may have two stitches on a needle when converting double bed fabric to the single bed, thus making your casting-off lumpy and tight.

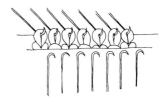

All stitches transferred to the main bed

(*1*) Transfer all your stitches from the ribber to the main bed. Make sure you have at least one loop on every needle.

(*2*) Leave alternate needles in W.P. on the ribber and knit one row on both beds.

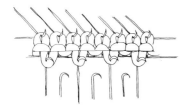

Alternate needles knit one row on the ribber

(*3*) Disconnect your ribber carriage and take it across the ribber bed, thus dropping all the loops on the ribber needles and leaving larger loops on the main bed needles. If you are not casting off the whole row, you will have to drop the stitches off the second bed by pushing the needles manually.

(*4*) Cast-off the work on the main bed using a preferred single bed cast-off technique.

II Transfer stitch cast-off for several stitches

This is a modified version of **I** above if you are doing shaping work. On the row before the cast-off row transfer the stitches from the ribber to the main bed opposite those stitches to be cast-off. Leave the empty ribber needles in W.P.

(*i*) On the same side as the carriage – after knitting the row, drop the loops off the 'extra' ribber needles manually and latch-off the required stitches on the main bed needles.

(*ii*) On the side opposite the carriage – after knitting the row, drop the loops off the 'extra' ribber needles manually and cast-off using the transfer tool technique.

III Ribber latch tool technique

This technique works very well on the Passap/Pfaff machines but is per-

haps a bit more difficult to master on the Japanese machines.

(*1*) After knitting the last row C.O.R. Transfer all stitches from the ribber to the main bed.

(*2*) Leave *all* the needles in W.P. on the ribber. Set the pitch lever so that the needles in W.P. on both beds will not hit each other.

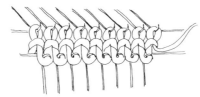

All needles knit one row on the ribber

(*3*) Knit one row from right to left. Drop the ribber or front bed slightly so that there is a gap between the two beds. Using a three-pronged transfer tool, push the 'heels' of the stitches from the previous row towards the front bed.

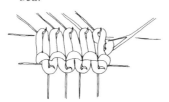

Using a latch tool to cast-off between the needle beds

(*4*) Using the latch tool, latch off the loops on the main bed, back bed needles. When you get to the last loop, break your M.Y. and pull it through. Special care must be taken to ensure that the correct loops are latched off otherwise you may find that you have not cast-off at all!

IV Double-eyed bodkin: working from the same side as the carriage

You may cast-off stitch by stitch using the double-eyed bodkin and the same method you would use for a single bed transfer tool except that you would be working alternately between the two beds and just casting-off the next stitch as you come to

it, regardless of which bed it is on. This method is time-consuming but can be quite loose. It is useful when shaping your garment.

V Needle bind-off

Although this method can be time-consuming it will give you a finished cast-off edge which is indistinguishable from the professional looking cast-on edge you get with the circular rows at the beginning of ribbed knitting.

Method A – 1 × 1 rib with waste knitting on the single bed

(*1*) When you have knit your last row of ribbed knitting, M.Y., C.O.L. Break off M.Y. and thread up W.Y. Transfer all stitches from the ribber needles to *empty* main bed needles.

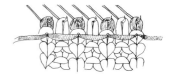

1 × 1 Bind-off with W.Y. (method A). Step (*2*)

(*2*) Push all main bed needles with transferred stitches on them to U.W.P. or H.P. Set the carriage to knit *only the needles selected to U.W.P. or H.P.* Set the carriage to slip, empty or part and make sure the pattern card is not connected to the needles. Knit one row with W.Y.

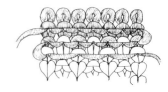

1 × 1 Bind-off with W.Y. (method A). Step (*3*)

(*3*) Re-set the carriage to knit all the needles and knit several rows with waste yarn. Remove the work from the machine.

(*4*) Press the waste knitting and turn it around so that the stocking stitch side is facing you. Fold the waste knitting down towards you over the work. The M.Y. 'tail' is at the right-hand side of the work and you will see two rows of M.Y. loops, a front row and a back row.

(5) Thread up your darning needle with the M.Y. 'tail' and pass the needle through the first M.Y. loop in the back row and through the first M.Y. loop in the front row (from back to front).

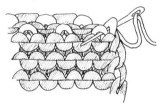

1 × 1 Bind-off with W.Y. (method A). Step (5)

(6) Take the needle to the back row M.Y. loops and pass the needle from back to front through the first back row M.Y. loop, then on from front to back through the next back row M.Y. loop.

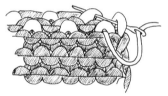

1 × 1 Bind-off with W.Y. (method A). Step (6)

(7) Return to the front row M.Y. loops. Pass the needle from front to back through the last front row M.Y. loop your yarn is coming out of and then from back to front through the next front row M.Y. loop.

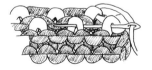

1 × 1 Bind-off with W.Y. (method A). Step (7)

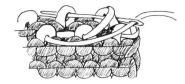

1 × 1 Bind-off with W.Y. (method A). Step (8)

(8) Repeat steps (6) and (7) until you have completed your bound off edge. Be very careful not to pull your stitches tight.

Method (B) – 2 × 2 rib with waste knitting on the single bed
(1)–(4) Follow the steps for method (A) above.

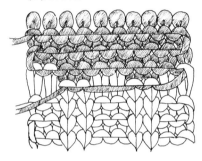

2 × 2 Bind-off with W.Y. (method B). Steps (1)–(4)

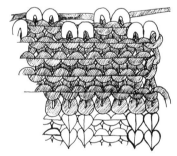

2 × 2 Bind-off with W.Y. (method B). Step (6)

(5) Thread up your darning needle with the tail of M.Y. You will see two rows of M.Y. loops in pairs. One row at the back and one row at the front.

2 × 2 Bind-off with W.Y. (method B). Step (6)

(6) Pass your needle through the first pair of M.Y. loops in the front row; through the first loop from front to back; and through the second loop from back to front.

(7) Then pass the needle from front to back through the first M.Y. loop in the front row and from front to back through the first M.Y. loop in the back row.

2 × 2 Bind-off with W.Y. (method B). Step (7)

(8) Return to the front row. Pass the needle from front to back through the last front row M.Y. loop your yarn came out of, and on from back to front through the next front row M.Y. loop.

2 × 2 Bind-off with W.Y. (method B). Step (8)

(9) Return to the back row M.Y. loops. Pass your needle from back to front through the last back row M.Y. loop your yarn came out of and on from front to back through the next back row M.Y. loop.

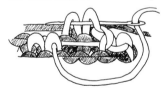

2 × 2 Bind-off with W.Y. (method B). Step (9)

(10) Repeat steps (8) and (9) until the binding-off is completed. Be careful not to pull your stitches too tight!

Method C – 1 × 1 rib with waste knitting on the double bed
(1) Knit the last row with M.Y. and break off the M.Y.

(2) Thread up the machine with W.Y. Set the carriage to knit only the needles on *one* bed. Increase the T.D. number to single bed main tension (about four numbers).

(3) Knit four rows on one bed.

(4) Knit four rows on the other bed only.

(5) Repeat steps (3) and (4) twice more, then knit several rows on both beds and remove the work from the machine.

(6) Press the waste knitting only and unravel the rows knit on both beds. Fold the two flaps of waste knitting down. You will see two rows of M.Y. loops, a top row and a bottom row.

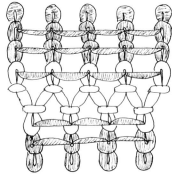

1 × 1 Bind-off with W.Y. (method C). Step (5)

(7) Thread up a darning needle with M.Y. and bind off last row of M.Y. loops.

(8) Pass the needle up through the first M.Y. loop in the top row, then up through the first M.Y. loop in the bottom row and on down through the next M.Y. loop in the bottom row.

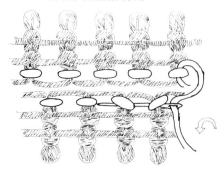

1 × 1 Bind-off with W.Y. (method C). Step (8)

(9) Return to the first M.Y. loop in the top row and pass the needle down through the first loop then up through the next M.Y. loop in the top row.

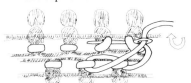

1 × 1 Bind-off with W.Y. (method C). Step (9)

(10) Continue to bind off the M.Y. loops always passing your needle alternately through the top and bottom rows of M.Y. loops returning to the last loop your yarn came out of. (The needle will make alternate u and n shaped movements.)

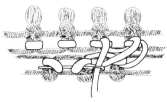

1 × 1 Bind-off with W.Y. (method C). Step (10)

Method (D) – 2 × 2 rib with waste knitting on the double bed

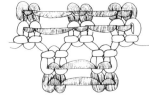

2 × 2 Bind-off with W.Y. (method D). Steps (1)–(7)

(1)–(7) as for method (C) above.

(8) Pass the needle down through the first M.Y. loop in the top row, then up through the next M.Y. loop in the top row.

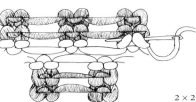

2 × 2 Bind-off with W.Y. (method D). Step (8)

(9) Pass the needle down again through the first M.Y. loop in the top row and down through the first M.Y. loop in the bottom row.

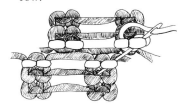

2 × 2 Bind-off with W.Y. (method D). Step (9)

(10) Return to the top row. Pass the needle down through the last left-hand M.Y. loop your yarn comes out of and up through the next M.Y. loop on the left in the top row.

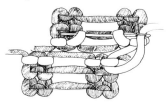

2 × 2 Bind-off with W.Y. (method D). Step (10)

(11) Return to the bottom row and pass your needle up through the last M.Y. loop your yarn comes out of then down through the next M.Y. loop.

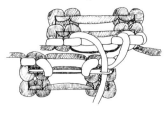

2 × 2 Bind-off with W.Y. (method D). Step (11)

(12) Repeat steps (10) and (11) until the binding off is completed. Be careful not to pull your stitches too tight!

8 Shaping: increasing and decreasing

Basically using the transfer tool enables you to move your stitches from one needle to another along the needle bed. You are usually supplied with a selection of transfer tools with your machine. These consist of a prong with an eye at either end of a handle. The tools are arranged either singly or in groups and are referred to as 1 × 2, 1 × 3, or 2 × 3 transfer tools. You can also purchase an adjustable multi-transfer 4.5mm ($\frac{1}{6}$ in.) tool that can have up to seven prongs in a row, which can be arranged in various ways.

The prongs of the transfer tools are spaced identically to the needles on your machine; thus tools are usually available for 4.5mm (standard gauge Japanese machines), 5mm (Passap and Pfaff machines), and 8mm and 9mm (chunky gauge Japanese machines). Be very careful that any tools you purchase for your machine in addition to the ones that come with the machine are the correct gauge. They are not interchangeable, although tools for the 4.5mm gauge may be used on the 9mm gauge machine as the needles are exactly twice as far apart. (You must remember that the needles are much bigger on the chunky machine than they are on the standard gauge machine.)

It is a fairly simple matter to increase or decrease stitches at the edge of your fabric. It is more difficult to alter the number of stitches in the middle of your work.

Increasing

I Simple increasing
You may increase *one* stitch at one edge of your work in one row by pushing an extra needle to W.P. at the edge of your knitting *between the work and the carriage only*. Do not push up a needle to W.P. at the other side of your work. You do not need a transfer tool to do this.

II Simple increasing using a transfer tool
You may increase one stitch at either or both ends of the row by using your transfer tool to pick up the heel of the stitch on the end needle (the loop from the row below) to an empty needle which you have pushed to W.P. at the edge of your work.

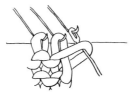

Picking up the heel of the edge stitch

III Fully fashioned increasing
You may use your multi-transfer tool to move two to three stitches simultaneously. You will then find you have an empty needle, not at the edge of your work but several needles in from the edge. You can use your single transfer tool to pick up the heel of the adjacent stitch (the loop from the row below) and transfer this loop onto the empty needle, thus preventing a hole from being formed.

Using the triple transfer tool

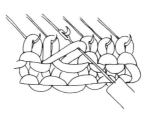

Picking up the heel of an adjacent stitch to place on an empty needle

IV Decorative fully fashioned increasing
In this method you proceed as in method *III* but do not transfer a loop onto the empty needle. The hole thus formed can provide a decorative feature. Remember to leave the newly emptied needle in W.P.

V Increasing more than one stitch at the edge of your work
In order to do this you are really casting-on; all the principles of casting-on will apply whether you are adding 2 stitches or 22 stitches.
(*1*) Simple 'E' wrap –
   (*a*) Between the knitting and the carriage, push the required number of needles to H.P. Set the carriage to knit all needles in H.P.
   (*b*) Using M.Y. wrap the needles as for an 'E' wrap cast-on.
   (*c*) Knit several rows, always pushing the cast-on needles to H.P. with one hand while pushing the knitting back against the machine with the other until you have some knitting on the new needles. Hang a claw weight on this knitting.

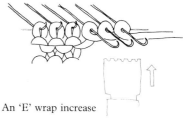

An 'E' wrap increase

(*2*) 'E' wrap with a waste swatch –
   (*a*) Between the knitting and the carriage, push the required number of needles to W.P. With the transfer tool mount a swatch of waste knitting on these empty needles.

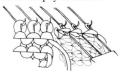

Picking up waste knitting using a triple transfer tool.

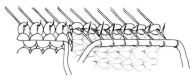

Laying-in the cast-on cord onto the needle hooks

(b) Push the needles to H.P. and knit one row by hand with the cast-on cord.

(c) Using M.Y. wrap the needles as for an 'E' wrap cast-on.

An 'E' wrap cast-on over the last row knit with the cast-on cord

(d) Continue to knit, hanging a comb or weight on the waste swatch. After you have finished your piece of knitting you can pull the cast-on cord out and the waste swatch will fall off.

(3) 'E' wrap with a comb –
(a) Between the knitting and the carriage, push the required number of needles to H.P. Set the carriage to knit needles in H.P.
(b) Using M.Y. wrap the needles as for an 'E' wrap cast-on very loosely.

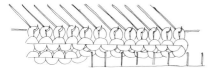

Cast-on comb hung onto the cast-on edge

(c) Knit one row and carefully hang the cast-on comb onto the new loops.

(4) 'E' wrap with a hanging cast-on comb –
(a) The hanging cast-on comb must be hung *first*, before the needles are pushed up to H.P.

Cast-on comb hung onto the gate pegs before beginning the 'E' wrap cast-on

(b) Between the knitting and the carriage, push the required number of needles to H.P. Set

the carriage to knit needles in H.P.

(c) Using M.Y. wrap the needles as for an 'E' wrap cast-on very loosely.

(d) Drop the comb onto the 'E' wrap cast-on and proceed to knit.

The main difficulty with this last method is in getting the comb to hang evenly on the work. If it is not symmetrical one end may tip up and foul the movement of the carriage.

These methods can also be used on the side of the work *opposite* the carriage by casting-on with a spare piece of M.Y. This means there will be no noticeable break in stitch patterning.

As well as mounting new stitches with an 'E' wrap edge, you can also use your latch tool to mount your new stitches on the needles. The same choices are open to you, using your latch tool instead of the 'E' wrap.

Decreasing

When doing a lot of decreasing at the edges of your work (even simple decreasing) you may find the edge of your knitting will become very tight and possibly even distort your garment. This is a common problem with raglan shaping that can be avoided by following these two measures.
(a) Hang claw weights at the edge of your work.
(b) Push up an empty needle to W.P. occasionally at the edge of the work between the knitting and the carriage. When you knit the following row, the empty needle will pick up a loop. Drop this extra loop and return the needle to N.W.P. before continuing your knitting. This will ensure the necessary elasticity at the edge of your work.

I Simple decreasing with a transfer tool
(A) Use the transfer tool to move the end stitch from the end needle to the adjacent needle with a stitch. Push the empty needle back to N.W.P. When you knit the next row you will automatically knit two stitches

together. This can be done at both edges of your work simultaneously. It is advisable to hang claw weights at the edges of your work.

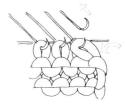

Edge stitch moved in one needle

(B) Use the transfer tool to move the second stitch from the end to the end needle – thus leaving the second needle from the end empty. Then transfer *both* stitches to the second needle from the end and push the end needle, which is now empty, back to N.W.P. This results in a more attractive edge, which is less lumpy and therefore easier to sew.

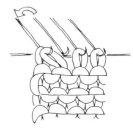

Second stitch from the edge moved out one needle

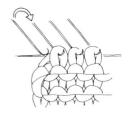

Both stitches moved back to the empty needle

II Fully fashioned decreasing
Instead of using a single-eyed transfer tool, you use a double, triple or

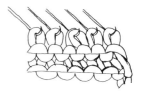

Fully fashioned decreasing purl side

multi-eyed transfer tool. You move several stitches at once; the needle with two stitches is not the end needle. This gives you a decorative feature in your knitting which can most plainly be seen in stocking stitch, lace or ribbed knitting as you get a continuous line of straight stitches at the edge of your work. It is not usually found in work using multi-coloured or very textured stitch patterns. It can be very effective in garments that require a great deal of shaping such as raglan sleeves and V necklines. With a band of plain stitches at the edge of your piece of knitting it then becomes much easier to make up the garment.

Fully fashioned decreasing stocking stitch side

III Multiple fully fashioned decreasing
This technique follows the same procedure as the simple fully fashioned decreasing, except that you may decrease more than one stitch at a time. In other words, with your triple transfer tool you may remove three stitches from three needles and then replace these stitches so that two of the stitches are transferred to needles with stitches already on them and only one stitch is transferred to an empty needle. You will then be able to push two newly emptied needles back to N.W.P. before knitting the next row.

IV Decorative fully fashioned
    decreasing
This technique is the same as method *III* – that is, you are using your triple transfer tool or your multi-eyed transfer tool to decrease two stitches, several stitches in from the edge of your work. However, if you put back one of the edge needles you have just made empty to W.P., you will get a decorative hole at the edge of your raglan shaping which will be a decorative feature when you come to make up your garment. This method is

most effective when you are decreasing fairly frequently, e.g. every other row.

V Decreasing several stitches
When you decrease several stitches you are really casting-off and, therefore, you must remember all the rules that apply to casting-off. For knitting plain fabric, i.e. stocking stitch, you need not take any special precautions. You may cast-off only at the side of your knitting which is next to your carriage; however, if you want to cast off on the opposite side simultaneously you must use a spare piece of yarn. Do not use the latch tool method for this decreasing as it is too tight.

For decreasing several stitches when you are doing stitch-patterned knitting the procedure is different. On machines with a pre-select row (the Jones/Brother and the Toyota) you can control the patterning of the edge stitches manually. If you are knitting a Fair Isle, tuck, or part/empty pattern on the row preceeding the cast-off row and on the side of the knitting opposite the carriage, push all the needles you wish to cast-off to U.W.P. This will ensure that they will all knit (or knit one colour) and thus be easier to cast-off on the following row.

If you are knitting a lace pattern and using a lace carriage push all the needles you wish to cast-off to W.P. on the rows preceeding the cast-off row and on the side of the knitting you wish to cast-off. This will ensure that the needles will all knit and thus be easier to cast-off on the following row.

On machines without a pre-select row you will have to use your stitch-pattern cams to isolate the edge needles, thus preventing them from knitting in a pattern.

On Passap and Pfaff machines you will be able to manually over-ride the pushers or use the positioning pins on the deco to isolate the edge needles and thus control the type knitting the edge needles do.

VI Decreasing several stitches at the edge of work opposite the carriage
This is a useful technique which is easily accomplished on any machine. Just introduce a separate spare piece of M.Y. and use this to do a loose transfer-tool cast-off on the edge of work which is opposite the carriage.

Increasing and decreasing evenly within a row

This technique can be very useful to control fullness in garments and is vital when knitting yoked garments. It is a bit time-consuming, however, and some skill plus a great deal of patience must be exercised.

The method is quite simple. You must remove your work from the machine onto either W.Y. or a garter bar and then return the stitches to a fewer or greater number of needles, depending on whether you want to increase or decrease the width of your knitting.

Some machines have deco combs or multi-transfer tools, which enable you to move as many as 30 stitches at one time. This makes it much easier to increase or decrease within your knitting and to make vertical darts. Some of the uses to which this technique can be put are:

- gathering of the garment into cuffs, hems or neck edges;
- decreasing evenly several times when knitting a yoke;
- gathering a skirt into a waistband or onto a bodice;
- gathering a full garment onto a fitted yoke;
- gathering a trim such as a ruffle which would then be applied to a garment;
- increasing after knitting a rib to produce more give in the body of a garment.

I Increasing evenly across the knitting

Knit the garment up to the row in which you wish to increase.

Using waste yarn
(1) Determine how many stitches you wish to increase across your row. Remember there is a limit to how far you can pull your knitting out.
(2) Knit several rows in W.Y. (at least eight).
(3) Remove the yarn from the carriage and knit one row, dropping the work off the machine.

Picking up the last row of M.Y. stitches

(4) Push up the required extra needles and replace the last row of M.Y. loops onto the needles. You will not have enough M.Y. loops to fill all the needles. *Pick up with your transfer tool, the heel of the stitch on the adjacent needle and put this loop onto the empty needle.* Repeat from * to * until all needles in W.P. have loops on them.

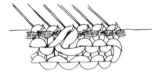

Picking-up the heel of the adjacent stitch onto the empty needle

Using the Garter Bar
(1) Determine how many stitches you wish to increase across your row. Remember there is a limit to how far you can pull your knitting out.
(2) Remove your work onto the garter bar.

Removing stitches onto the garter bar

(a) You may remove all your stitches directly onto the garter bar, putting each stitch directly onto a needle.
(b) You may remove your stitches in groups onto your garter bar, leaving gaps on the bar to correspond to the stitches you wish to increase. A transfer tool hung onto the hook of the needle next to the last needle in the group of stitches you are transferring to the bar will prevent stitches being dropped.

Removing stitches in groups onto the garter bar

(3) Push up the required extra needles and replace the stitches from your garter bar onto the needles in groups, leaving an empty needle at fixed intervals across the bed so that you have evenly spaced your stitches across the width of the working needles.

II Decreasing evenly across the row

Decreasing evenly across the row before removing the work
Firstly, decide how many stitches you need to delete.

Secondly, calculate how many needles you will have between each decrease. *See* the Magic Formula on page 177. Subtract the number of stitches you require from the number of stitches you have: this is equivalent to the number of times you must put two stitches on one needle. Divide the number of stitches you require by the number of times you must decrease. This will give you the number of stitches you will have between each decrease. If this number is not even you may distribute the decreasing evenly across the row by using the magic formula or you may be a bit more casual by approximating the distribution of decreasing. It will

only be critical if you are knitting a Fair Isle yoke and require the pattern to be evenly spaced. You can avoid this problem by using a pattern with a small stitch repeat in the rows just before and after the shaping row.

Thirdly, use the transfer tool or the lace carriage* to transfer stitches to adjacent needles.

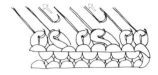

Transferring stitches before removing work from the machine

Either:
(1) Push the needles you wish to transfer the stitches from to U.W.P.
(2) Then pass the lace carriage across the bed. The stitches will be transferred.
(3) Remove the lace carriage and push all needles back to W.P.
(4) Push empty needles to N.W.P.
Or:
(1) Pass the lace carriage from L. to R. (with not punch card in the machine all needles are selected to U.W.P.).
(2) Push back to W.P. all needles except the needles of the stitches you wish to transfer.
(3) Pass the lace carriage from L. to R. The stitches will be transferred.
(4) Remove the lace carriage and push all needles back to W.P.
(5) Push empty needles to N.W.P.

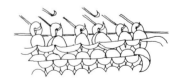

Knit one row with empty needles in N.W.P.

Fourthly, knit one row M.Y. across needles in W.P. (only needles with loops on them.)

Fifthly, remove the work from the machine. Either knit eight to ten rows with W.Y., then knit one row without any yarn in the carriage and drop the work off the machine or remove the work onto a garter bar.

Finally, push the required needles to W.P. Replace the last row of M.Y. loops onto the needles.

Decreasing evenly across the row after removing the work
Firstly, decide how many stitches you need to delete. Secondly, calculate how many needles you will have between each decrease. (The magic formula.) Subtract the number of stitches you require from the number of stitches you have. This gives you the number of times you must put two stitches on one needle (decrease). Divide the number of stitches you require by the number of times you must decrease. This gives the number of stitches you will have between each decrease. If this number is not even you may distribute the decreasing evenly across the row by using the magic formula (p. 177) or you may be more casual by approximating the distribution of decreasing. It will be critical only if you are knitting a Fair Isle yoke and require the pattern to be evenly spaced. Avoid this problem by using a pattern with a small stitch repeat in the rows just before and after the shaping row.

Thirdly, remove the work from the machine. Knit eight to ten rows with W.Y. Knit one row with no yarn in the carriage and drop the work off the machine. Remove the work onto the garter bar. At this point you have the option to place one stitch on every eye of the bar or you may wish to decrease at this time by placing your stitches on the bar with the stitches already doubled-up the required number of times.

Finally, push the required number of needles to W.P. Replace the last row of M.Y. loops onto the needles, doubling-up the stitches on the needles where necessary. (**NB** At cuffs of full sleeves you may wish to place three or more stitches on every needle.)

You may also find this method of gathering your work useful at the hem edge of your garment. Start knitting the body of your garment on W.Y. When you finish, turn the knitting upside down to replace the *first* row of M.Y. loops on the machine, decreasing evenly across the row.

9 Partial knitting

In addition to increasing, decreasing, casting-on and casting-off you can also shape your garment by using the technique of partial knitting. With partial knitting you 'ignore' the stitches on some needles and knit only the stitches on other needles. You keep the unknitted stitches on the needles rather than fasten them off and delete them completely. The advantage of this technique is that you can knit these stitches at a later point in the garment without having to cast them on again.

You can use partial knitting when shaping gradually, as in the shoulder slope or on a sideways knitted skirt. You can also use the technique within a garment shape to give it form, as in knitting bust darts or the heel of a sock. Once you have grasped the concept there is no limit to its possibilities, e.g. for hoods, sideways knitted sleeves, etc. Partial knitting can also be used as a means of introducing

Uses of partial knitting
Skirts – shaping hems   sideways knit skirts

Tops – batwing styles with
      shoulder shaping
      neck inserts
      shoulder inserts
      bust darts
      shoulder shaping
      neck shaping

Effects – bobbles
      larger cables
      producing large
        blocks of colour
      changing stitch
        patterns

flat, coloured shapes into your garment and also to create three dimensional effects like bobbles and cables.

Method
Basically there are three ways of knitting only some of the needles in working position (needles with stitches).
(1) Push those needles you do not wish to knit to hold position and set the carriage so that it doesn't knit those needles. The disadvantage of this method is that the brushes on the sinker plate repeatedly brush across the surface of the fabric and mark it. To solve this problem you can either:
● put adhesive or masking-tape onto the knitting below the needles in hold position;

Attach adhesive tape on knitting below needles in H.P.

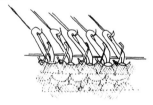

Curtain fabric hung onto gate pegs after stitches have been knit back to N.W.P. with the cast-on cord

● hang a scrap of waste knitting or net curtain over the gate pegs in front of the knitting to protect it. You must remember to do this before you push your needles into hold position.
(2) Use the ravel cord to knit those needles of the stitches you wish to hold back to N.W.P. by hand. To help keep those needles back in N.W.P. you can put a piece of adhesive or masking-tape on the needle bed in front of the needle butts. The problem of protecting the knitting on the needles in

H.P. remains the same as in method (*1*) and can be solved in the same way, but because your needles are not sticking out it is easier to hang a bit of waste knitting or net curtain on the gate pegs.

When you leave your work on the machine – that is, you either push needles to H.P. or knit them with the ravel cord back to N.W.P., you must ensure you do not mark the knitting you are holding by constantly passing the carriage across it. It will not mark if you only knit a few rows, but if your yarn is delicate (e.g. soft lambswool) or light coloured (e.g. white) you must take extra precautions.

(*3*) Take the stitches you wish to hold off the needles by one of the following methods.
- Knit only those stitches off onto waste yarn (in which case you would have to put the remaining stitches into H.P.).
- Put the stitches you wish to hold onto a knitting needle by hand.
- Use a holding comb (which is similar to a multi-transfer tool with 30 teeth and a lid for retaining stitches) or a garter bar.
- Take the stitches to be held off onto a garter bar which can then be hung onto the gate pegs. The garter bar will prevent the work from being marked by the repeated passage of the brushes on the front of the carriage.
- On the Passap machine which is a double-bed machine that works without weights, you are always knitting with both carriages (locks) and the ribber is always in position. On these machines it is a simple matter to transfer the stitches to the bed that is not is use.
  The advantage of method (*3*) is that your work is never marked by the brushes on the front of the carriage.

Wrapping

When you use method (*1*) or (*2*) at the end of each row you must be careful to wrap the yarn at the edge of the needles which are in working position or you will get holes in your fabric. There are two methods of wrapping.
(*1*) *Manual wrap:* when you have brought the carriage across the needles in holding position, you must take the yarn underneath the last needle in holding position next to the working needles and then bring it up over the rest of the needles in holding position ready to bring the carriage back to knit the next row.

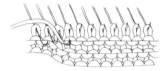

Manually wrapping the last needle in H.P.

(*2*) *Automatic wrap:* when you have brought the carriage across the needles in holding position, you must push the last needle in working position (next to the group of needles in holding position) to holding position as well, thus automatically bringing the yarn underneath the last needle in holding position.

When pushing needles to holding position always remember to push the knitting back against the machine with one hand while you push the needle butts forward with your other hand. With this method you must remember you will be adding an additional needle to those in holding position at the *end* of the row.

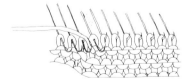

'Automatic' wrap

Changing from holding position back to working position

There are three ways of doing this
- Push the needles back to U.W.P. They will then knit without altering the carriage setting. Be careful to push them back just so that the open latches are aligned with the gate pegs – If you push them too far, your stitches will drop off.
- Alter the carriage setting to knit all needles.
- Return the stitches to the needle hooks by hand using a transfer tool. This may be necessary if you wish to continue in pattern knitting.

When you wish to return needles to W.P. in order to continue with pattern knitting the easiest way to do this is to knit the needles back using the ravel cord for one row. You can then unravel it, thus leaving all needles in W.P.

10 Hems

Hems are an integral part of garment design and associated with the beginning of your garment. Deciding on what sort of hem to use before you begin is very important, as is the realisation that many hems are unsuitable for some garments. Hems are closely related to edges and therefore often interchangeable with them.

I Basic turned-up hem on all machines

Basic turned-up hem (front)

Basic turned-up hem (back)

(*1*) Cast on with W.Y. M.T. Knit 9 rows. C.O.L.
(*2*) Remove W.Y. from feeder and replace with the cast-on-cord. Hold the cord by hand, (hand-feed) and knit 1 row. C.O.R.
(*3*) Remove the cord from the feeder and replace with M.Y.

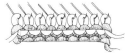

One row knit with the cast-on cord

(*4*) Knit ten rows. M.T.–2. C.O.R. R.C.10.
(*5*) Knit one row M.T.+1. C.O.L. R.C.11.
(*6*) Knit ten rows M.T.–2. C.O.L. R.C. 21.
(*7*) Knit one row M.T.+1. C.O.R. R.C.22.
(*8*) Turn up hem. Pick up the first row of M.Y. loops after the row knit with the cast-on-cord.

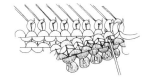

Turning up a hem

(*9*) Knit one row M.T.+1.

Continue to knit the garment. After knitting, pull the cast-on cord out and the waste knitting will fall off. The depth of the hem can be increased or decreased by altering the number of rows knit in steps (*4*) and (*6*). In order to ensure the hem does not flip up you could knit step (*4*) at a smaller number than you will use in step (*6*). The smaller your tension dial setting (stitch size) the neater and tighter your hem will be.

II Basic turned-up hem on all machines with an 'E' wrap cast-on

Basic turned-up hem with 'E' wrap cast-on (front)

Basic turned-up hem with 'E' wrap

(*1*) Select required needles to H.P. Set carriage to knit all needles.

Thread up carriage with M.Y. C.O.R.
(*2*) Place a slip knot on the first needle at the left in H.P., with M.Y. and do an 'E' wrap cast-on on all needles in H.P.
(*3*) Knit ten rows, M.T.–2, C.O.R. On the first few rows carefully push all needles to H.P. with one hand on the needle butts, being sure to push the knitting down and back against the machine behind the needle latches with the other hand. This will help to ensure that the first few rows are knit properly without problems.
(*4*) Knit 1 row M.T.+1, C.O.L.
(*5*) Knit 10 rows M.T.–2, C.O.L.
(*6*) Knit 1 row M.T.+1, C.O.R.

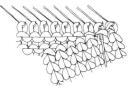

Turning up a hem with 'E' wrap cast-on edge

(*7*) Turn up hem. Pick up the loops from the 'E' wrap cast-on. *Either:* place one loop onto each needle; *or:* place one loop onto every fourth needle.

III Basic turned-up hem on machines with hanging cast-on comb

Basic turned-up hem on machines with hanging cast-on comb (front)

7.6
Basic turned-up hem on machines
with hanging cast-on comb (back)

(1) Hang the cast-on comb carefully
so that the comb hooks sit at the
base of the turn up of the gate
pegs.

(2) Push alternate needles to W.P.
C.O.R.

(3) Thread up M.Y. Knit one row.
C.O.L. R.C.1.

(4) Drop the comb by turning the
hooks at each end of the comb
towards you.

(5) Release the yarn between the
last needle in W.P. and the carriage from under the hooks on
the comb.

(6) Push all needles to W.P.

(7) Pull down the yarn behind the
yarn brake to prevent any slack.
Check all needle butts are lined
up evenly in W.P.

(8) Knit 9 rows M.T.–2, C.O.R.
R.C.10.

(9) Knit 1 row M.T.+1, C.O.L.
R.C.11.

(10) Knit 11 rows, M.T.–2, C.O.R.
R.C.22.

(11) Knit 1 row M.T.+1, C.O.L.
R.C.23.

(12) Push alternate needles to H.P.
Set carriage to knit all needles.
Turn up a hem by swivelling the
cast-on comb up and over towards you and slipping the large
loops which are hanging in the
hooks of the comb up and over
onto the needles in H.P. Continue to swivel the comb up and

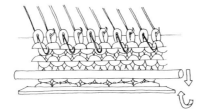

Hem III. Step (12). Turning up a hem
using the cast-on comb.

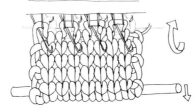

Dropping the first row of loops onto the
needles. Make it easier by using a dowel
stick

over away from you until the
loops drop off onto the needles.
Be very careful not to drop these
loops over the gate pegs.

Side view of the dowel stick

If you should fail to transfer a
loop or two onto needles in H.P.
it doesn't matter because this
edge is a closed-edge cast-on
and the stitches will not run
back. The loops are easy to see
and can be picked up manually
after you have removed the
comb before you continue with
knitting your garment.

In order to make turning up
the hem easier when you have a
large number of stitches to deal
with, you may weight the knitted hem when turning it up by
placing a rod (e.g. a thin length
of wooden doweling or metal
curtain rod or one of the extension rails from your machine)
onto the knitting before you fold
it over by bringing up the comb.

(13) Knit one row. M.T.+1 on all
needles. Proceed to knit the
garment.

Two variations at this point
would be as follows.

(i) Lift the first row of M.Y.
loops onto the needles in
H.P. as above and set your
carriage not to knit needles
in H.P. for one row. Knit one
row M.T.+1. Re-set the
carriage to knit needles in
H.P. and then proceed to
knit the garment. The purpose of this is to discourage
the hem from flipping up.

Variation (front) (i)

Variation (back) (i)

(ii) Lift the first row of M.Y.
loops onto the needles in
H.P. as above and set your
carriage to slip/part/empty.

Knit one row on M.T. + 1. Re-set the carriage to knit and proceed to knit the garment. Only the needles with two loops on them knit for one row. The purpose of this is to discourage the hem from flipping up.

Variation (front) (*ii*)

Variation (back) (*ii*)

IV Basic turned-up hem on machines with non-hanging cast-on comb

These are machines with combs without clips at either end for hanging onto gate pegs.

(*1*) Push alternate needles to W.P. C.O.R.

(*2*) Thread up M.Y. Knit one row. C.O.L. R.C.1

(*3*) Hang the comb onto the M.Y. loops either from behind or by pushing the comb onto the loops from the front of your work.

(*4*) Push *all* needles to W.P.

(*5*) Pull down the yarn behind the yarn brake to prevent any slack. Check all needle butts are lined up evenly in W.P.

(*6*) Knit 9 rows M.T.–2, C.O.R. R.C.10.

(*7*) Knit 1 row M.T. + 1, C.O.L. R.C.11

(*8*) Knit 11 rows, M.T.–2, C.O.R. R.C.22.

(*9*) Knit 1 row M.T. + 1, C.O.L. R.C.23.

(*10*) Push alternate needles to H.P. Set carriage to knit all needles. Turn up a hem by swivelling the cast-on comb up and over towards you and slipping the large loops which are hanging in the hooks of the comb up and over onto the needles in H.P. Continue to swivel the comb up and over away from you until the loops drop off onto the needles. Be very careful not to drop these loops over the gate pegs. If you should drop a loop or two it doesn't matter because this edge is a closed-edge cast-on and the stitches will not run back. The loops are easy to see and can be picked up manually after you have put away the comb before you continue with knitting your garment.

In order to make turning up the hem easier when you have a large number of stitches to deal with, you may weight the knitted hem when turning it up by placing a rod (e.g. a thin length of wooden doweling, metal curtain rod or an extension rail from your machine) onto the knitting before you fold it over by bringing up the comb.

(*11*) Knit 1 row M.T. + 1 on all needles. Proceed to knit the garment.

A variation at this point would be to lift the first row of M.Y. loops onto the needles in H.P. as above and set your carriage not to knit needles in H.P. for one row. Knit one row M.T. + 1. Re-set the carriage to knit needles in H.P. and then proceed to knit the garment. The purpose of this is to discourage the hem from flipping up.

V Basic turned-up hem – variation to avoid bulky edge

Avoiding bulky edge (front)

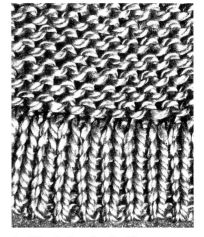

Avoiding bulky edge (back)

(*1*) In hem **I**:

(*a*) Step (*3*) Knit 1 row with sewing thread, 9 rows with M.Y.

(*b*) Step (*7*) Pick-up the sewing thread loops.

Knit one row with sewing cotton

(2) In hem **II**:
  (a) Step (3) Knit 1 row with sewing thread instead of M.Y.
(3) In hem **III**:
  (c) Step (2) Knit 1 row with sewing thread instead of M.Y.

VI Hem with purl stitch on reverse

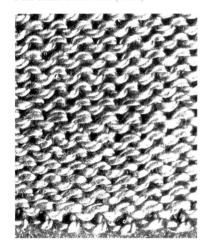

Purl stitch on reverse (front)

Purl stitch on reverse (back)

This hem can be useful to stop any flipping up and also if you are knitting a garment where the reverse (or purl) side of the knitting is the right side.
(1) Cast on with W.Y. M.T. Knit 9 rows. C.O.L.
(2) Remove W.Y. from feeder and replace with the cast-on cord. Hold the cord by hand (hand-feed) and knit one row. C.O.R.
(3) Remove the cord from the feeder and replace with M.Y. Knit 7 rows. M.T.–2, C.O.L. R.C.7.
(4) Knit 1 row M.T. + 1, C.O.R. R.C.8.
(5) Remove the knitting from the machine:
  (a) Knit 8–10 rows with W.Y., remove the yarn from the carriage and knit one row. Drop the work from the machine.
  (b) Remove the work onto a garter bar.
(6) Place C.O.L. R.C.8. Turn the work so the stocking stitch side of the work is facing you and the purl side is facing the machine. Replace the work onto the needles.

Reversing the work on the machine

(7) Knit 5 rows. M.T. – 2, C.O.R. R.C.13.
(8) Knit 1 row, M.T. + 1, C.O.L. R.C.14.
(9) Turn up hem. Pick up the first row of M.Y. loops after the row knit with the cast-on cord.
(10) Knit one row M.T. + 1.
Continue to knit the garment. After knitting, pull the cast-on cord out; the waste knitting will then fall off. The depth of the hem can be increased or decreased by altering the number of rows knit in steps (3) and (5). To ensure that the hem does not flip up you could knit step (3) at a smaller number than you will use in step (5). The smaller your tension dial setting

the neater and tighter your hem will be.

VII Hem with one row of purl stitch on the edge

Purl stitch on edge (front)

Purl stitch on edge (back)

This hem is a bit fiddly; it is much easier if you use the garter bar for it as the work must be turned twice. The hem has a very neat, crisp finish.
(1)–(2) as in hem **IV**.
(3) Remove the cord from the feeder and replace with M.Y.
(4) Knit 7 rows M.T.–2. C.O.L.
(5) Knit 1 row M.T. + 1. Turn the work as in step (5) for hem **VI**. C.O.L.
(6) Knit 1 row M.T. + 1. Turn the work as in step (5) for hem **VI**. C.O.L.

(7) Knit 8 rows M.T.–2. C.O.L.

(8) T.U.H. as steps (9) and (10) for hem **VI**.

VIII Picot edge with mock rib backing

Picot edge with mock rib backing (front)

Picot edge with mock rib backing (back)

This hem can be done with a hanging cast-on comb, with a cast-on comb that does not hang on the gate pegs or by starting the knitting by casting-on with W.Y. However, when you are using the comb care must be taken because the edge is not a locked edge – the stitches will run if you loose them before you hook them up on the needles.

(1) Begin hem.

(a) Hanging comb –
  (i) Hang comb onto gate pegs.
  (ii) Select alternate needles to W.P.
  (iii) Thread up carriage. C.O.R. Knit 1 row.
  (iv) Drop comb onto yarn loops.

(b) Cast-on comb without end clips.
  (i) Select alternate needles to W.P.
  (ii) Thread up carriage. C.O.R. Knit one row.
  (iii) Hang comb onto yarn loops.

(c) Cast-on with waste yarn:
  (i) Select alternate needles to W.P.
  (ii) Cast-on an open edge or 'E' wrap cast-on over alternate needles with waste yarn.
  (iii) Knit several rows with waste yarn.
  (iv) C.O.L. Thread up carriage with cast-on cord. Knit 1 row.
  (v) With C.O.R., thread up with M.Y. Knit one row.

(2) Knit 10 rows M.Y. M.T.–2.

(3) Select all needles to W.P.

(4) Knit 1 row. M.Y. M.T.+1.

(5) Knit 12 rows M.Y. M.T.–2.

(6) Turn up hem. The method used will depend on how you started your knitting.

(a) Hanging cast-on comb
  (i) Select alternate needles to H.P.
  (ii) Turn up hem by swivelling comb up and over the needles in H.P. so the loops on the comb drop onto the needles.

(b) Cast-on comb – as in method (a).

(c) Cast-on with waste yarn – pick up the first row of M.Y. loops after the waste knitting with your transfer tool and lift them onto alternate needles.

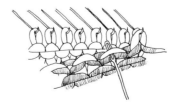

Picking up a row of stitches knit on alternate needles

IX Picot hem using the lace carriage or transfer tool

Picot hem using lace carriage/transfer tool (front)

Picot hem using lace carriage/transfer tool (back)

(1) Cast-on as for applicable hem.
  (a) Hem **I**; steps (1)–(3). C.O.L.
  (b) Hem **II**; steps (1)–(6). C.O.L.
  (c) Hem **III**; steps (1)–(4). C.O.L.

(2) Knit 8 rows M.Y. M.T.–2 C.O.L.

(3) Knit 1 row M.Y. M.T.+1 C.O.R.

(4) Make a row of holes:
  (a) With the lace carriage on Jones/Brother punch card or electronic, or Toyota machines:
    (i) Place lace carriage onto

needle bed at the left. Do not program the electronic machine and do not put a punch card in the punch card machines.

(ii) Take the lace carriage from the left to the right across the needles in W.P. All needles are selected to U.W.P.

(iii) Push alternate needles back to W.P.

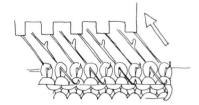

Using the pusher to push alternate needles back to W.P.

(iv) Take the lace carriage from the right to the left across the needle bed. Alternate stitches are transferred leaving alternate needles empty. All needles are left in U.W.P. They will all knit as normal on the next row and needn't be pushed back to W.P. Remove the lace carriage.

(b) With the lace carriage on Jones/Brother push button machines and Toyota 858:

(i) Place the lace carriage onto the needle bed at the left.

(ii) Push alternate push buttons, e.g. 1,3,5,7, and pull the set lever. Alternate needles are selected to U.W.P.

(iii) Take the lace carriage from the left to the right of the needle bed. Alternate stitches are transferred leaving alternate needles empty.

(iv) Remove the lace carriage from the machine.

(c) Using the transfer tool:

(i) With the transfer tool,

transfer alternate stitches to adjacent needles;

(ii) Leave the empty needles in W.P.

(5) Knit 9 rows M.Y. M.T.–2 C.O.L.

(6) Knit 1 row M.Y. M.T. + 1. Turn up hem.

X Mock 1 × 1 rib

Mock 1 × 1 rib (front)

Mock 1 × 1 rib (back)

(1) Begin hem.

(a) Hanging comb –

(i) Hang comb onto gate pegs.

(ii) Select alternate needles to W.P.

(iii) Thread up carriage. C.O.R. Knit 1 row.

(iv) Drop comb onto yarn loops.

(b) Cast-on comb without end clips –

(i) Select alternate needles to W.P.

(ii) Hang comb onto yarn loops.

(c) Cast-on with W.Y.

(i) Select alternate needles to W.P.

(ii) Cast-on an open edge (with cast-on cord) or 'E' wrap cast-on over alternate needles with W.Y.

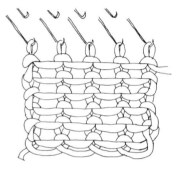

'E' wrap cast-on and knitting on alternate needles

(iii) Knit several rows with W.Y.

(iv) C.O.L. Thread up carriage with cast-on cord. Knit 1 row.

(v) With C.O.R. Thread up M.Y. Knit 1 row.

(d) Cast-on with M.Y.

(i) Select alternate needles to W.P.

(ii) Cast-on in M.Y. with the 'E' wrap technique over alternate needles.

(iii) To ensure the first few rows knit successfully, you may:

(a) push working needles to H.P. for the first 4 rows;

(b) place your cast-on cord between the needle hooks and the gate pegs and hold down firmly while knitting the first 4 rows.

(2) Knit 11 rows M.Y. M.T.–2 R.C.12 C.O.R.

(*3*) Knit 1 row M.Y. M.T.+1 R.C.13 C.O.L.

(*4*) Knit 11 rows M.Y. M.T.−2 R.C.24 C.O.R.

(*5*) Knit 1 row M.Y. M.T.+1 R.C.25 C.O.L.

(*6*) Turn up hem. Select all needles to W.P. and pick up the first row of M.Y. loops onto *empty needles*.

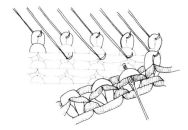

Picking up M.Y. loops for a mock 1 × 1 rib

XI Mock 2 × 1 rib (continental rib)

Mock 2 × 1 rib (front)

(*1*) Select all needles to W.P., then push every third needle back to N.W.P.

(*2*) Cast-on with W.Y. and knit several rows. C.O.L.

(*3*) Thread up with cast-on cord and knit one row. C.O.R.

(*4*) Thread up with M.Y. and knit 1 row C.O.L.

(*5*) Follow steps (*2*)–(*5*) for Hem **X**.

(*6*) Turn up hem. At the right hand

Mock 2 × 1 rib (back)

edge of your work, using your transfer tool, pick up the first (little) M.Y. loop after the W.Y. and place onto the second needle with a stitch. Pick up the next (bigger) M.Y. loop after the W.Y. and place onto the next empty needle. Skip a needle (with a stitch). Little loop onto the second needle with a stitch. Big loop onto the empty needle, etc.

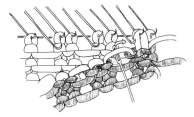

Picking up M.Y. loops for a mock 2 × 1 rib

XII Hem with a basted effect

This hem is useful for skirts as it does not give a bulky turn-up.

(*1*) Begin hem.

　(*a*) Hanging Comb –

　　(*i*) Hang comb onto gate pegs.

　　(*ii*) Select alternate needles to W.P.

　　(*iii*) Thread up carriage. C.O.R. Knit 1 row.

　　(*iv*) Drop comb onto yarn loops.

Hem with a basted effect (front)

Hem with a basted effect (back)

　(*b*) Cast-on comb without end clips:

　　(*i*) Select alternate needles to W.P.

　　(*ii*) Thread-up carriage. C.O.R. Knit 1 row.

　　(*iii*) Hang comb onto yarn loops.

　(*c*) Cast-on with W.Y.

　　(*i*) Select alternate needles to W.P.

　　(*ii*) Cast-on an open edge (with cast-on cord) or 'E' wrap cast-on over alternate needles with W.Y.

　　(*iii*) Knit several rows with W.Y.

　　(*iv*) C.O.L. Thread up carriage with cast-on cord. Knit one row.

(*v*) With C.O.R. Thread up M.Y. Knit one row.
(*2*) Push all needles to W.P.
(*3*) Knit 11 rows M.Y. M.T.–2 R.C.12 C.O.R.
(*4*) Knit 1 row M.Y. M.T.+1 R.C.24 C.O.L.
(*5*) Knit 11 rows M.Y. M.T.–2 R.C.24 C.O.R.
(*6*) Knit 1 row M.Y. M.T.+1 R.C.25 C.O.L.

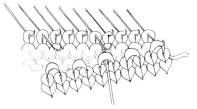

Picking up alternate loops for a less bulky edge

(*7*) Turn up hem. Place alternate large loops from the first row of M.Y. loops onto every fourth needle. If you have used a cast-on comb you may select every fourth needle to H.P. and swivel-up your comb to place the loops onto the needles. If you have cast-on with W.Y. you will have to use your transfer tool to do this job.

XIII Decorative tuck hem

(*1*) Begin hem.
  (*a*) Hanging comb –
    (*i*) Hang comb onto gate pegs.

Decorative tuck-hem (front)

Decorative tuck-hem (back)

(*ii*) Select alternate needles to W.P.
(*iii*) Thread up carriage. C.O.R. Knit 1 row.
(*iv*) Drop comb onto yarn loops.
  (*b*) Cast-on comb without end clips –
    (*i*) Select alternate needles to W.P.
    (*ii*) Thread up carriage. C.O.R. Knit 1 row.
    (*iii*) Hang comb onto yarn loops.
  (*c*) Cast-on with W.Y.
    (*i*) Select alternate needles to W.P.
    (*ii*) Cast-on an open edge (with cast-on cord) or 'E' wrap cast-on over alternate needles with W.Y.
    (*iii*) Knit several rows with W.Y.
    (*iv*) C.O.L. Thread up carriage with cast-on cord. Knit one row.
    (*v*) With C.O.R., thread up M.Y. Knit 1 row.
(*2*) Push all needles to W.P.
(*3*) Knit 4 rows M.Y. M.T.–2 R.C.5 C.O.L.
(*4*) Introduce pattern on edge.
  (*a*) Punch card and electronic machines with a pre-set row. (e.g. Jones/Brother and Toyota) –

(*i*) Insert card for tuck stitch pattern, e.g. Jones/Brother card 2J, etc. Lock card on row 1 or program machine to read only one row.
(*ii*) Set carriage to connect pattern card to needles.
(*iii*) Knit 1 row. C.O.R. Set carriage to tuck.
(*iv*) Knit 4–6 rows in pattern. Set carriage to knit.
  (*b*) On Knitmaster machines –
    (*i*) Insert card for tuck stitch pattern, e.g. Knitmaster card 3, etc. Lock card on row 1.
    (*ii*) Push the side levers on the carriage to the back.
    (*iii*) Knit 1 row. C.O.R. Set carriage to tuck.
    (*iv*) Knit 4–6 rows in pattern. Set carriage to knit.
  (*c*) On push button machines (e.g. Jones/Brother 710, Toyota 858) –
    (*i*) Knit 1 row M.T.+1. C.O.R.
    (*ii*) Push buttons for a tuck stitch pattern, e.g. 1, 2, 3, 5, 6, 7.
    (*iii*) Set carriage to tuck. *Pull the set lever. Knit 1 row.* Repeat from * to *, 4–6 times. C.O.R.
  (*d*) On push button machines (an alternative method) –
    (*i*) Knit one row M.T.+1. C.O.R.
    (*ii*) Push buttons for a pull-up stitch pattern, e.g. (*1*) and (*4*). Pull the set lever.
    (*iii*) Set both holding cam levers on the carriage to III.
    (*iv*) Knit 4–6 rows. Set holding cam levers on the carriage to I. C.O.R.
  (*e*) On manual machines (or manually on automatic machines) –
    (*i*) Knit 1 row M.T.+1 C.O.R.
    (*ii*) Select one needle at intervals: e.g. every third, fourth or fifth needle, to H.P.

(*iii*) Set the carriage not to knit needles in H.P.

(*iv*) Knit 4–6 rows. C.O.R. Set carriage to knit all needles.

(5) Knit 5 rows. M.T.–2 C.O.L.

(6) Knit 1 row M.T. + 1 C.O.R.

(7) Turn up hem.

XIV Decorative tuck edge

Decorative tuck edge (front)

Decorative tuck edge (back)

(*1*) Begin edge

(*a*) Waste yarn –

(*i*) Push needles required to W.P. C.O.R.

(*ii*) Thread up with W.Y. Knit 1 row. Place cast-on cord between hooks of needles and gate pegs.

Knit several rows. C.O.L. Pull out cast-on cord.

(*iii*) Remove W.Y. Thread up carriage with cast-on cord and knit 1 row. C.O.R.

(*iv*) Push all needles to H.P.

(*v*) Do an 'E' wrap cast-on over needles with M.Y.

(*b*) Hanging cast-on comb with end clips –

(*i*) Hang cast-on comb.

(*ii*) Push needles required to H.P. C.O.R.

(*iii*) Do an 'E' wrap cast-on over needles with M.Y.

(*iv*) Drop comb onto the cast-on loops.

(*c*) Cast-on comb without end clips:

(*i*) Push needles required to H.P. C.O.R.

(*ii*) Do an 'E' wrap cast-on over needles with M.Y.

(*iii*) Drop comb onto the cast-on loops.

(*2*) Introduce pattern on edge:

(*a*) Punch card and electronic machines with a pre-set row (e.g. Jones/Brother and Toyota) –

(*i*) Insert card for tuck stitch pattern e.g. Knitmaster card 3, etc. Lock card on row 1 or program machine to read only one row.

(*ii*) Set carriage to connect pattern card to needles.

(*iii*) Knit 1 row. C.O.R. Set carriage to tuck.

(*iv*) Knit 4–6 rows in pattern. Set carriage to knit.

✕	✕	✕
✕	✕	✕
✕	✕	✕
✕	✕	✕
✕	✕	✕
✕	✕	✕
✕	✕	✕
✕	✕	✕

Tuck stitch card

(*b*) On Knitmaster machines –

(*i*) Insert card for tuck stitch pattern, e.g. Knitmaster card 3. Lock card on row 1

(*ii*) Push the side levers on the carriage to the back.

(*iii*) Knit one row. C.O.R. Set carriage to tuck.

(*iv*) Knit four to six rows in pattern. Set carriage to knit.

(*c*) On push button machines (e.g. Jones/Brother 710, Toyota 858) –

(*i*) Knit one row M.T. + 1. C.O.R.

(*ii*) Push buttons for a tuck stitch pattern, e.g. 1, 2, 3, 5, 6, 7.

(*iii*) Set carriage to tuck. *Pull the set lever. Knit one row.* Repeat 4–6 times from * to *. C.O.R.

(*d*) On push button machines (an alternative method) –

(*i*) Knit 1 row M.T. + 1. C.O.R.

(*ii*) Push buttons for a pull-up stitch pattern, e.g. (*1*) and (*4*). Pull the set lever.

(*iii*) Set both holding cam levers on the carriage to III.

(*iv*) Knit 4–6 rows. Set holding cam levers on the carriage to I. C.O.R.

(*e*) On manual machines (or manually on automatic machines) –

(*i*) Knit one row M.T. + 1 C.O.R.

(*ii*) Select one needle at intervals: e.g. every third, fourth or fifth needle, to H.P.

(*iii*) Set the carriage not to knit needles in H.P.

(*iv*) Knit 4–6 rows. C.O.R. Set carriage to knit all needles.

(*3*) Continue to knit the garment.

This hem can also be done substituting a crochet-edge cast-on for the 'E' wrap cast-on.

XV 'Stained glass window' hem

Stained glass window hem

(*1*) Cast-on for a basic hem with W.Y. Knit several rows. C.O.L. Thread up carriage with cast-on cord. Knit one row. C.O.R.

(*2*) Thread up carriage with contrast yarn.

(*3*) Knit 11 rows M.T.–2. Con. Y. C.O.L.

(*4*) Take out Con.Y. and thread up M.Y. Knit 1 row M.T.+1. C.O.R. Place a basic simple lace card in the pattern card feeder.

(*5*) With M.Y. knit 12 rows M.T.–1 in the lace pattern.

(*6*) Turn up the hem.

XVI Manual latch-up 1 × 1 rib on a single bed machine

This is, in fact, a true rib. It is an alternative for those who do not have a ribber, who want a knit one, purl one rib, and who do not wish to do this on a standard pair of knitting needles, then transfer the rib onto the machine needles one by one.

(*1*) Select the required number of needles to W.P. Push alternate needles back to N.W.P. except for the two edge needles at the right hand edge of the work which must *both* be in W.P.

(*2*) Do an 'E' wrap cast-on in W.Y. and knit several rows. C.O.L.

(*3*) Remove W.Y. and thread up with

Manual latch-up 1 × 1 rib (front)

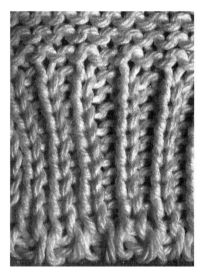

Manual latch-up 1 × 1 rib (back)

the cast-on cord. Knit 1 row. C.O.R.

(*4*) Thread up with M.Y. Knit 3 rows M.Y., M.T.–2. C.O.L.

(*5*) Pick up the first M.Y. loop in the

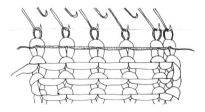

Latch up 1 × 1 rib. Step (*3*)

first row after the W.Y. knitting at the right edge of the work and place it onto the needle in W.P. at the right hand edge of the work. Push all needles to W.P.

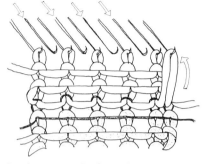

Latch up 2 × 1 rib. Step (*5*)

(*6*) Knit the required number of rows for the rib.

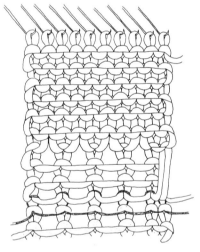

Latch up 1 × 1 rib. Step (*6*)

(*7*) Drop the stitches from the needles that were originally in N.W.P. and run the stitches back to the W.Y. knitting.

(*8*) From the side of the work facing you latch up the dropped stitches. Hook the latch tool into the first M.Y. loop after the W.Y. knitting. Skip two M.Y. loops. Latch the next and each following M.Y. loop through until you arrive back at the needle bed. Hook the last loop back onto the empty needle.

Although this seems time-

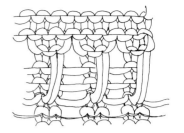

Latch up 1 × 1 rib. Step (5)

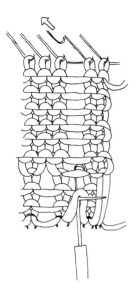

Latch up 1 × 1 rib. Step (8)

Manual latch-up 2 × 1 rib (front)

Manual latch-up 2 × 1 rib (back)

Latch up 1 × 1 rib. Step (8)

(6) Knit the required number of rows for the rib.
(7) Drop the stitches from the needles that were originally in N.W.P. and run the stitches back to the W.Y. knitting.
(8) From the side of the work facing you, latch-up the dropped stitches. Hook the latch tool into the first M.Y. loop after the W.Y. knitting. Skip two M.Y. loops. Latch the next and each following M.Y. loop through until you arrive back at the needle bed. Hook the last loop back onto the empty needle.

This will give you quite a quick and acceptable true rib.

This is only a basic introduction to making hems. Once you get the hang of it there is no reason why you should not be as inventive in creating new hems as you are in designing garments. Try using various stitch patterns in your hems as well as in your garments. If you want a hem which will be a firm neat edge to your garment try the basic bird's eye or 1 × 1 pattern as a Fair Isle and place one strand of your main yarn in both Feeder A and feeder B.

11 Finishing hems

You may want to have a hem at the end of your garment if you are knitting a skirt with a knitted-in waistband. Or you may wish to knit the garment 'upside-down' so it is important to know how to put a hem on the finishing edge of the garment as well as the beginning.

consuming, you can work up quite a speed doing this and the advantage is that it does give a very professional finish to the garment.

XVII Manual latch-up 2 × 1 rib on a single bed machine

This rib is the same in principle as the preceeding rib. However, being a 2 × 1 rib it is quicker to do and yet still gives a similar professional result.
(1) Select the required number of needles to W.P. Push every third needle back to N.W.P. Ensure the two edge needles at the right hand edge of the work are *both* in W.P.
(2) Do an 'E' wrap cast-on in W.Y. and knit several rows. C.O.L.
(3) Remove W.Y. and thread up with the cast-on cord. Knit 1 row. C.O.R.
(4) Thread up with M.Y. Knit 3 rows M.Y., M.T.–2. C.O.L.
(5) If you look at the first row of M.Y. knitting carefully you will see a little loop alternating with a big loop. The little loops appear between the two adjacent needles in W.P. Pick up each of these little loops and place them onto the right hand needle in W.P.

I Basic hem for a machine with a hanging cast-on comb

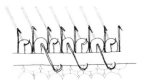

Hang cast-on comb before selecting needles to H.P.

(*1*) Hang the comb on the gate pegs in front of your knitting.
(*2*) C.O.R. Select alternate needles to H.P. (If you have a Jones/Brother 710 or Toyota 858 you can push buttons 1,3,5,7, etc. and pull your set lever to bring the needles forward.) Set carriage to knit all needles in H.P. Push both part buttons.
(*3*) Knit 1 row. C.O.L. Drop the cast-on comb. Cancel the patterning buttons.

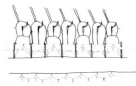

Drop comb after knitting one row on alternate needles

(*4*) Knit the hem you require, e.g.: 10 rows M.T.–2, 1 row M.T. +1, 10 rows M.T. –2.
(*5*) Turn up hem. Push alternate needles to H.P. Set carriage to knit all needles. Pick up the loops you made on the patterned row which are hanging on your cast-on comb by swivelling the comb up and over the needles in H.P., dropping the loops onto the needles.
(*6*) Knit one row very loosely and cast off.
N.B. If this hem is a waistband, you need a *very loose* cast-off to be able to pull the skirt over your hips.

II Basic hem for all machines

(*1*) C.O.R. Select alternate needles to H.P. Set the carriage to knit all needles in H.P. Set the carriage to part/slip/empty. (Do not have the carriage connected to the pattern card – i.e. on Jones/Brother automatic machines the change knob is on N.L.; on Toyota machines the side lever is back; and on Knitmaster automatic machines the side levers are forward to o.)
(*2*) Knit 1 row. C.O.L. Cancel the patterning. (Return the carriage to normal knitting.)
(*3*) Knit the hem you require, e.g.: 10 rows M.T.–2, 1 row M.T. +1, 10 rows M.T. –2.
(*4*) Turn up the hem. Pick up the loops you made on the patterned row with your transfer tool and place them onto alternate needles. Knit one row and cast-off very loosely.

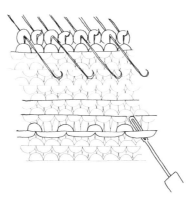

Pick up loops from the row knit on alternate needles

III Basic hem for machines with a weaving facility

(*1*) C.O.R. Select alternate needles to H.P. Set the carriage to knit all needles in H.P. Put the weaving brushes into working position. (Do not have the carriage connected to the pattern card – i.e. on Jones/Brother automatic machines the change knob is on N.L., on Toyota machines the side lever is back and on Knitmaster automatic machines the side levers are forward to o.)
(*2*) Lay a length of very thin yarn or contrast thread across the needles in H.P. to act as a marker for this row.
(*3*) Knit 1 row. C.O.L. Cancel the

weaving brushes, and return to normal knitting.
(*4*) Knit the hem you require e.g.: 10 rows M.T.–2, 1 row M.T. +1, 10 rows M.T.–2.
(*5*) Turn up hem. Pick up the loops from the row marked by the weaving yarn with your transfer tool and place them onto alternate needles. Knit one row and cast-off very loosely.

If you decide to introduce a mock 1 × 1 or 2 × 1 rib at the end of your knitting, it is a very easy matter to identify which stitches need to be picked up after the hem is knitted to make a doubled edge.

If your hem is to be knit in a contrast colour you can see again quite easily where the loops are to make your doubled edge.

Edges

The edges of a garment can make or break its appearance. If the edges are neat, well finished and appropriate they can give a true professional look to the garment. Some edges are described for the single bed and some are described for the ribber. The first two edges are the very basic ones. The instructions for edges done on the single bed assume that all needles are in working position. However, they can be altered to produce a continental or mock rib edge too.

I Basic pick-up edge with cast-off finish

(*1*) Select the required number of needles to W.P. C.O.R. Thread up with M.Y.
(*2*) Pick up the edge of the garment onto all the needles with the right

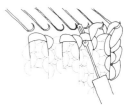

Basic pick up edge I. Step (*2*): pick up the edge of the garment

Basic pick-up edge (front)

Basic pick-up edge (back)

side of the garment facing the machine. Push all needles to H.P. to help knit the row. Set the carriage to knit all needles in H.P.

(3) Knit the required depth of the hem at M.T.–2 (or tighter to achieve a neater hem).

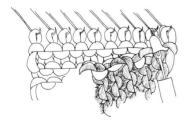

Basic pick up edge I. Step (6): pick up the edge again.

(4) Knit 1 row M.T. + 1 (to achieve a neat fold line).
(5) Repeat step (3).
(6) Pick up the first row of hem loops (two loops on every needle). Push all needles to H.P. to help knit the row. Set the carriage to knit all needles in H.P. Knit 1 row T. 10 and cast-off.

II Basic pick-up edge with catch-stitch finish on the wrong side (a variation of **I**)

Pick-up edge with catch-stitch finish (front)

Pick-up edge with catch-stitch finish (back)

(1) Select the required number of needles to W.P. C.O.R. Thread up with M.Y.
(2) Pick up the edge of the garment

onto all the needles with the right side of the garment facing the machine. Push all needles to H.P. to help knit the row. Set the carriage to knit all needles in H.P.

(3) Knit the required depth of the hem at M.T.–2 (or tighter to achieve a neater hem).
(4) Knit 1 row M.T. + 1 (to achieve a neat fold line).
(5) Repeat step (3).
(6) Pick up the first row of hem loops (two loops on every needle). Push all needles to H.P. to help knit the row. Set the carriage to knit all needles in H.P.
(7) Knit 4 rows M.T., M.Y.
(8) Knit several rows with W.Y. and strip work off the machine.
(9) Fold the W.Y. knitting back and catch-stitch the last row of M.Y. loops down invisibly onto the wrong side of the garment.

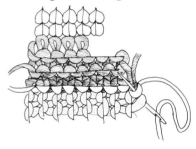

Catch stitch the last row of M.Y. loops.

III Basic pick-up edge with back-stitch finish

(1) Select the required number of needles to W.P. C.O.R. Thread up with M.Y.
(2) Pick up the edge of the garment onto all the needles with the wrong side of the garment facing

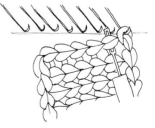

Pick up the edge of the garment onto the machine, wrong side facing the machine

Basic pick-up edge with back-stitch finish (front)

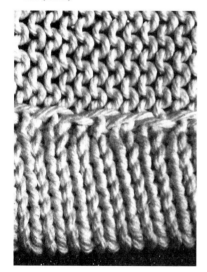

Basic pick-up edge with back-stitch finish (back)

the machine. Push all needles to H.P. to help knit the row. Set the carriage to knit all needles in H.P.

(3) Knit the required depth of the hem at M.T.–2 (or tighter to achieve a neater hem).

(4) Knit one row M.T. + 1 (to achieve a neat fold line).

(5) Repeat step (3).

(6) Remove the M.Y. from the feeder and thread up W.Y.

(7) Knit several rows in W.Y. and strip off work from the machine.

(8) Fold the hem over onto the right

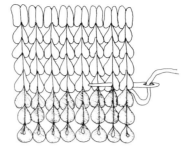

Fold the hem over onto the right side of the garment

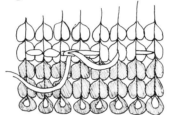

Back stitch through the last row of M.Y. loops

side of the garment and back stitch through the last row of M.Y. loops. Remove the waste knitting.

IV Edge knitted separately with waste knitting

(1) Select the required number of needles to W.P. C.O.R. Thread up with W.Y. and knit several rows. C.O.R.

(2) Remove the W.Y. and thread up M.Y.

Edge knitted separately with waste knitting (front)

Edge knitted separately with waste knitting (back)

(3) Knit the required depth of the hem at M.T.–2 (or tighter to achieve a neater hem).

(4) Knit 1 row M.T. + 1 (to achieve a neat fold line).

(5) Repeat step (3).

(6) Pick up the first row of M.Y. loops after the waste knitting onto all needles. Knit one row M.Y. and M.T.

(7) Pick up the edge of the garment onto the needles with the right side of the garment facing the machine. Push all needles to H.P. to help knit the row. Set the carriage to knit all needles in H.P.

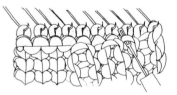

After picking up the hem, pick the garment up onto the needles with the right side facing the machine

(8) Knit 1 row T. 10 and cast-off. Remove the waste knitting.

V Edge knitted separately with 'E' wrap

(1) Select the required number of needles to W.P. C.O.R.

(2) Do an 'E' wrap cast-on and thread up carriage with M.Y.

Edge knitted separately with 'E' wrap (front)

Edge knitted separately with 'E' wrap (back)

(3) Knit the required depth of the hem at M.T.–2 (or tighter to achieve a neater hem).

(4) Knit 1 row M.T. + 1 (to achieve a neat fold line).

(5) Repeat step (3).

(6) Pick up the loops of the 'E' wrap

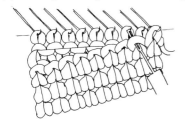

Edge knitted separately: pick up the loops of the 'E' wrap cast-on

cast-on. Knit one row M.Y. and M.T.

(7) Pick up the edge of the garment onto the needles with the right side of the garment facing the machine.

(8) Knit 1 row T. 10 and cast-off.

VI Edge knitted separately and sewn on

Edge knitted separately and sewn on (front)

Edge knitted separately and sewn on (back)

(1) Select the required number of needles to W.P. C.O.R.

(2) Do an 'E' wrap cast-on and thread up the carriage with M.Y.

(3) Knit 4 rows M.Y. 6 M.T.

(4) Transfer stitches for a mock rib (e.g. 1 × 1 or 2 × 1 – every alter-

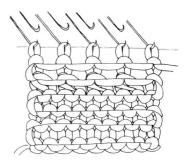

After an 'E' wrap cast-on and several rows, transfer stitches for a mock rib

nate or third needle empty and in N.W.P.)

(5) Knit the required depth of the hem at M.T.–2 (or tighter to achieve a neater hem).

(6) Knit 1 row M.T. + 1 (to achieve a neat fold line).

(7) Repeat step (5).

(8) Push all needles to W.P. and pick up the loops from the row where the stitches were transferred at the beginning of the mock rib.

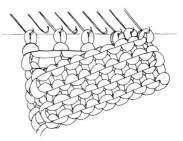

Pick up loops from the row where stitches were transferred for the mock rib

(9) Knit four rows M.Y. and M.T. Remove M.Y. Thread up W.Y.

(10) Knit several rows of waste

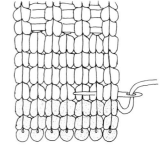

Back-stitching through the last row of M.Y. loops

knitting and remove the band from the machine.

(*11*) Back stitch the band onto the right side of the garment through the last row of M.Y. loops before the waste knitting. Catch-stitch the 'E' wrap cast-on edge down onto the wrong side of the garment.

This edge would be a simple edge suitable for a cut-and-sew neckline.

VII Mock rib edge with back stitch finish (a variation of VI)

Mock rib edge with back stitch finish (front)

Mock rib edge with back stitch finish (back)

(*1*) Select the required number of needles to W.P. C.O.R.

(*2*) With the right side of the garment facing you pick-up the edge onto the needles. Push all needles to H.P. and set the carriage to knit all needles (the first row is easier to knit).

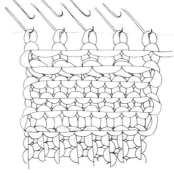

The picked-up edge of the garment (purl side facing) and several rows of plain knitting before transferring for a mock rib

(*3*) Thread up M.Y., M.T. + 1. Knit one row.

(*4*) M.T. Knit 3 rows. C.O.R.

(*5*) Transfer stitches for a mock rib – e.g. transfer every second (or third) stitch to the adjacent needle and push the empty needles back to N.W.P.

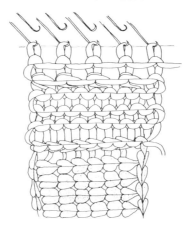

The picked-up edge of the garment (stocking stitch side facing) and several rows of plain knitting before transferring for a mock rib

(*6*) Knit the edge: e.g.
   10 rows   M.T.–2
   1 row   M.T. + 1
   10 rows   M.T.–2 C.O.L.

(*7*) Push all needles to W.P.

(*8*) Pick up loops from the first row of mock ribbing onto the empty needles now in W.P.

(*9*) Knit 3 rows M.T.

(*10*) Remove M.Y. and thread up with W.Y. Knit ten rows and drop the work from the machine.

(*11*) Back stitch the edge of the band down onto the right side of the garment, stitching through the last row of M.Y. loops.

This edge can also be applied in the same manner as the hem following.

VIII Edge knitted separately and applied to garment on the machine

This is an alternative for those who don't like to sew.

(*1*) Select the required number of needles to W.P. C.O.R. Thread up with W.Y. and knit several rows (or do an 'E' wrap cast-on). C.O.R.

(*2*) Remove the W.Y. and thread up M.Y.

(*3*) Knit the required depth of the hem at M.T.–2 (or tighter to achieve a neater hem).

(*4*) Knit one row M.T. + 1 (to achieve a neat fold line).

(*5*) Repeat step (*3*).

(*6*) Remove the M.Y. from the feeder and thread up W.Y.

(*7*) Knit several rows in W.Y. and strip the work off the machine.

Edge knitted separately (front)

Edge knitted separately (back)

(8) Pick up the edge of the garment onto the needles with the wrong side facing the machine. Push the garment behind the latches and push the needles to H.P.

(9) *Optional – you may do an up-side-down 'E' wrap cast-on with M.Y. on the needles in H.P. in front of the garment.*

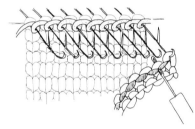

An upside-down 'E' wrap on needles in H.P. before picking up the loops from the last row knit in M.Y. of the edge

(10) Pick up the first row of M.Y. loops after the waste knitting on the separate band. Ensure these loops are in the hooks of the needles in front of the latches.

(11) Pull the needles back to W.P. *by*

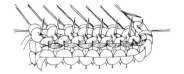

Edge knitted separately and applied by machine. Stitches in the needle hooks being pulled through the 'E' wrap cast-on and the garment

hand (putting your thumb on the needles butts) and pulling the loops of the band which are in the hooks of the needles through (the 'E' wrap cast-on and) the garment.

(12) Pick up the first row of M.Y. loops on the hem after the waste knitting (two loops on every needle).

(13) Knit one row T. 10 and cast-off.

IX Single bed edge applied upside-down

Single bed edge applied upside-down (front)

Single bed edge applied upside-down (back)

This edge is suitable for a cut-and-sew edge.

(1) The hem can be started either with waste knitting or an 'E' wrap cast-on. Select the needles required to W.P. and begin the hem.

(2) Knit the required depth of the hem at M.T.−2 (or tighter to achieve a neater hem).

(3) Knit 1 row M.T. + 1 (to achieve a neat fold line).

(4) Repeat step (2).

(5) Place the garment *upside down* on top of the machine with the edge placed over the needles and the wrong side of the garment facing the machine. (The garment can be positioned on the gate-pegs.)

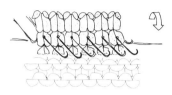

Cut edge of the garment pushed onto the needles from above the needle bed

(6) Push the needles through the edge of the garment. This can be done either by pushing the needle butts with the hand reaching under the garment or by pushing the transfer tool through the edge of the garment, catching the needles and pulling them through the edge.

(7) Push the work behind the open needle latches. Pick up the first row of the M.Y. loops of the knitted hem and place them into the hooks of the needles in front of the latches.

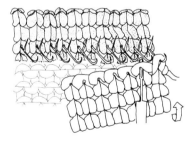

'E' wrap cast-on of the edge picked-up onto the needles after the garment edge is pushed behind the latches

(8) Gently pull the needles back until the latches close over the stitches in the needle hooks.

(9) Pull the stitches through the work.

(10) Pick up the garment from the

top of the needle bed and hang it down in front of the bed.

(*11*) Knit 1 row loosely and cast-off.

Alternative edge 1 × 1 (front)

Alternative edge 1 × 1 (back)

ALTERNATIVELY

(*7*) Push the work behind the open needle latches. Pick up the first row of the M.Y. loops of the knitted hem. Push all work back behind the open latches.

(*8*) Knit 1 row M.Y. by hand laying the yarn into the needle hooks and pulling the needles back by hand (thumb on the needle butts).

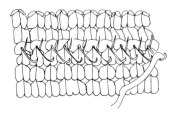

Knit one row in M.Y. by hand. Step 8

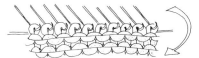

After pulling through the loops of the edge, lift the garment and edge over and hang down in front of the machine. Step 9

(*9*) Pick up the garment from the top of the needle bed and hang it down in front of the bed and cast-off.

X Trim with built in buttonhole

Trim with built-in buttonhole (front)

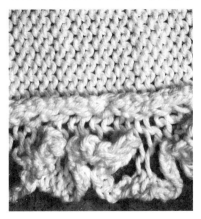

Trim with built-in buttonhole (back)

This trim is knit as a strip and attached to the edge of the garment afterwards.

(*1*) Select needles to W.P. as follows:
I I O I I I
1.2.3.4.5.6.

(*2*) C.O.R. Do an 'E' wrap cast-on with M.Y. over five (out of six) needles in W.P. (leaving the third needle in N.W.P.).

(*3*) Knit two rows. M.Y. M.T. C.O.R. Set carriage so that it doesn't knit needles in H.P.

(*4*) Push needles 1, 2, and 4. to H.P.

(*5*) Knit eight rows on needles 5 and 6 only.

(*6*) Return needles 1, 2, and 4 to U.W.P. and knit two rows on all needles.

(*7*) Repeat steps (*4*)–(*6*) until the strip is to the required length. Cast-off.

XI Cable-effect edge

Cable effect edge (front)

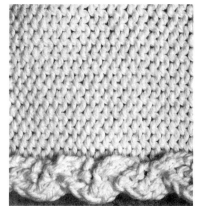

Cable effect edge (back)

(*1*) With the right side of the garment facing the machine, pick up three stitches from the right-hand end

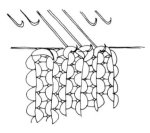

Pick up three edge stitches

of the piece onto the centre three needles.

(2) C.O.R. Thread up carriage with M.Y. Knit 8 rows on these three needles.

(3) Pick up three loops from the edge of the garment (to the left of the original three loops picked up) and place these loops onto the three needles with stitches on them in W.P.

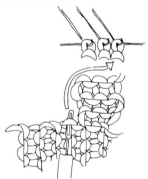

Pick up the next three edge stitches

(4) Knit 8 rows.

(5) Repeat steps (3)–(4) until you have finished edging the garment.

(6) Repeat step three and cast-off.

XII Decorative scalloped edge

This edge would be used mainly in conjunction with stitches picked up from waste yarn.

(1) C.O.L. Pick up the required number of stitches at the edge of the garment onto the needles.

(2) M.Y., M.T. Knit one row. C.O.R.

Decorative scalloped edge (front)

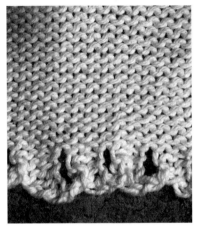

Decorative scalloped edge (back)

The number of stitches used in this pattern repeat can vary according to the effect you wish to achieve. This is dependent on the type of garment and the thickness of the yarn. The following is only an example.

---

(3) Push all needles to H.P. except the six needles at the right hand edge of the work (nearest to the carriage). Set the carriage not to knit needles in H.P.

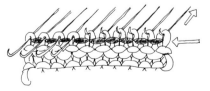

Decorative scalloped edge. Step (3)

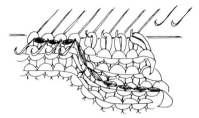

Decorative scalloped edge. Step (4)

(4) *Knit 1 row. C.O.L. Decrease one stitch at the right edge of the work. Knit 1 row. C.O.R.* (You are decreasing one stitch every other row).

(5) Repeat from * to * until you have one needle left in W.P. at the right edge of your work and the C.O.R. Push another six needles to W.P. at the right edge of your knitting.

(6) Continue until you have finished off all your knitting.

XIII Decorative edge with a cable

This edge would be used mainly in conjunction with stitches picked up from waste yarn.

(1) C.O.L. Pick up the required number of stitches at the edge of the garment onto the needles.

(2) M.Y., M.T. Knit 1 row. C.O.R.

(3) Push all needles except the five needles at the right edge of the work to H.P. Set the carriage not to knit needles in H.P.

Decorative edge with cable (front)

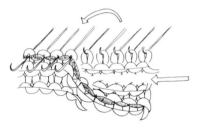

Decorative edge with cable (back)

(4) Knit 8 rows on five needles. C.O.R.
(5) *Push the adjacent five needles next to the needles in W.P. to U.W.P. Knit 1 row. C.O.L.

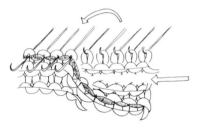

Decorative edge with a cable. Step (5)

(6) Transfer the five stitches at the right to the five needles in working position at their left and push the empty needles back to N.W.P. (two loops on each of five needles).
(7) Knit 7 rows. C.O.R.*
(8) Repeat from * to * until you have only five stitches left.
(9) Pick up the loops from the row where you made the last cable. Knit 1 row and cast-off.

XIV Attaching a knitted edge to fabric with a sewing machine

(1) Wind a sewing machine bobbin by hand with a fine knitting yarn. You may have to adjust the tension on the bobbin thread.

Attaching knitted edge to fabric with sewing machine (front)

(2) Loosen the tension on the top thread of the sewing machine. Use ordinary sewing cotton or top stitching thread in the needle of the machine. In your stitching line, the bobbin thread should lie on the surface of the fabric.
(3) Stitch around the edge where the knitting will be attached with the largest possible stitch. Have the wrong side of the garment on top and the right side of the garment (where the knitting yarn will be) underneath when you are stitching on the machine.
(4) After you have stitched a line around the edge of the garment, pick up the stitches formed by the knitting yarn onto your knitting machine and knit your edge.

Picking up sewn stitches onto the machine

(5) After knitting the edge, knit several rows of W.Y. and strip the work off the machine. Fold the edge over and catch-stitch the last row of M.Y. loops down onto the sewing line.

XV A knitted edge sewn onto a fabric garment

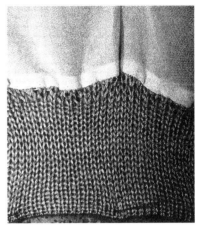

A knitted edge sewn onto a fabric garment

Any edging can be knitted on the machine, cast-off and then sewn onto the edge of a fabric garment with the sewing machine. The advantage of sewing the edge on after completion is that you have more control of the amount of gathering of the fabric. You can ease the fabric onto the elastic edge ensuring a better fit.

XVI Braided effect edge

This edge can be done for a garment where the right side is either the stocking stitch or purl side. However, a slightly different technique is used in each case.

Braided effect edge (front)

Braided effect edge (back)

Stocking stitch as the right side –

(*1*) (If you have a cast-on comb with end clips hang it at this stage.) Push the number of needles required for the edge of the garment to H.P. (If you do not use a comb, it might be wise to cast-on and knit a few rows in W.Y. at this point.) C.O.R.

(*2*) Starting at the L.H. edge using two yarns (contrasting colour can be very effective, or you could use two strands of the same yarn), 'E' wrap cast-on from L. to R. Use each strand alternately and always bring the next strand in behind the back of the strand you just used to wrap the needle. You are twisting the strands every time you wrap a needle and when you get to the R.H. edge, you will find the two strands quite twisted!

Two colour 'E' wrap

(*3*) Now that you have finished going in one direction, repeat the procedure, going back again in the other direction. In other words you will do a reverse 'E' wrap, twisting the yarn as you go and alternating the two strands. You will find when you have arrived

back at the L.H. edge that you have untwisted the two strands again. Be careful not to wrap the needles too tightly. If you have used contrasting colours for your wrapping, you may wrap the needle the second time with the opposite colour from the one used the first time.

(*4*) (If you are using a cast-on comb, drop it on the 'E' wrap edge at this point.) Thread up the carriage with M.Y. and proceed to knit your garment.

Purl stitch as the right side –

(*1*) (If you have a cast-on comb with end clips hang it at this stage.) Push the number of needles required for the edge of the garment to H.P. (If you do not use a comb, it might be wise to cast-on and knit a few rows in W.Y. at this point.) C.O.R.

(*2*) Starting at the L.H. edge using two yarns (contrasting colour can be very effective, or you could use two strands of the same yarn) do an upside-down 'E' wrap cast-on from L. to R. Use each strand alternately and always bring the next strand in behind the back of the strand you just used to wrap the needle. You are twisting the strands every time you wrap a needle, and when you get to the R.H. edge you will find the two strands quite twisted!

Two colour upside-down 'E' wrap

(*3*) Now that you have finished going in one direction, repeat the procedure going back again in the other direction. In other words you will do an upside-down reverse 'E' wrap, twisting the yarn as you go and alternating the two strands. You will find when you have arrived back at the L.H. edge that you have untwisted the two strands again. Be careful not to wrap the needles too tightly. If you have used contrasting colours

for your wrapping, you may wrap the needle the second time with the opposite colour from the one used the first time.

(*4*) (If you are using a cast-on comb, drop it on the 'E' wrap edge at this point.) Thread up the carriage with M.Y. and proceed to knit your garment.

XVII Use of a separately knitted braid added on

Separately knitted braid (front)

Separately knitted braid (back)

(*1*) Knit a strip of fabric from 6–12 stitches wide (depending on the thickness of the yarn and the thickness of the edge desired. Knit the strip the same length (or longer as it is a simple matter to ravel back any excess) as the piece to be edged. This strip can be in plain knitting or in a pattern e.g.

Fair Isle or tuck, etc. The stocking stitch side of the strip will be the right side.

(2) If starting the garment with a braided edging push up the number of needles required for the width of the garment. Pick up the edge of the braid. The purl side of the braid is facing you if the purl side of the fabric is the right side. The plain side of the braid is facing you if the stocking stitch side of the fabric is the right side. Proceed to knit the garment.

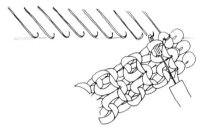

Picking up the edge of a knitted strip

(3) If attaching the braid to the cast-off edge of the garment, after finishing the knitting and before casting the piece off pick up the edge of the braid onto the needles in W.P. with the purl side of the braid facing you. Knit one row on a very loose tension and cast-off. The strip will roll over onto the stocking stitch side of the knitting.

(4) If attaching the braid to the edge of the garment pick up the edge of the garment with the right side facing you. Pick up the edge of the braid with the purl side facing you. Then knit 1 row on a very loose tension and cast-off. The braid will roll over onto the wrong side of the garment.

XVIII Plaited edge

(1) Knit two strips: cast-on with an 'E' wrap. The number of stitches will depend on the width of strip required (e.g. 6–10 sts). The length of the strip should be approximately twice the length of the knitting to be edged. The strip need not be cast-off. The

Plaited edge (front)

Plaited edge (back)

strips can be in M.Y., contrast yarn or two contrasting colours.

(2) Pick up the edge of the garment onto the needles with the right side facing you.

(3) Pick up the edge of the strips: use the triple transfer tool to pick up three loops at a time onto the needles, with the right side of the strip facing the machine. Alternate picking up the strips. First pick up three loops from one strip, then three loops from the second strip. Always take the next

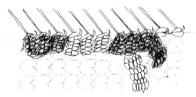

Picking up the edge of two knitted strips for a cable effect

strip to be picked up behind the strip you have just picked up, plaiting (twisting) them as you go.

(4) When you have finished picking up the two strips you may have to unravel rows and finish off the ends of the strips. You can fold these edges over and pick up the loose stitches onto the end needles.

(5) Knit 1 row T. 10 and cast off.

XIX Bias knitted edge

Bias knitted edge (front)

Bias knitted edge (back)

This edge can be knitted separately and then sewn onto the edge of the garment.

(1) Start at the extreme L.H. side of the machine. With M.Y. cast-on 10–16 sts., depending on the width of edging desired. C.O.R.

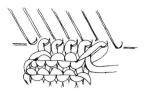

Bias knitted strip

(2) Knit 1 row. C.O.L. Decrease one stitch at the L.H. edge of the knitting.

(3) Knit 1 row, C.O.R. Push to W.P. one additional needle at the R.H. edge of the knitting. (Increase 1 st.)

(4) Repeat steps (2) and (3) until the desired length of edging is knitted. You will find you will be moving gradually from left to right along the needle bed. If you reach the other end of the needle bed before you have completed the required length of braid, you will have to remove the strip from the machine and replace it at the L.H. edge of the needle bed.

(5) Sew the strip to the edge of your garment, allowing it to roll over onto the right side of the garment.

XX Bias edge knitted onto the garment

This is a variation of **XIX**; however, instead of sewing the strip onto the garment after it is completed, this edging is knitted onto the edge of the garment. It is particularly suitable for a neckband as the beginning and end of the band can be invisibly grafted into a circle.

(1) Pick up the edge of the garment with the right side of the garment facing you. C.O.L.

(2) At the L.H. edge of the work 'E' wrap cast-on the number of sts. required for the width of the bias strip (e.g. 10–16 sts.) in M.Y. (or the band may be started by mounting waste knitting onto the required needles). Thread up the carriage.

(3) Set the carriage so that it does not knit needles in H.P.

(4) Push all needles to H.P., except those needles which have been used for the cast-on.

(5) Push two needles at the left of the needles in H.P. back to U.W.P. Knit 1 row. C.O.R.

(6) At the left, decrease 1 st. Knit 1 row. C.O.L.

(7) At the left, decrease 1 st.

(8) Repeat steps (5)–(7) until you reach the other end of your picked-up edge. Cast-off (or remove by hand onto waste knitting, and graft the end onto the beginning).

Bias edging knitted onto the garment with squared ends

This edging will have a diagonal beginning and end. To even off the beginning and end of this edging you will have to use an additional shaping technique. This edging can be used on a straight edge of the garment (i.e. not a curved neckband).

(1) Pick up the edge of the garment onto the needles with the right side of the garment facing you. C.O.R. Thread up the carriage with M.Y. Set the carriage not to knit needles in H.P.

(2) Knit 1 row C.O.L. Push all needles except the two needles at the left edge of the knitting to H.P. (On the next row two needles will be knitting.)

(3) Knit 2 rows. C.O.L. Push one additional needle at the left of the knitting from N.W.P. to W.P. Push one needle at the right of needles in W.P. from H.P. to U.W.P. (on the next row two more needles will be knitting).

(4) Repeat step (3) until the required number of needles for the width of the band are brought to W.P.

(5) Push two needles at the left of the needles in H.P. back to U.W.P. Knit 1 row. C.O.R.

(6) At the left, decrease 1 st. Knit one row. C.O.L.

(7) At the left, decrease 1 st.

(8) Repeat steps (5)–(7) until you reach the other end of your picked-up edge. C.O.R.

(9) On the next and every following row decrease 1 st. at each end every row until no sts. are left. (Decrease two sts. on every row).

This shaping will give you an edging with 'squared' ends.

XXI Vertical knitted band

(1) 'E' wrap cast-on for the required number of stitches for a vertical band – that is, twice the number needed to give the required width as the band will be folded in half before being attached to the edge of the garment.

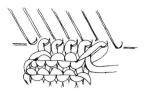

2 row repeat

Punch card for fold line in a vertical knitted band

(2) Leave the centre needle in N.W.P. – this will give you a fold line. Alternatively you may choose a punch card (or arrange your needles manually) to enable you to tuck or slip the centre needle on alternate rows. This will also give you a neat fold line.

(3) Knit the number of rows required to make a band long enough to fit the garment. If the band is too long it is a simple matter to unravel the excess rows.

(4) Attach the band to the garment by your preferred method. You may fold the band over and hand stitch it; you may prefer to attach it by linking on the knitting machine or the linker or you may sew it on the sewing machine.

12 Edges knitted with a ribber

I Ribbed edge – pick up method

This method is suitable for neck edges where the shaping has been done by putting the needles into H.P. and where no casting-off has been done. This is the most elastic finish possible for a neck edge and, therefore, it is especially suitable for small children's garments. With this edge there will be no casting-off at all.

(1) Join the seams at the neck edge of your garment leaving one seam open.

(2) C.O.L. On the M.B. push the required number of needles to W.P. and, with the right side of

Ribbed edge – pick-up method (front)

Ribbed edge – pick-up method (back)

the garment facing you, pick up the stitches for the neck edge which have been held on W.Y. onto the needles.

(3) If you have knit a round-neck garment, pick up the stitches from the straight rows knit at the side of the neck onto the needles and, with a spare piece of M.Y., knit these stitches by hand. If you

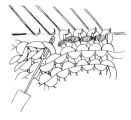

Picking up the stitches around the neck

have knit a raglan garment you may not have knit any straight rows in your shaping.

(4) Push all needles to H.P. and set carriage to knit all needles in H.P. Thread up M.Y. Knit 1 row M.T. on the M.B. C.O.R. Push up the ribber. Transfer alternate stitches to the ribber.

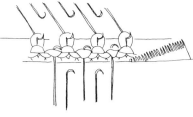

Re-hanging the ribber comb

(5) Hang the ribber comb and weights. This can be difficult. Remove the wire from the ribber comb. Then drop the ribber bed slightly and push the needles of the main bed forward a little to U.W.P. (being careful not to let the stitches slip back behind the latches) in order to slip the comb up between the needles on the main bed. Replace the ribber wire into the comb. Push the needles on the main bed back to W.P. Push the ribber back up to working position and drop the comb onto the knitting, pushing any needles brought up on the ribber back to W.P.

(6) Proceed to knit the edge in rib. Knit twice the number of rows required to get the depth of rib in main rib tension.

(7) If a turn row is required in the middle of your rib you may: Knit one row M.T. + 2 and then set your main bed carriage to slip/part/empty for one row in the

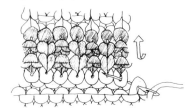

Back stitching the last row of M.Y. loops

middle of your rib. Knit one row only on the ribber. This will give you an automatic turn row.

(8) Remove M.Y. and thread up with W.Y. Knit several rows in W.Y. and strip work off the machine.

(9) Fold the rib band down onto the inside of the garment and catch-stitch down through the last row of M.Y. loops.

II Ribbed edge – 'pocket' method

Ribbed edge – 'pocket' method (front)

Ribbed edge – 'pocket' method (back)

(1) Cast-on and knit a ribbed band to

the required length and depth for your edge.

(2) Push all needles on both beds to W.P.

(3) *Optional* Pick up the heel of the adjacent or opposite stitch onto empty needles to prevent holes. This can be done on one bed or both beds.

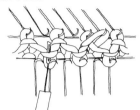

Picking up the heel of the stitch on the needle opposite to put onto the empty needle

(4) Set the ribber to half pitch. Knit 1 row on *all* needles at main rib tension.

(5) Set the machine to knit only on the main bed. Knit 4 rows, gradually bringing up the tension to the main single bed garment tension.

(6) Set the machine to knit only on the ribber bed. Knit 4 rows, gradually bringing up the tension to the main single bed garment tension.

(7) Remove the M.Y. from the feeder and replace with W.Y. Repeat steps (5) and (6).

(8) Knit several rows on both beds together with W.Y. and strip knitting off the machine.

(9) Carefully steam *only the waste knitting*.

(10) Unravel *only* the full needle rib in waste yarn, leaving the rest of the waste knitting on the band.

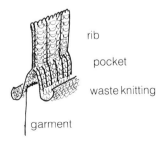

rib

pocket

waste knitting

garment

Attaching a 'pocket' band

(11) Carefully pin the pocket of single bed knitting over the edge of the garment and stitch down carefully, back stitching through the last row of M.Y. loops onto the right side of the garment and catch-stitching down the last row of M.Y. loops onto the wrong side of the garment.

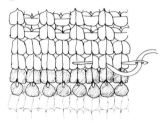

Back stitching through the last row of M.Y. loops on a pocket band.

III Ribbed edge – pocket method

This method applies the edge to the garment on the machine.

(1) Cast-on and knit a ribbed band to the required length and depth for your edge.

(2) Push all needles on both beds to W.P.

(3) *Optional* Pick up the heel of the adjacent or opposite stitch onto empty needles to prevent holes.

(4) Set the ribber to half pitch. Knit one row on *all* needles at main rib tension.

(5) Set the machine to knit only on the main bed. Knit four rows gradually bringing up the tension to the main single bed garment tension.

(6) Set the machine to knit only on the ribber bed. Knit four rows, gradually bringing up the tension to the main single bed garment tension.

(7) Lower the ribber bed slightly.

(8) With the right side facing you, drop the garment edge to be attached down into the pocket of the band from above the machine.

(9) Gently push the needles from the main bed through the edge of the knitting.

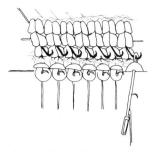

Transferring the stitches from the ribber side of the pocket band to the hooks of the main bed needles

(10) Place the stitches from the ribber into the hooks of the needles of the main bed.

(11) Push all the needles of the main bed to H.P. and drop the ribber.

(12) Knit one row by hand. Carefully lift the garment off the main bed and drop it down in front of the machine. Cast-off.

IV Double ribbed edge – sewn into garment

(1) Cast-on and knit ribbed edge. Knit twice the number of rows required to get the depth of rib in main *rib* tension.

(2) If a turn row is required in the middle of your rib you may knit one row M.T. + 2 and then set your main bed carriage to slip/part/empty for one row in the middle of your rib. Knit one row only on the ribber. This will give you an automatic turn row.

(3) Transfer all stitches to the main bed and knit 1 row M.T.

(4) Knit several rows with W.Y. and strip knitting off the machine.

(5) Pin the band onto the right side of

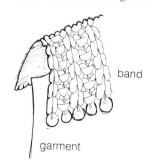

band

garment

A ribbed band applied over the edge of the garment

the garment and back-stitch down or graft rib-wise through the last row of M.Y. loops. Turn the ribbed band down over the edge and catch-stitch the cast-on edge down onto the wrong side of the garment.

V Double ribbed edge – applied to the garment on the machine

(1) Cast-on and knit ribbed edge. Knit twice the number of rows required to get the depth of rib in main rib tension.
(2) If a turn row is required in the middle of your rib you may knit 1 row M.T. + 2. Then set your main bed carriage to slip/part/empty for 1 row in the middle of your rib and knit one row only on the ribber. This will give you an automatic turn row.
(3) Transfer all stitches to the main bed and knit 1 row M.T.
(4) Knit several rows with W.Y. and strip knitting off the machine.
(5) With the right side of the garment facing you, pick up the edge onto the same number of needles you used to knit the ribbed band. Push the garment back behind the latches.
(6) Replace the last row of M.Y. loops from the band onto the needles, making sure you have put the stitches carefully into the hooks of the needles *in front of the latches*. (Turn the band around so that the purl side of waste knitting is now facing the machine.)

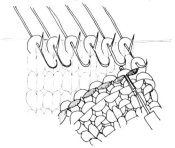

Replace the last row of M.Y. loops from the band onto the needle hooks

(7) Pull the loops of the band through the knitting of the garment.

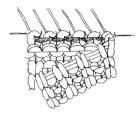

Pick up the cast-on edge of the band

(8) Pick up the cast-on edge of the ribbed band onto the needles.
(9) Knit 1 row very loosely (by hand) and cast-off.

VI Double ribbed edge – applied to the garment on the machine

(1) Cast-on in W.Y. and knit several rows. Join M.Y.
(2) Knit ribbed edge. Knit twice the number of rows required to get the depth of rib in main rib tension.
(3) If a turn row is required in the middle of your rib you may knit one row M.T. + 2 and then set your main bed carriage to slip/part/empty for one row in the middle of your rib. Knit 1 row only on the ribber. This will give you an automatic turn row.
(4) Transfer all stitches to the main bed.

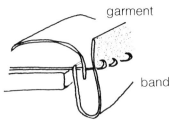

garment

band

Drop the garment onto the machine from above. Pull the needles through the edge

(5) With the right side of the garment facing you, 'drop' the edge to be attached down in front of the main bed.
(6) Gently push the needles from the main bed through the edge of the knitting. Push all work back against the machine.
(7) Pick up the first row of M.Y. loops after the waste knitting of

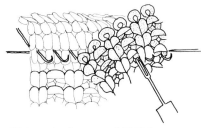

Pick up the first row of M.Y. loops

the rib and place them onto the needles.
(8) Knit 1 row loosely by hand.
(9) Gently lift the garment off the needle bed and drop down in front of the machine. Cast-off.

VII Mock pocket edge

(1) Cast-on and knit a ribbed band to the required length and twice the depth for your edge.
(2) Transfer all stitches from the ribber to the main bed.
(3) Drop the ribber and pick up the edge of the garment onto the main bed needles with the right side of the garment facing you.

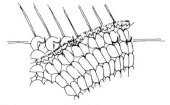

Pick up the edge of the garment

(4) Knit 4 rows M.Y., M.T. Remove M.Y. and thread up W.Y.

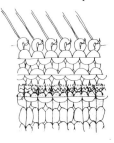

Knit four rows M.Y.

(5) Knit several rows W.Y. and strip work off the machine.
(6) Steam W.Y. and fold edge down over the front of the garment. Back stitch down onto the front of the garment through the last row of M.Y. loops. Remove the W.Y.

VIII Picot neck
(from New Zealand)

This is a neck shaped with needles in H.P.

(*1*) Pick up the neck edge of the garment onto the main bed with the wrong side of the work facing the machine.

(*2*) Knit 1 row. Transfer alternate stitches to the ribber. Hang the ribber comb and weights.

(*3*) Select all needles on both beds to W.P. and set the ribber to half pitch. Set the machine to circular knitting.

(*4*) Knit 8 rows circular knitting in M.T. (4 rows on each bed).

(*5*) Transfer stitches on both beds for a 1 + 1 rib.

(*6*) Knit rib twice as deep as the band required at rib tension (e.g. M.T.–2 or –3), with the middle row at M.T. + 1 to give a crisper fold line.

(*7*) Remove M.Y. from feeder. Thread up W.Y. and knit 10 rows.

(*8*) Remove W.Y. and knit 1 row with empty feeder. (Drop work off the machine.) Fold the rib band down to the wrong side of the garment and catch stitch down through the last row of M.Y. loops.

13   Single bed buttonholes

These buttonholes are designed to go into a fold-over band or edging on the garment. They are not suitable for a single thickness of single bed fabric – e.g. a buttonhole in a double breasted garment. Because the edging is double you will have to make two holes for the button.

These buttonholes can be made on vertical or horizontal knit bands.

I Simple transfer

Determine whether you will knit a vertical or horizontal band. Begin knitting the band.

Simple transfer buttonhole

Vertical band

(*1*) 'E' wrap cast-on for the required number of stitches for a vertical band (twice the number to give you the necessary width).

(*2*) Leave the centre needle in N.W.P. to give you a neat fold line.

(*3*) Knit the number of rows required to the position of the first buttonhole.

(*4*) Transfer the centre stitch in each group of working needles to the adjacent needle. (You have now made two holes.) Leave the empty needles in W.P.

Horizontal band

(*1*) Bring into W.P. the required number of needles to give a band of sufficient length.

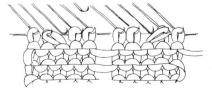

Simple transfer buttonhole, vertical band

(*2*) Begin knitting the band, choosing a preferred method – e.g. picking up the edge of the garment and knitting the band or knitting the band first and then attaching it to the garment after it is finished.

(*3*) Knit half the number of rows required for the depth of the band M.T.–2 (one quarter the total number of rows required).

(*4*) At regular intervals along the needle bed transfer a stitch to the adjacent needle. Leave the empty needle in W.P.

(*5*) Knit the remaining number of rows required for the depth of the hem. (M.T.–2) Knit 1 row M.T. + 1, Knit half the number of rows required for the depth of the band M.T.–2 (three quarters the total number of rows required).

(*6*) Repeat step (*4*), transferring the same stitches you transferred previously.

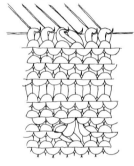

Simple transfer buttonhole, horizontal band

(*7*) Finish knitting the band. Fold over. The buttonholes will be opposite one another.

II Two stitch transfer

The procedure is similar to a simple transfer buttonhole.

Vertical band

(*1*) 'E' wrap cast-on for the required number of stitches for a vertical band (twice the number to give you the necessary width).

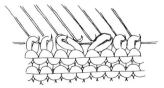

Two stitches transferred

(2) Leave the centre needle in N.W.P. to give you a neat fold line.

(3) Knit the number of rows required to the position of the first buttonhole.

(4) Transfer the two centre stitches in each group of working needles to the adjacent needle. Transfer one to the right and one to the left. Leave the empty needles in W.P.

(5) Knit 1 row, making a long loop across the two empty needles. Take this loop off one of the needles and twist it with the transfer tool. Replace this loop on the empty needle. (It is not necessary to twist the loop for *both* needles.)

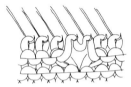

One loop of yarn on two needles

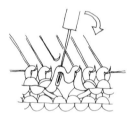

Twist the loop on one of the needles

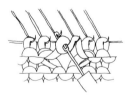

Place the twisted loop back onto the needle

Horizontal band

(1) Bring into W.P. the required number of needles to give a band of sufficient length.

(2) Begin knitting the band, choosing a preferred method – e.g. picking up the edge of the garment and knit the band, or knit the band first and then attach it to the garment after it is finished.

(3) Knit half the number of rows required for the depth of the band M.T.–2 (one quarter the total number of rows required).

Buttonholes using H.P. Step (3)

(4) At regular intervals along the needle bed transfer two stitches to the adjacent needles. Leave the empty needles in W.P.

(5) Knit 1 row, making a long loop across the two empty needles. Take this loop off one of the needles and twist it with the transfer tool. Replace this loop on the empty needle. It is not necessary to twist the loop for *both* needles.

(6) Knit the remaining number of rows required for the depth of the hem (M.T.–2). Knit 1 row M.T.+1, Knit half the number of rows required for the depth of the band M.T.–2 (three quarters the total number of rows required).

(7) Repeat steps (4) and (5), transferring the same stitches you transferred previously.

(8) Finish knitting the band. Fold over. The buttonholes will be opposite one another.

III Buttonholes using holding position

These buttonholes are found mainly in horizontal knitted bands.

(1) 'E' wrap cast-on the required number of needles for the band, leaving the centre needle in N.W.P. Cast-on an even number of stitches for each side of the band, e.g. 12 stitches over 13 needles.

(2) Knit the number of rows required to reach the position of the first buttonhole. Set the carriage so that it does not knit needles in H.P. C.O.R.

(3) Push all the needles to the left and

half the needles to the right of the needle in N.W.P. to H.P. Leave just half the needles at the right hand edge of the right hand band in W.P.

(4) Knit 3–5 rows on the needles at the right hand edge only. Finish with C.O.L.

(5) Push all needles to H.P. Pass the carriage to the right. C.O.R. Pull the yarn down below the last stitch to be knitted to make a loop before the next stitch is knitted.

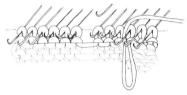

Buttonholes using H.P. Step (6)

(6) Push the centre half of the needles back to U.W.P.

(7) Knit 3–5 rows on the centre needles only. C.O.L.

(8) Push all needles to H.P. Pass the carriage to the right. C.O.R. Pull the yarn down below the last stitch to be knitted to make a loop before the next stitch is knitted.

(9) Push the left hand half of the needles to the left of the needle in N.W.P. back to U.W.P.

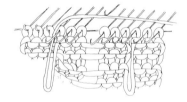

Buttonholes using H.P. Step (9)

(10) Knit 3–5 rows on the needles at the left hand edge of the knitting only. The buttonhole is now complete.

(11) Re-set the carriage and continue knitting the band. Upon completion the loops must be cut and threaded back into the band. They may be used to catch together the two buttonholes opposite each other when the band is folded in half and attached to the garment.

IV Machine-finished buttonhole on a horizontal band

Machine-finished buttonhole on a horizontal band

(*1*) Cast-on or pick up from the edge of the garment, the required number of stitches for the band.

(*2*) Knit half the number of rows required for the depth of the band – i.e. one quarter the total number of rows required for the whole band.

(*3*) Select groups of needles for the band spaced evenly across the needle bed. Using short lengths of contrast yarn, knit these groups of needles by hand.

(*a*) Push the needles forward so that the stitches fall behind the latches.

(*b*) Lay the contrast yarn in the needle hooks.

Machine finished buttonhole on a horizontal band. Step (*3b*)

(*c*) Pull the needles back just far enough for the latches to close over the contrast yarn.

(*d*) Pull the needles back one by

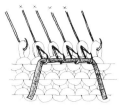

Machine finished buttonhole on a horizontal band. Step (*3c*)

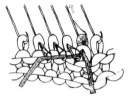

Machine finished buttonhole on a horizontal band. Step (*3d*)

one to form the contrast yarn stitches.

(*4*) Knit the other half of the band depth, one loose row to give a crisp fold line then half the number of rows required for the return of the band (three quarters of the entire number of rows required for the band).

(*5*) If you look carefully at the knitting of stitches in waste yarn you will see that there is an additional loop of M.Y. above the W.Y. stitches (*Fig. i*).

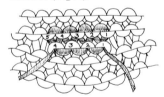

Machine finished buttonhole on a horizontal band. Step (*5*)(*i*)

At this point there are several ways of completing the buttonhole, which are described below.

A Cast-off with the transfer tool
Using a transfer tool, place the first row of loops in the main yarn (above the stitches knit by hand in step (*3*) in contrast yarn) onto the same needles that were originally used in step (*3*) (*Fig. ii*). You will have one additional loop. Place this loop onto an extra

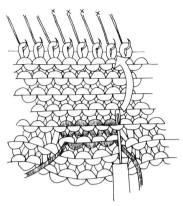

Machine finished buttonhole on a horizontal band. Option A(*ii*)

needle at the left. You have two loops on each needle.

Push the needles forward so that the original stitches fall behind the latches and the transferred stitches remain in the hooks of the needles (*Fig. iii*).

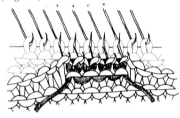

Machine finished buttonhole on a horizontal band. Option A(*iii*)

Pull the transferred stitches through. You now have one stitch on each of the 'buttonhole' needles (*Fig. iv*).

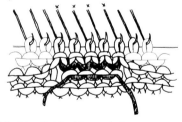

Machine finished buttonhole on a horizontal band. Option A(*iv*)

If they are numbered from right to left starting at 1 on the right-hand edge button hole needle, transfer the stitch from the needle 2 to the needle 1 (*Fig. v*).

Push needle 1 forward so that the first stitch falls behind the latch while

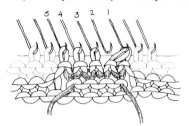

Machine finished buttonhole on a horizontal band. Option A(*v*)

the transferred stitch remains in the needle hook. If you find this difficult and both stitches fall behind the latch, use your transfer tool to lift the second stitch over the latch into the hook so that it can be pulled through the first stitch (*Fig. vi*).

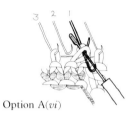

Option A(*vi*)

Transfer this stitch back to needle 2, leaving needle 1 empty and in W.P. (*Fig. vii*).

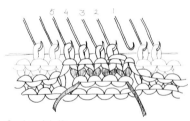

Option A(*vii*)

Repeat this 'casting-off' until you have all the original buttonhole needles empty.

B Cast-off with the latch tool

Using a transfer tool, place the first row of loops in the main yarn (above the stitches knit by hand in step (*3*) in contrast yarn) onto the same needles that were originally used in step (*3*). You will have one additional loop. Place this loop onto an extra needle at the left. You have two loops on each needle.

Push the needles forward so that the original stitches fall behind the latches and the transferred stitches remain in the hooks of the needles. Pull the transferred stitches through. You now have one stitch on each of the 'buttonhole' needles.

If the needles are numbered consecutively starting at the right hand edge with number 1, push needle number 1 forward so that the stitch falls behind the latch (*Fig. viii*).

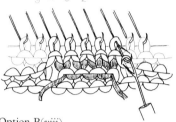

Option B(*viii*)

Put the hook of the latch tool into the hook of the needle and pull the needle back so that the stitch is transferred onto the latch tool (*Fig. ix*).

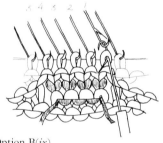

Option B(*ix*)

Push the tool up so that the stitch falls behind the latch. Transfer the stitch from needle 2 onto the tool in the same way keeping the second stitch in the hook of the tool (*Fig. x*).

Option B(*x*)

Pull the tool so that the second stitch is pulled through the first stitch. You now have two empty

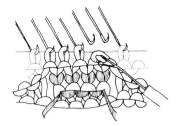

Option B(*xi*)

needles and one stitch in the hook of the latch tool (*Fig. xi*).

Continue until all the original buttonhole needles are empty.

C Cast-off with spare piece of M.Y.

Using a transfer tool, place the first row of loops in the main yarn (above the stitches knit by hand in step (*3*) in contrast yarn) onto the same needles that were originally used in step (*3*). You will have one additional loop. Place this loop onto an extra needle at the left. You have two loops on each needle.

Push the needles forward so that the original stitches fall behind the latches and the transferred stitches remain in the hooks of the needles. Pull the transferred stitches through. You now have one stitch on each of the buttonhole needles.

Starting at the right hand end of the buttonhole needles, with a spare length of M.Y., cast-off the stitches from the buttonhole in the standard manner (*Figs. xii and xiii*). Hook both ends of the spare piece of W.Y. over the needles adjacent to each end of the empty buttonhole needles (*Fig. xiv*).

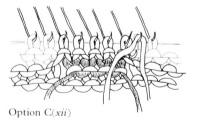

Option C(*xii*)

Option C(*xiii*)

Option C(*xiv*)

D Loose latch-off

Put the latch tool through the first M.Y. loop at the right hand top edge of W.Y. stitches. Let the stitch fall behind the latch of the tool (*Fig. xv*).

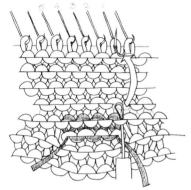

Option D(*xv*)

If the original buttonhole needles are numbered from 1 consecutively, starting at the right hand edge, push needle 1 forward so that the stitch falls behind the latch (*Fig. xvi*).

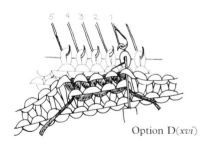

Option D(*xvi*)

Place the hook of the tool into the hook of the needle and pull the needle back so that the stitch is transferred into the hook of the tool.

Pull the tool so that the transferred stitch is pulled through the stitch on the tool behind the latch.

Slip this stitch behind the latch and swivel the tool around so that it is pointed down in the direction of the knitting (*Fig. xvii*).

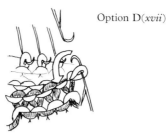

Option D(*xvii*)

Push the tool through the next M.Y. loop at the top of the W.Y. stitches and pull this loop through the stitch behind the latch on the tool (*Fig. xviii*).

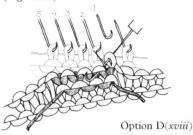

Option D(*xviii*)

Swivel the tool around again so that it is pointing towards the needle bed again.

Repeat, latching off the stitches and alternating between those on the needles and those at the top of the W.Y. stitches until you have all the original buttonhole needles empty.

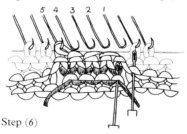

Step (6)

(6) You now have to place the M.Y. loops from the bottom of the row of W.Y. stitches onto the empty needles.

(7) Pick up one extra loop at the right hand edge onto a needle, making a stitch to prevent a hole.

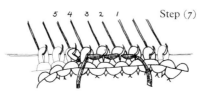

Step (7)

Knit the remaining required rows (one quarter the total number and one half the number required for the depth of the band). Finish off the band.

Remove the W.Y.

V Machine-finished buttonhole vertical band

Machine-finished buttonhole on a vertical band

Lengthwise bands are often knit double the width, leaving one centre needle in N.W.P., and then folded in half and applied to the garment. This band is knitted double the length and folded as it is knitted.

(1) You may knit the button band first to determine the number of rows you require and to decide where the buttonholes should be.

(2) Cast-on in W.Y. and knit one side of the band first. Knit the buttonhole needles at the required rows in W.Y. as in buttonhole **IV**.

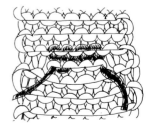

Four stitches knit in contrast yarn by hand

(*3*) When you have completed the required number of rows, knit one row M.T. + 1 for a fold row.

(*4*) As you knit back up the other side of the band pick up the first and every following alternate edge loop onto the edge needles every alternate row, thus knitting the front of the band and joining it to the back at the same time.

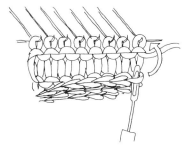

Picking up an edge loop of the band onto the edge needle

(*5*) When you arrive at the stitches knit in contrast yarn indicating the buttonholes, you may complete them as for any of the methods described in buttonhole **IV**.

VI Hand-finished buttonholes

Buttonholes may be made in any single bed fabric by knitting the required stitches in W.Y. by hand.

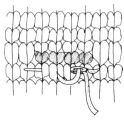

Back stitch through the M.Y. loops at the edge of the stitches in W.Y. to finish off the buttonhole

Upon completion of the garment, the loops of the M.Y. are secured either by hand sewing in a back stitch, buttonhole stitch or by crocheting through the M.Y. loops with a latch tool or crochet hook. The W.Y. knitting may then be safely removed. This type of buttonhole may be used on an unfaced piece of knitting. That is, it does not have to be an integral part of a garment band but may be in

the body of the garment – e.g. the front of a double-breasted cardigan.

14 Double bed buttonholes

These buttonholes are usually much neater if knitted vertically rather than horizontally as they tend to disappear into the ribbed fabric rather than distort it. However, on manufactured garments ribbed bands are often faced with gros-grain ribbon of a similar colour and width to the band itself and then the buttonholes can be executed on a domestic sewing machine.

It is easier to gauge the number of rows you will need between each buttonhole if you knit the button band first, making careful note of the number of rows required to make the band the correct length. (Remember that it is always easier to unravel knitting and shorten it than to pick it back up on the machine to lengthen it!)

I Simple transfer buttonhole

In a ribbed band you can transfer stitches as follows: transfer C to A, and B to D.

Simple transfer buttonhole

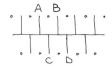

Simple transfer buttonhole, diagram

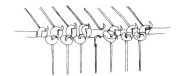

Simple transfer buttonhole, stitches on needles

II Vertical band buttonhole using holding position

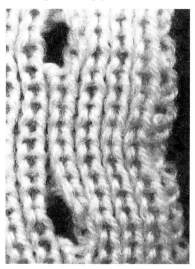

Vertical band buttonhole

(*1*) Cast-on and knit the band to the position of the first buttonhole. C.O.R. Disconnect the row counter.

Vertical band buttonholes using H.P. Step (*2*)

(*2*) Push all needles on both beds to the left of the centre to H.P. Set both carriages not to knit needles in H.P.

(3) Knit the required number of rows for the buttonhole – i.e. the diameter of the button, remembering that knitting stretches! Make this number an *odd* number and finish with the carriage on the *left*.

(4) Push all needles to H.P. Take the carriage to the right. With the aid of a hook or a latch tool, pull a loop of yarn down between the needle beds next to the last stitch knitted.

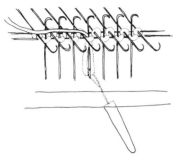

Vertical band buttonholes using H.P. Step (4)

(5) Push all the needles to the left of the centre to U.W.P.

(6) Knit the same number of rows on these stitches as were knit for the first half of the buttonhole. C.O.R.

(7) Reset both carriages to knit all needles and move the row counter on the same number of rows you used to knit the buttonhole.

III Horizontal buttonhole in a vertical band (hand-finished)

(1) Cast-on and knit the band to the position of the first buttonhole. Be sure to cast-on enough stitches to make the band wide enough to allow the buttonhole to be made

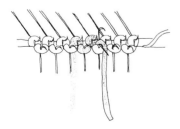

Horizontal buttonhole in vertical band. Step (2)

Horizontal buttonhole in a vertical band

without distorting the band and having enough stitches at either edge of the buttonhole.

(2) Knit three to four stitches by hand in W.Y. over the centre needles. This will be your buttonhole. With the aid of a hook or latch tool pull the ends of the W.Y. down between the needle beds.

(3) Continue to knit the band repeating step (2) wherever a buttonhole is required.

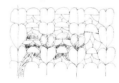

Horizontal buttonhole in vertical band. Step (4)

(4) When the band is completed cast-off and attach the band to the garment. Complete the buttonholes by one of these methods.
- Back-stitch through the M.Y. loops at either side of the W.Y. loops.
- Buttonhole stitch through the M.Y. loops at either side of the W.Y. stitches.
- Crochet through the M.Y. loops at either side of the W.Y. loops.

IV Horizontal buttonhole in vertical ribbing (cast-off method)

Horizontal buttonhole in vertical ribbing

(1) Cast-on band and knit to the first buttonhole position. (Make sure the band is wide enough so that the buttonhole does not distort the band.)

(2) Using a spare piece of M.Y., cast-off the centre three to four stitches. Use the transfer tool method with the double-eyed bodkin and alternate, first casting-off a stitch on the main bed, then casting off the next stitch on the ribber, etc.

Horizontal buttonhole in vertical ribbing (cast-off method). Step (2)

(3) Take the end of this piece of spare yarn when you have completed the casting-off and wind it back around the empty needles (under and then up and over the needles as in the 'E' wrap method, alternating first with a needle on the main bed, then the next empty needle on the ribber).

Horizontal buttonhole in vertical ribbing (cast-off method). Step (*3*)

(4) To ensure the needles knit on the next row, push them all to H.P. and set both carriages to knit all needles. If possible try to hang the wire-loop type weight hangers.

Horizontal buttonhole in vertical ribbing (cast-off method). Step (*4*)

(5) Continue to knit the band, re-peating for additional button-holes. After the band is attached to the garment, the edge of the buttonhole can be reinforced by your stitching it with a button-hole stitch if desired.

15   Pockets

Pockets are not difficult to insert in a garment; they can be a very useful addition to a warm jacket or chil-dren's clothes or a decorative feature in a fashion garment. Pockets can, of course, always be added in the side seams, but you must be careful that a filled pocket does not spoil the line of a garment. If you are placing a pocket on the front of a cardigan, the outside edge of the pocket must be a hand's width away from the side seam.

Three of the most common types of pockets are described in the following exercises.

One

(1) Cast on 60 sts. using the 'E' wrap method.
Knit 10 rows M.T. − 2,

Knit 1 row M.T. + 1,
Knit 10 rows M.T. − 2.
Turn up hem. C.O.R.
(2) K. 30 rows, M.Y., M.T. Set carriage not to knit needles in H.P. C.O.R.
(3) Push 15 nds. at opp. edge of knitting to H.P. Knit one row. C.O.L.
(4) Push 15 nds. at opp. edge of knitting to H.P. K. 1 rw. C.O.R.
(5) Working on *only* the centre 30 nds., push alt. nds. to U.W.P. Set carr. to part/slip/empty. K. 1 rw. C.O.L. Cancel patterning and return carriage to stocking stitch knitting but leave carriage not knitting needles in H.P.
(6) K. 6 rws. M.T.−2 C.O.L. K. 1 rw. M.T. + 1 C.O.R. K. 6 rws. M.T.−2 C.O.R. Pick up loops from slipped row. (Hem for pocket.) Knit 1 row. C.O.L.
(7) K. 41 rws. C.O.R. Push 15 nds. at opp. edge of knitting back to U.W.P. Knit 1 rw. Set carr. to knit all nds. back to W.P.
(8) K. 11 rws. Cast off. Sew up pocket sides. Neaten top edge of pocket.

Two

(1) Cast on 40 sts, using the 'E' wrap method.
Knit 10 rows M.T.−2, C.O.R.
Knit 1 row M.T. + 1, C.O.L.
Knit 10 rows M.T.−2, C.O.L.
Turn up hem. Knit one row. C.O.R.
(2) K. 10 rws. C.O.R. Set carriage not to knit needles in H.P.
(3) Push 10 nds. at opp. side of knitting to H.P.
K. 30 rws. Break M.Y. C.O.R.
(4) Push all nds. to H.P. Place C.O.L.
(5) Put 10 nds. at left side of knitting to U.W.P. Join M.Y. K. 30 rws. C.O.L. Set carriage to knit all nds. back to W.P.
(6) K. 10 rws. Cast-off.
(7) With purl side of pocket edge facing you and right side of gar-ment folded over towards you, pick up back pocket edge. K. 40 rws.

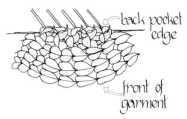

Pocket two. Step (*7*)

(8) With right side of pocket edge facing you, pick up other side of pocket edge (the front of the garment).
K. 6 rws. M.T.−2
K. 1 rw. M.T. + 1
K. 6 rws. M.T.−2. Break M.Y. Join W.Y. K. 10 rws. Strip off the machine. Fold edges over onto right side of garment and back-stitch into place.

These two exercises can be repeated using a pattern card instead of plain knitting for the main fabric of the garment. This will give you practice in re-establishing your stitch pattern.

Three

(1) Make a closed edge cast on over 30 nds.
(2) K. 20 rws. M.Y., M.T. Break M.Y., join W.Y. K. 10 rws. strip off the machine.
(3) Cast on 60 sts. using the 'E' wrap method.
Knit 10 rows M.T.−2, C.O.R.
Knit 1 row M.T. + 1, C.O.L.
Knit 10 rows M.T.−2 C.O.L.
Turn up hem. Knit one row. C.O.R.
(4) Set the machine for two-colour Fair Isle knitting. Join con. col.
(5) K. 30 rws. in a Fair Isle pattern. Make a note of card row number. Lock card. Cancel pattern knit-ting. Remove con. col.
(6) Set carr. not to knit needles in H.P. Push 15 nds. at both edges of work to H.P.
(7) On centre 30 sts. arrange nds. for 2 × 1 mock rib. Transf. every 3rd. st. to the adjacent needle. Nds. arranged as follows:
1 o 1 1 o 1 1 o 1 1 . . . . . 1 1 o 1
Push empty nds. back to N.W.P.
(8) K. 6 rws. M.T.−2

K. 1 rw. M.T. + 2

K. 6 rws. M.T.–2. T.U.H. Cast off loosely.

(9) Place piece made in steps (1) and (2) onto empty centre nds., picking up last row of M.Y. loops before W.Y.

(10) Place C.O.R. Set carr. to K. all nds. back to B. Pos. K. 1 rw. W.Y. Unravel W.Y. (All nds. W.P.)

(11) Set carr. to re-register pattern. With carr. set to part/slip/empty, all nds. in W.P. card locked, take carr to R. C.O.R. Unlock card and resume pattern knitting.

(12) K. 10 rws. Cast-off.

16 Necklines

Necklines can be a problem. You have to consider the design of the neckline in relation to: the garment, the size and shape of the 'hole'; and the type of finishing you will require – e.g. collar, ribbed band, crochet edge, etc. Once having designed the neckline you then have to decide on how you are going to go about actually constructing it. On a cardigan or jacket where you have a front opening it is simply a matter of calculating your decreases and shapings. However, on any other type of garment you will be knitting on only one side of the garment to shape the hole and you will be 'holding' the rest of the garment to be knitted later.

Let us look more closely at the mechanics of knitting a neckline. You can hold the unwanted section of work while knitting one of the sides of the neckline in the following ways.

I Removing half the knitting from the machine

Removing the work onto waste yarn

(1) Push the needles of the section of work you wish to knit to H.P. Set the carriage not to knit needles in H.P.

(2) Thread up the carriage with W.Y. and knit several rows on the stitches you wish to remove.

(3) Strip these stitches off the machine. Re-set the carriage to knit all needles. Re-thread the carriage with M.Y. and continue to knit one side of the neck.

(4) When you have finished one side of the neck and removed your work from the machine, you may pick up the last row of M.Y. loops from the other half of your garment and knit the other side of the neck reversing your shaping.

The disadvantage of this method is that you may find it difficult if you are knitting in a stitch pattern because you will have to reset the patterning every time you re-start knitting in your M.Y. (twice).

Removing the work onto a hand-knitting needle:

Take a circular needle and slip all the stitches you wish to hold onto the needles. Push all empty needles to N.W.P. Secure the stitches on the needle with two rubber bands wrapped around the needle, one at each end.

Removing the work onto an attachment

Use one of the alternatives below.

● The work can be transferred onto a garter bar and the garter bar can then be hung on the gate pegs. As it hangs in front of the work, the work will not be marked by the passage of the carriage.

● Alternatively, use holding combs: these look like multi-fingered transfer tools mounted on a bar with a removable 'lid' which goes over the top after you have collected the stitches. They are usually available with 30 eyelets. You will need several if you decide to use them. They can also be used to transfer groups of stitches and can be cut up into smaller sections.

● On a Passap or Pfaff machine, remove the stitches you don't want to knit onto the opposite bed. You always have both beds in working position when knitting, even if you are only knitting on one of the beds.

II Pushing needles to hold position

You can push needles to holding position providing you do not want to knit a very deep neckline. The disadvantage of this method is that if you are using a very light coloured yarn or the purl side of the knitted fabric is the right side, continual passage of the knitting carriage may mark your work. You can protect the 'held' knitting by putting a card or net fabric on the gate pegs in front of the knitting before you push your needles to H.P. or you can put masking tape over the knitted fabric just below the needles in H.P.

III Push needles to N.W.P.

You can manually knit the needles you wish to hold back to N.W.P. using a cast-on cord. You must then take similar precautions as in **II** against marking your work by the passage of the carriage. You can also place tape on the needle bed in front of the needle butts in N.W.P. to ensure that they don't get pulled forward, thus allowing the stitches to be knitted.

IV Knitting two sides simultaneously

This method can be used for stocking stitch or lace knitting.

Using two main yarns and the Fair Isle setting

(1) Make sure your patterning information is not being transferred to the needles. On machines with pre-set rows the needles are not being brought forward by the passage of the carriage or by pulling the set lever. On machines with pattern drums, the side levers are forward.

(2) Set the machine to Fair Isle/colour. Thread up one main yarn in feeder A and the other main yarn in feeder B. Set the carriage to knit all needles including the needles in H.P.

(3) Push the needles on one side of the neck to U.W.P. or H.P. Knit

one row. Push the same needles again to U.W.P. or H.P. Knit one row. Continue in this way, always pushing the appropriate needles forward before every row, and continue to shape the neck on both sides.

Using two main yarns and slip/part/empty
(1) Make sure your patterning information is not being transferred to the needles. On machines with pre-set rows the needles are not being brought forward by the passage of the carriage or by pulling the set lever. On machines with pattern drums, the side levers are forward.
(2) Set the machine to part/slip/empty. Thread up the tension mast with two strands of main yarn. Thread up one main yarn in feeder A. Set the carriage to knit all needles including the needles in H.P.
(3) Push the needles on one side of the neck to U.W.P. or H.P. Knit one row. Push the same needles again to U.W.P. or H.P. Knit one row. You have knit two rows on one side of the neck. Repeat the procedure with the second main yarn, pushing to U.W.P. or H.P. the needles that were previously **not** knit. Knit two rows on these needles.
Continue in this way always pushing the appropriate needles forward before every row and continue to shape the neck on both sides.

Knitting two sides simultaneously using the eye
If you have the intarsia feeder or plaiting feeder, which enables you to get a better look at your needles while you are knitting, and if you have a gap of several needles in N.W.P. in the centre of your neck, you can thread up your tension mast with the two yarns or hand feed them into the carriage. With a little practice you will be able to change the yarn in mid-row. This could be a useful technique if you are doing a complicated lace pattern.

Using the intarsia carriage
Because the carriage is designed to knit more than one yarn in a row, once you have mastered the technique you can use it to knit the two sides of your neckline simultaneously.

V Cut and sew

This technique can also be known as sew and cut and sew. I prefer to ensure that there can be no stitches to run and tend to be over cautious. This technique can be used quite successfully, no matter how thick or chunky the yarn and the knitting.

The whole neckline
(1) Knit the garment without any neck shaping.
(2) Mark carefully with a strand of contrast yarn the line you will stitch on. You can mark the fabric inside or outside your proposed stitching line.
(3) Using a zig-zag sewing machine and polyester thread stitch along your marked line using a medium stitch width and a medium stitch length. Allow the knitting to 'spread out' under the sewing foot and allow it to 'splay'. This is very important. Your stitching line, even though it is a zig-zag stitch, is *not elastic*. If the stitching is too tight it will break. Your garment band will pull the knitting in and prevent it from appearing ruffled and ugly so don't worry if the stitching line looks rather ungainly.
(4) Cut the unwanted knitted fabric away and discard it. You may run another line of zig-zag stitching over the cut edge if you wish. Remember to stretch the edge slightly as you sew to prevent the stitching from constricting the neckline. You are now ready to cover over your ugly edge with a band. No-one will ever know you took the easy way out!

Using transferred stitches to mark the neckline
(1) If you wish to mark the neckline while knitting the garment on the

machine, cast off the centre stitches onto a spare piece of yarn if they are required in the shaping.
(2) Transfer the unwanted stitches as you would if you were shaping the neckline.
(3) Push the empty needles back to N.W.P.
(4) Continue to knit the garment. You will have strands of yarn being carried across the space of the neckline. When you have completed the knitting and removed the work from the machine you can cut these floats and tie them off. Then you can deal with the band as you would for a 'cut and sew' neckband. This technique can be useful in pattern knitting if you haven't got a zig-zag sewing machine.

There is no doubt that the most elastic neckline can be achieved when you keep your casting-off to a minimum. If you put your stitches onto waste yarn or 'holding position', knit them straight into the band, and then catch-stitch the band down onto the wrong side of the garment you will be amazed at the elasticity of the neckline. This is especially important with children's garments because, although their necks are not wide, their heads are, and it is difficult to make a neckline which will fit neatly around a small neck and still be stretchy enough to go over the head.

Sample necklines

Round neck shaping using holding position
(1) Cast-on 62 stitches with an 'E' wrap cast-on.
(2) Knit 10 rows. C.O.R.
(3) Push all needles to the Left of O and 7 needles to the Right of O to H.P. Set the carriage not to knit needles in H.P.
(4) Knit 1 row. (C.O.L.) Push one needle at the left of the needles in W.P. to H.P.

(5) Knit 1 row. (C.O.R.). Push three needles at the left of the needles in W.P. to H.P.

(6) Knit 1 row. (C.O.L.) Push one needle at the left of the needles in W.P. to H.P.

(7) Knit 1 row. (C.O.R.) Push two needles at the left of the needles in W.P. to H.P.

(8) Knit 1 row. (C.O.L.) Push one needle at the left of the needles in W.P. to H.P.

(9) Knit 1 row. (C.O.R.) Push one needle at the left of the needles in W.P. to H.P.

(10) Knit one row. (C.O.L.) Push one needle at the left of the needles in W.P. to H.P.

(11) Repeat (9) and (10) once more.

(12) Knit 5 rows straight and cast off the shoulder.

(13) Take the carriage to the left. Leaving seven needles to the left of O in H.P., push the remaining needles to the left of the work to U.W.P.

(14) Repeat steps (4)–(12) reversing the shaping.

(15) You now have all the centre stitches on needles in H.P. Pick up the straight sides of the neckband at either edge of the needles in H.P. up to the shoulder. (You are picking up the stitches at the edge of the five straight rows.) Push all needles to H.P. for the first row.

(16) Knit one row M.Y. M.T. Knit the neckband. If you wish to knit a 2 × 1 mock rib at this point you may transfer every third stitch to the adjacent needle and push the empty needles back to N.W.P.

(17) If you wish to graduate the tension at which you knit the neckband you would proceed as follows –
Knit 2 rows M.T.
Knit 2 rows M.T.–1
Knit 2 rows M.T.–2
Knit 2 rows M.T. + 1
Knit 2 rows M.T.–2
Knit 2 rows M.T.–1

(18) Push all needles (including those at N.W.P.) to W.P. Knit two rows M.Y., M.T. Knit several rows in W.Y. and remove work from the machine.

(19) Catch stitch the last row of M.Y. loops down loosely onto the wrong side of the garment.

Round neck shaping using needles knit back to N.W.P.

The above neckline can be repeated exactly except that instead of pushing needles forward to H.P. you may knit them back to N.W.P. manually using the cast-on cord. When you are ready to knit the neckband, pull gently on the cord until the needles are pulled forward and return to W.P. Then you can unravel the cord, leaving the stitches in the needle hooks ready to knit the band.

'V' neck

(1) Cast on 61 stitches using the 'E' wrap method.

(2) Knit 12 rows. (C.O.L.).

(3) Put the centre stitch on a safety pin. (Push the empty needle back to N.W.P.)

(4) Push all needles to the right of O to H.P. Set the carriage not to knit the needles in H.P.

(5) Thread up the carriage with W.Y. and knit several rows on the stitches remaining in W.P. Release these stitches from the machine and return the empty needles to N.W.P.

(6) Return the carriage to right. Reset the carriage to knit all needles. Thread up carefully with M.Y.

(7) Continue to knit on the 30 stitches to the R. of O.

(8) Decrease one stitch at the neck edge on the next and every following second row 20 times. (Ten stitches remain.)

(9) Cast-off.

(10) Put the carriage on the left. Pick up the last row of M.Y. loops next to the waste knitting on the other half of the knitting. Place these loops on the 30 needles to the left of O.

(11) Thread up with M.Y. and knit the second half of the 'V' neck reversing the shapings. Cast-off.

17 Making-up

This section is basically concerned with putting two pieces of knitted fabric together. Various techniques can be used to make your garment look really professional and it is often worth spending a bit more time to perfect your garment, even though you may be anxious to see the whole thing finished. If you consider the garment as a sum of *all* the parts, the making-up techniques will not only include putting the front and back together and then setting-in the sleeves, but also may include attaching garment bands at the hem, neck, sleeve and front border.

It pays to always separate your main yarn knitting from any waste yarn knitting by knitting *one* row with the cast-on cord or a length of sewing cotton in a contrast colour.

Using markers

When putting two pieces of knitting together securely and neatly, there are several methods of ensuring that pieces are joined evenly.

Take a tip from dressmaking and knit in markers – that is, small pieces of contrast yarn tied in to the edge of the pieces you are knitting at fixed points. These markers correspond to the notches found on dressmaker's paper patterns. They can be indicated on your knit tracer/knit radar/knit leader sheet to remind you as you knit or you can knit them in after a fixed number of rows at regular intervals.

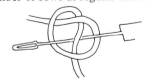

Slip knot on transfer tool

To make a yarn marker use a slip knot loop. Make a slip knot in a small piece of W.Y. Slip the loop onto the transfer tool; remove the edge stitch onto the tool. Then slip the yarn loop over the end of the tool, hang it onto the stitch and replace the stitch onto the needle.

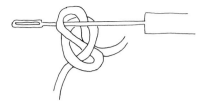

Pull the yarn marker down towards the handle of the tool

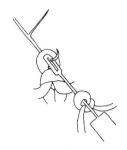

Remove the stitch onto the tool

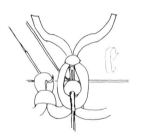

With the stitch on the tool, pull the marker up and over the stitch

An alternative method is to make a loop with a spare piece of W.Y. and hang the loop onto the edge needle(s). Attach a bull-dog clip to keep the loop from popping off.

Basting methods

Basting the seam with contrast yarn

Baste the two pieces by hand with a contrast piece of yarn. Pin the two pieces together with *large* glass-headed pins placed at frequent intervals and at right angles to the edge. *Or* use the basting wire included with the

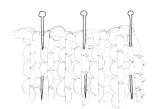

Putting in pins at right angles to the edge

Jones/Brother Knitleader or a wire from a ribber cast-on comb. (Glue a piece of plasticine or similar substance to the end to prevent the wire tangling in the knitting or pulling through). *Or* hold the two pieces together using hair-grips, small bull-dog clips or other similar clips.

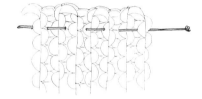

Using the basting wire

I Back-stitch or crochet seam

You work this seam with the wrong side of the fabric facing you.
(1) Put both sections of the garment to be joined with right sides together and fix using one of the above methods.
(2) Join.
  (a) Sew together working one stitch in from the edge.
  (b) Sew together with a loose over-sewing stitch matching ridge to ridge.
  (c) Crochet together working one stitch in from the edge.

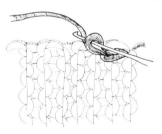

Crochet seam

II Mattress stitch seam

You work this seam with the right side of the fabric facing you.
(1) Place the two sections of the garment to be joined together side by side with the right side of the fabric facing you.

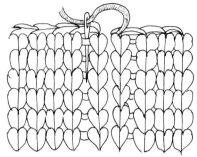

Mattress stitch (stocking stitch facing)

  (a) Stocking stitch facing: sew together, alternating first one side then the other. Sew down a 'channel' between two ridges of stitch in stocking stitch. You can catch either one cross bar each time or two.

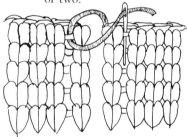

Mattress stitch (stocking stitch facing)
Mattress stitch (stocking stitch facing)

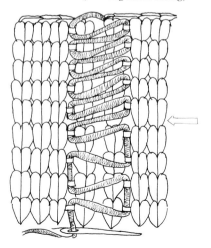

(*b*) Purl stitch facing: sew together alternating first one side then the other. Catch up the 'loops' of the stitches.

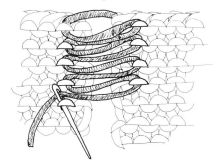

Mattress stitch (purl stitch facing)

III Sewing machine seams

Seams can be sewn on the sewing machine, but be careful not to allow the edge of the knitting to become stretched or fluted. Carefully fix the two pieces of work together by one of the above means. The wire method is recommended, but use the method you find most suitable to the way you work. Use a stitch suitable for stretchy fabric – e.g. a zig-zag stitch at width approximately $1\frac{1}{2}$, length approximately $1\frac{1}{2}$.

Care must be taken to ensure that the fabric feeds evenly into the machine. Some machines have special feet for dealing with knitted fabric. You might also find your seams more successful if you release the pressure on the presser foot. Consult your sewing machine manual. Ribbed and thicker fabrics such as tuck stitch require more care to prevent fluting.

IV Grafting

This is a method of sewing by hand with the main yarn to make an invisible join. If I am careful I find this the most satisfactory way of joining two pieces of knitting end to end. This technique will not only give you an invisible join at the shoulder between the front and back of a garment but can also be used to add ribbing to the main section of knitting invisibly. In other words, you need never have a cast-off edge again! It is very impor-

tant to knit one row with the cast-on cord or sewing cotton before doing any waste knitting.

It will take some practice to perfect the technique and to 'get your eye in'. It helps if you practise on sample pieces which are knit in thick yarn and light in colour (even the waste yarn) so that you will not strain your eyes. A white yarn and a mid-colour contrast yarn for W.Y. would be easiest. Do not practise on a finished garment. Develop confidence before tackling your final work. If you are successful you will find your perfect garment an ample reward. However, if you are allergic to hand-finishing or are producing garments where time is an important factor, this technique is not for you.

(*1*) Finish the sections of knitting to be grafted as follows.
　(*a*) All shaping to be done by putting needles into H.P.
　(*b*) Knit one row over all needles with M.Y. Before cutting the M.Y. ensure you leave a 'tail' three times the width of the knitting.
　(*c*) Knit 1 row with the cast-on cord or sewing thread in main feeder.
　(*d*) Knit several rows of W.Y. and strip knitting off the machine.
(*2*) Press the W.Y. (only) firmly to lock the stitches.
(*3*) Place the two sections to be joined together with the right sides facing you.
(*4*) Sew together using a blunt-ended tapestry needle and M.Y. Follow the cast-on cord with your sewing needle, alternating between the two pieces of work.

Grafting: Stocking stitch to stocking stitch

Waste Knitting Folded away from You
(*1*) Place the two sections to be joined together with the right sides facing you. Fold the waste knitting down between the two sections of knitting. Hold the two sections

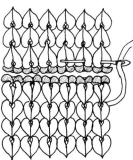

Grafting stocking stitch (W.Y. folded away). Step (*3*)

together with the join horizontally placed towards you. It will help if you can slip the two sections of waste knitting between the fingers of the hand holding the knitting.

(*2*) Thread up a blunt-ended tapestry needle with a tail of M.Y. preferably from one of the knitted sections.
(*3*) Push the needle into the first stitch at the right of the top section from the front, then up out through the next stitch from the back.

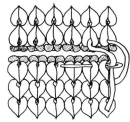

Grafting stocking stitch (W.Y. folded away). Step (*4*)

(*4*) Take the needle to the bottom section of knitting. Push the needle down into the first stitch at the right and up out of the next stitch.

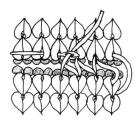

Grafting stocking stitch (W.Y. folded away). Step (*6*)

(5) Return to the top section. With the needle, go down into the stitch you came out of and up through the next stitch.

(6) Repeat, alternating from one section to another, always going into the last stitch you came out of on the section you are working on. You will find that you are following the last row that was knitted in the cord or sewing thread.

(7) It is very important not to pull the yarn tight otherwise you will distort your stitches. When the grafting is complete the W.Y. may be removed.

Waste Knitting Folded Towards You

(1) Place the two sections to be joined together with the right sides facing you. Fold the waste knitting up over the top of the two sections of knitting. Hold the two sections together with the join horizontally placed to you.

(2) Thread up a blunt-ended tapestry needle with a tail of M.Y. preferably from one of the knitted sections.

(3) Push the needle into the first stitch at the right of the top section from the front, then up out through the next stitch from the back.

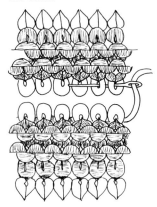

Grafting stocking stitch (W.Y. folded towards). Step (3)

(4) Take the needle to the bottom section of knitting. Push the needle down into the first stitch at the right and up out of the next stitch.

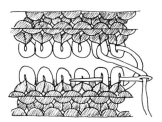

Grafting stocking stitch (W.Y. folded towards). Step (4)

(5) Return to the top section. With the needle, go down into the stitch you came out of and up through the next stitch.

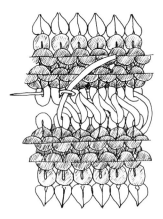

Grafting stocking stitch (W.Y. folded towards). Step (5)

(6) Repeat, alternating from one section to another, always going into the last stitch you came out of on the section you are working on. You will find that you are following the last row that was knitted in the cord or sewing thread.

(7) It is very important not to pull the yarn tight, otherwise you will distort your stitches.

Grafting: Purl stitch to purl stitch

(1) Place the two sections to be joined side by side with the right side (purl side) facing you. Fold the waste knitting down between the two sections away from you. Place the join horizontally to you.

(2) Thread a blunt-ended tapestry needle with the tail of M.Y. from one of the sections of knitting.

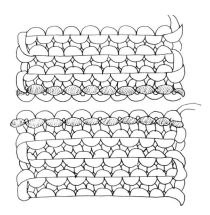

Grafting purl stitch. Step (1)

(3) Push the needle up (from the back) of the first stitch at the right edge of the top section and then back down through the next stitch.

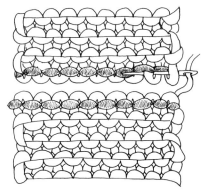

Grafting purl stitch. Step (2)

(4) Then push the needle up through the first stitch at the right edge of the bottom section and down through the next stitch.

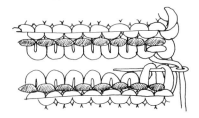

Grafting purl stitch. Step (4)

(5) Return to the top section. Push the needle up through the last stitch your needle went down into, then down through the next stitch.

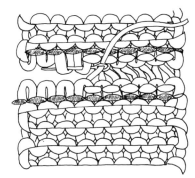

Grafting purl stitch. Step (5)

(6) Repeat, alternating between the top section and the bottom section. You will find that you will be following the last rows knitted in W.Y. or sewing thread.

(7) It is very important not to pull the sewing tight as you will distort the stitches. When the grafting is complete the W.Y. may be removed.

Grafting: Stocking stitch to rib

This technique may seem overly elaborate but it is one of the most effective ways of gathering knitted fabric onto a ribbed edge. It has the enormous advantage (in my opinion) of joining two sections of the garment effectively, without the restricting of elasticity that would happen if the two were cast-off together on the machine. It has the disadvantage of taking longer but gives a better result. Both sections to be joined must be removed from the machine onto a cast-on cord or sewing thread and waste knitting.

This technique is particularly useful in that you can attach a 2 × 2 industrial or half-pitch rib to a single bed fabric without *reducing* the number of stitches (which you would do if you were just continuing to knit the garment directly after completing the rib). With an industrial or 2 × 2 half-pitch rib, the needle arrangement on each bed consists of two needles in W.P. opposite one needle in N.W.P. on the opposite bed. Traditionally when transferring stitches to continue in single bed fabric you find two stitches on every third needle. With

the grafting method you begin the garment on W.Y. You knit the rib separately and remove the knitting on W.Y.; then you can join the two pieces stitch by stitch thus achieving a gathered effect.

Waste Knitting folded away from you

(1) Place both sections to be joined side by side with the right side facing you and the join placed horizontally. The rib section should be the bottom section (closest to you).

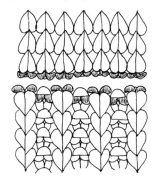

Grafting stocking stitch to 1 × 1 rib. Step (1)

(2) Fold the waste knitting down between the two sections away from you. It will be easier if you can slip the waste knitting between the fingers of the hand supporting the knitting.

(3) Take a blunt-ended tapestry needle threaded with the tail of M.Y. (preferably from the rib) and insert it into the first stitch at the right edge of the top section of knitting (stocking stitch). Bring the needle out through the adjacent stitch.

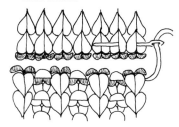

Grafting stocking stitch to 1 × 1 rib. Step (3)

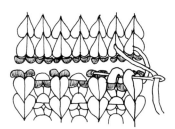

Grafting stocking stitch to 1 × 1 rib. Step (4)

(4) Take the needle to the bottom section of knitting (rib). Insert the needle into the first plain stitch at the right edge of the knitting. *Insert* the needle into the second stitch (purl) stitch at the right edge.

(5) Return to the top section and insert the needle into the last stitch your needle came out of. Bring the needle out through the following stitch.

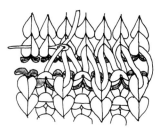

Grafting stocking stitch to 1 × 1 rib. Step (5)

(6) Return to the rib section. Push the needle *up* through the last stitch you went down into (purl stitch) and again up through the next (plain) stitch. In other words follow the last row knitted in cast-on cord/sewing thread.

(7) Repeat alternating from the plain to the rib section until you have completed the grafting. Do not pull your sewing too tight or you will distort your stitches. When the grafting is complete the W.Y. may be removed.

Waste Knitting Folded Towards You
This method requires a different technique when you are removing the ribbing from the machine onto waste knitting; it is not suitable for any ribs knit on the half-pitch setting. All stitches must be transferred singly to

the main bed – This is not possible on ribs knit on a half-pitch setting.

(*1*) After completing the ribbing, transfer all stitches to the main bed. C.O.R.

(*2*) Push all needles which have rib stitches on them to U.W.P.

(*3*) Set the carriage to part/slip/empty (Knitmaster machines must disconnect the pattern drums by pushing the side levers forward). Knit one row. C.O.L. (Only the rib stitches will knit.)

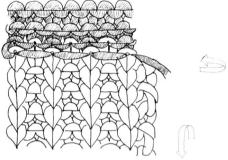

Grafting stocking stitch to rib (W.Y. folded towards you). Step (*3*)

(*4*) Cancel the patterning of the carriage and continue to knit in W.Y. Strip the work off the machine and press the W.Y.

(*5*) Turn the section of ribbed knitting around so that the stocking stitch side of the waste knitting is facing you; fold this waste knitting down over the top of the ribbing so that the loops of the last row knitted in M.Y. stick out at the top.

Grafting stocking stitch to rib (W.Y. folded towards you). Step (*5*)

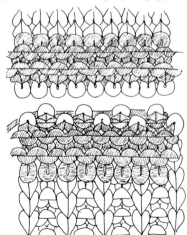

(*6*) On the stocking stitch section, fold the waste knitting back over the top so that the purl side of the waste knitting is facing you.

(*7*) Place both sections to be joined side by side with the right side facing you and the join placed horizontally. The rib section should be the bottom section (closest to you).

(*8*) Take a blunt-ended tapestry needle threaded with the tail of M.Y. (preferably from the stocking stitch section) and insert the needle into the first purl stitch at the right edge of the bottom section of knitting (rib). Insert the needle into the adjacent (plain) stitch.

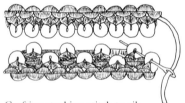

Grafting stocking stitch to rib (W.Y. folded towards you). Step (*8*)

(*9*) Take the needle to the top section of knitting (stocking stitch). Insert the needle into the first stitch at the right edge of the knitting. Bring the needle out of the second stitch.

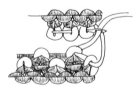

Grafting stocking stitch to rib (W.Y. folded towards you). Step (*9*)

(*10*) Return to the bottom section and push the needle up through the last stitch your needle came out of. Push the needle up through the following stitch.

Grafting stocking stitch to rib (W.Y. folded towards you). Step (*10*)

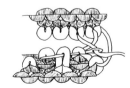

Grafting stocking stitch to rib (W.Y. folded towards you). Step (*11*)

(*11*) Return to the stocking stitch section. Insert the needle into the last stitch you came out of and down into the next stitch.

(*12*) Repeat, alternating from the plain to the rib section until you have completed the grafting. Follow the last rows knitted in cast-on cord/sewing thread. Do not pull your sewing too tight or you will distort your stitches. When the grafting is complete the W.Y. may be removed.

V Grafting on a machine

For this you can use a knitting machine or linker, e.g. Belinky or Hague Linker. This method of joining two sections of knitting stitch to stitch is not as elastic as the method involving hand sewing. However, it is quicker. There are two factors which control the amount of ease.

(*a*) The distance between each stitch when it is picked up. That is, the gauge of the machine (whether linker or knitting machine). The further apart the needles or points (on a linker) the more ease there is in the seam.

(*b*) The amount of ease you are able to introduce into the linking or casting-off itself. This is controlled by the size of the stitch. (The looser your cast-off row, the 'holier' your join!)

Grafting on a Knitting Machine (stitch to stitch)

(*1*) Pick up the last row of M.Y. loops of one section of the knitting onto needles with the right side of the work facing you. Push the needle to H.P. and push the knitting back behind the latches.

(*2*) Pick up the last row of M.Y. loops

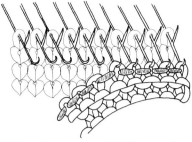

Pick up the last row of M.Y. loops of the second section

of the second section onto the needles with the wrong side facing you. (The right sides of the knitting face each other.) Make sure the loops are in the hooks of the needles in front of the open latches.

(3) Pull the needles back so that the latches will close over the second set of stitches and pull them through the first set of stitches.

(4) You now have one loop on every needle. C.O.R. Knit one row on the loosest possible tension and cast off using your preferred method. When the grafting is complete the W.Y. may be removed.

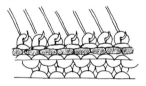

Pull the second set of loops through the first set

Grafting on a Linker Stitch to Stitch

This can be done in the same way by transferring the last row of M.Y. loops onto the points of the linker. Be sure to put the right sides of both sections together.

VI Grafting side seams together

Because you are not joining the fabric stitch to stitch you can introduce more ease into this kind of seam by stretching the sections out across the needles or points as you pick them up onto the machine. Next to mattress stitching, this is the most effective way of joining up two sections of knitting.

(*1*) Pick up the edges of the sections to be joined onto the needles or points of the linker with the right sides of both sections together.

(*2*) Knit one row on the loosest possible tension and cast-off or link.

18 Decorative making-up techniques

This section is a continuation from the previous making-up section. However, in the previous section we have concentrated on techniques which will take a back seat in garment construction. They endeavour to remain as unobtrusive as possible. There may be times when you will want your joins to be not only obvious but, in fact, a design feature. When it is impossible to disguise the fact that you are joining two sections of knitting together it is often more politic to focus attention on the join and make it as striking and attractive as possible. In other words you are not just making the best of a bad job, you are using it to advantage.

Some of these techniques must be planned in advance because they require alterations to the knitting of the garment shapes. Others may be included as an after thought.

I Latch-up join

(*1*) When casting-off the two sections of the garment to be joined by this method, the two or three edge stitches of the side to be joined must not be cast-off but taken off the machine onto a separate piece of W.Y. Alternatively, you can leave the needle next to the edge needle in N.W.P. All increasing and decreasing of the knitting must be carried out three to four stitches in from the edges.

(*2*) Place the two sections to be joined next to each other and the right side of the fabric (stocking stitch) facing you. Remove the W.Y. from the stitches that were not included in the cast-off, thus releasing those stitches.

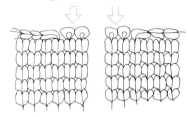

Latch-up join. Step (*2*)

(*3*) Using the blunt end of the latch tool, push against the released stitches allowing them to unravel.

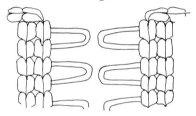

Latch-up join. Step (*3*)

Latch-up join

This will give you loops at the edge of your work. Repeat on the second piece of knitting.

(4) Starting at the bottom, take two to three loops from the edge of one piece of knitting onto the latch tool. Let these loops slip behind the latch. Take two to three loops from the edge of the second piece of knitting into the hook of the tool and let the first group of loops slip over them off the tool. Push these loops behind the latch.

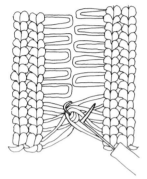

Latch-up join. Step (4)

(5) Return to the first piece of knitting and repeat, taking the next two to three loops into the hook and pulling them through the loops behind the latch.

(6) Continue to repeat this process, alternating from the first piece of knitting to the second until you reach the top. Fasten off the last group of loops.

(7) When dealing with sections which commence with knitted hems, the stitches in question must be taken off onto W.Y. after the hem is turned and before knitting the rest of the garment. Those empty needles must be cast-on again as the stitches from them will be used to make the loops. With any type of stitch pattern where needles are left in N.W.P. (such as open tuck lace) or lace, at least three to four stitches at the edge must always knit.

II Two sections joined with decorative strip knitting

Two sections joined with decorative strip

(1) When knitting the two sections concerned, make a hole at fixed intervals on the edge to be joined by moving the third stitch from the edge to the second needle from the edge every fourth row. Leave the empty needle in W.P.

(2) Knit both sections in this way making sure the holes occur at the side to be joined.

(3) When you are ready to join the two pieces 'E' wrap cast-on four needles on the machine. Place the two pieces side by side with the wrong sides facing you.

(4) Knit 3 rows on the four needles. C.O.L.

(5) Insert the double-eyed transfer tool through the bottom hole on the right hand piece of knitting. Remove the two right-hand stitches of the strip of knitting from the machine. Pull the piece

Joining two sections with a decorative strip

of knitting over the two stitches and replace them on the needles.

(6) Knit 1 row C.O.R.

(7) Repeat step (5) on the left with the left-hand piece of knitting.

(8) Knit 1 row.

(9) Repeat steps (4) to (7) until the two pieces are joined.

You can experiment by not only joining straight pieces of knitting but also using this method to insert decorative shapes in a garment piece. Remember any increasing and decreasing must take into consideration that you will be making a 'hole' two stitches in from the edge every four rows.

III Piping

You can always make a decorative feature of a seam by 'sandwiching' a strip of knitting in between two sections of knitting when joining them together. Take advantage of the fact that knitting naturally 'rolls' and knit a strip of four to eight stitches wide and as long as necessary. The strip need not be plain: a small Fair Isle pattern is very effective, especially if you are joining two sections knit in two different yarns. When picking up the seam to be joined, you need only include *one* edge of the strip. The other edge will roll over and hide the join.

Piping

IV Invisible join row to row – pick up as you knit

This join should be very unobtrusive indeed and can be used when you wish to marry two sections which have been knit consecutively. You can achieve the effect of mirror imaging a punch card pattern, thus give the impression of a 48 stitch repeat instead of a 24 stitch repeat. In fact, you can knit any number of sections in different Fair Isle patterns and colours and give the impression that they were all knit simultaneously.

If you are introducing this technique in the middle of a piece of knitting you must remove the section you wish to knit afterwards onto W.Y.

(*1*) Ensure the section you wish to knit is positioned accurately on the needle bed to ensure the pattern will be knitted correctly according to the pattern repeat. Set the machine to begin pattern knitting with two yarns in the two feeders ready to knit and needles selected to pattern if necessary. C.O.R.

(*2*) Knit one row in your pattern. C.O.L.

(*3*) Hang the cast-on cord very loose-

Invisible join

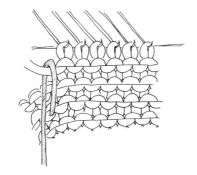

Invisible join on the machine. Step (*3*)

ly over the yarn leading from the knitting to the carriage.

(*4*) Knit two rows. C.O.L.

(*5*) Repeat steps (*3*) and (*4*) until the pattern desired is completed.

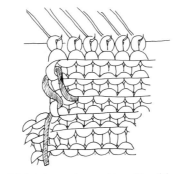

Invisible join on the machine. Step (*5*)

(*6*) Remove the stitches onto W.Y.

(*7*) Replace the second side on the

needles making sure the pattern will be reproduced correctly as desired. (The punch card will have to be replaced in the card-reading mechanism.) Set the machine to begin pattern knitting with two yarns in the two feeders ready to knit and needles selected to pattern if necessary. C.O.L.

(*8*) Knit two rows C.O.L. Pick up the first left-hand loose end stitch of the first part of knitting which is around the cast-on cord and place this on the edge needle of the second section of knitting.

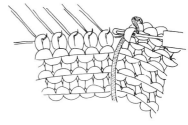

Invisible join on the machine. Step (*7*)

(*9*) Repeat step (*8*) until the motif is finished.

(*10*) Replace all stitches on the machine, repositioning the knitting on the needles if necessary, and continue knitting the piece.

V Insertions

When assembling your garment you may insert a decorative braid, cable or

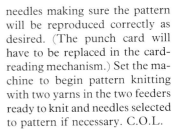

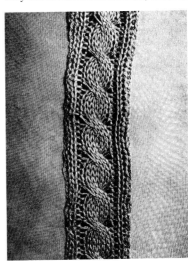

Insertions

strip of Fair Isle or pattern knitting. Sections of knitting may also be combined with fabric by using the sewing machine in assembling the garment.

VI Use of woven fabric

Woven fabric may be used in many ways when making up your garment. You may decide to have whole sections in fabric such as sleeves or yokes. On the other hand you may decide that one part of the garment would be more effective in fabric such as the front bands of a cardigan (button band and buttonhole band). You may also decide that a small touch of fabric on a top, e.g. bias binding around the neckline, could effectively echo the skirt with which it is worn.

19 Use of techniques

You now have a library of techniques available. They aren't any good unless you *use* them. Where can they be used?

Decorative hems and edges

Increasing evenly after knitting the hem

Ribbed edges

Decreasing evenly within a row

Simple increasing

Edges, casting on

Seams, adding several stitches

Decreasing

Decorative shaping

Shaping with partial knitting

Decorative borders

VII Design Possibilities

1 Introduction to designing

With the modern machine and all its labour-saving attachments, you are now freed from patterns. The punch card takes care of the stitch pattern automatically and the knit leader/tracer/radar/forma releases you from the chore of calculating how many stitches and rows you need to knit a particular shape.

All knitting, hand and machine, is logical. It is based on the measurement of your tension square – that is, your stitches and rows. For example, if 20 sts. = 10cm (4in.), then 40 sts. = 20cm (8in.), etc. Alternatively, if you want to use a printed knitting pattern, providing you can draw the shape out on your attachment, you no longer have to knit half a dozen tension squares and hope one will come close to the specifications in the pattern. Nowadays, you make a tension square and the machine 'writes' the pattern to fit your sample swatch. Machine knitters are now released to concern themselves with more exotic flights of fancy. You are only limited by your imagination, patience and vision. But you must cultivate all three!

Rule 1: Don't be a defeatist! When you see an attractive garment don't say 'but I couldn't knit that!' or you've been beaten before you start.

Rule 2: Learn to look carefully at garments you admire. Note the direction of the knitting, e.g. is it knit from hem to neck or sideways or a combination of several different techniques? What sort of stitch was used – look closely at the fabric and the way the loops are formed – is it knitted on a single bed machine or is it knit on a machine with a ribber? If your machine can't do the exact stitch can you achieve a similar effect?

If the garment is not a knitted garment at all but a garment sewn from a woven fabric there is no law that says you cannot make a similar garment, only knit your fabric to the right shape instead of buying it by the metre and cutting it out!

Rule 3: Using colour. Don't forget that often the most striking effects are achieved by using simple techniques with effective colours and that the colour must be right! So take a bit of extra time to try and find the colours which will blend together to give the effect you want.

Rule 4: Try out new ideas quickly. Rush home and try out your ideas *on the machine*. If you don't try them out straight away, you may find that your notes will not give you enough information to re-create the idea and by then you may have forgotten some crucial detail.

Rule 5: Most important – don't be discouraged. If you don't succeed the first time all your samples will prove useful references in the future. After all flaky pastry was only invented because some young lad forgot to add the butter at the right time. Mistakes can always be design features!

Garment design

It is a sad fact of life that if you are cube-shaped, pear-shaped, or sack-of-potato shaped no garment, however beautifully knit, will alter your basic shape. You can wear a large brown paper bag but inside it you will remain a cube, pear, etc.

The art of designing is to maximise your positive points and minimize your negative ones and with a bit of crafty engineering this is really quite easy to do.

Tape measures never lie and it pays dividends to believe them. The smaller your garment, the tighter the fit and the more revealing it will be. The question is how much do you want to reveal? When you are creating a garment pattern or shape you are not, in fact, drawing. What you are doing is *drafting* a shape. You are making an outline of a shape with the aid of a ruler and a set square. The measurements of this shape have been dictated by a simple set of guidelines from measurements taken as accurately as possible with a tape measure. This is one step towards designing your own garment.

If you find it difficult to visualize your garment a useful design aid is to take a large photo from a fashion magazine, paste it onto a stiff piece of card and, with a sharp knife, cut-out

Garment cut outs

the outline of the garment from the picture leaving only the outline and the face etc. of the original model. After you have knit your sample fabrics you can place this 'cut-out' over the samples and that will give you some idea of the effect of the finished garment.

When approaching an individually designed garment you can think of a child's colouring book. There is the outline, which is like a picture frame you can fill in, like painting on a canvas. Your garment pattern or your shape is your canvas. Try to think of this shape in a fluid, imaginative way; for example, subdivide it into smaller shapes which you might knit separately and then assemble like a jigsaw.

Garment knit in layers

Cotton lace top with picot edging, cord threaded and tied at the waistline

Lace pattern integrated into garment shape

Firm edges added later to a garment knit sideways in fine yarn

Garment gathered into a rib at the wrist and waist with a frilled neck band

Trims: knitted fringes and triangles

Dress knit from hem to neck with sideways knit stitch (inspired by a commercial sewing pattern)

Shaping at the yoke by decreasing within the row; open tuck stitch for lace effect

Plain edges on a Fair Isle jacket

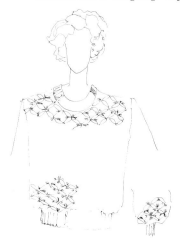

Ribbed bands added later to a fabric in a difficult stitch pattern

> When designing your garment you have three components to consider.
> (*1*) The outline: the garment pattern or shape.
> (*2*) The filling in: the type of fabric you use to make the garment.
> (*3*) The framing: the finishing and the edges.

Cables and bobbles on a chunky knit

Garment 'sliced' up the middle

Fabric quilted at yoke and waistband combined with a knitted bodice

Garment top in lace; skirt and shirt in tuck stitch. Layers in linen contrast in colour and stitch

Knitted drape added

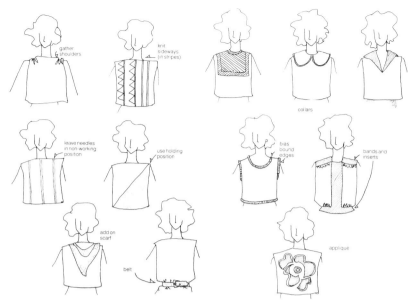

Design ideas for a simple garment based on a square

Knitting combined with woven fabric

Garment knit in sections

The filling in

When considering the type of fabric you wish to use to make your garment you must consider:

(*1*) The yarn you intend to use –
   - colour or colours;
   - type of yarn e.g. wool, acrylic, cotton, or a combination;
   - texture and/or weight of yarn, e.g. smooth, mohair, bouclé, etc.

(*2*) The stitch pattern you intend to use – you must remember that if you use more than one type of stitch pattern you will have to do a tension swatch for each pattern. However, you can use an unexpected combination of stitch patterns to produce an unusual and interesting garment. You may decide to use:
   - manual patterning, cables, picked-up stitches, intarsia, etc.
   - Punch card patterns.

(*3*) 'Knitmanship' techniques – you can approach the garment in any way you choose. There are no rules and regulations when designing your knitted garments, only the final result counts. As long as you can master the techniques well enough to achieve your desired result you have done the right thing. Knitmanship techniques are only the tools that permit you to achieve this desired result. Get out of the tram-lines of conventional thinking about knitting.

(*a*) 'Start at the beginning, stop when you reach the end, and leave the middle for in-between' said Lewis Carrol. That may be all very well for Alice but in machine knitting you can be much more versatile. You can knit from the middle out. As long as the garment is planned in a logical way and you know where you are going you can start virtually anywhere. You can knit the garment from the bottom to the top (hem to neck); sideways; upside-down (neck to hem) or up and over; or, middle out – sub-dividing the garment shape into separate sections and knitting each one individually or in different directions or both.

(*b*) Manipulation of the fabric within the garment shape – this can be achieved if you understand what the machine can do for you. *Alternative one:* shape each pattern piece while knitting by using the holding position to 'knit in' darts. *Alternative two:* gather the fabric by removing your work from the machine and replacing it on fewer needles, thus reducing the number of stitches in a row. *Alternative three:* use stitches to shape your pattern pieces: e.g. a tuck stitch will produce a fabric which is much shorter and wider than a slip stitch, although both stitches are knit on the same number of needles with the same yarn and at the same stitch size. *Alternative four:* use graduated stitch sizes to make your pattern piece larger or smaller.

(*c*) Finishes – detailing on a garment can often make or break its success. You must decide on the final effect you wish to achieve. There is no reason why you can't think as creatively when you decide what kind of finishing you will use as you did in designing the garment shape or the type of fabric you were going to use. Hems and bands can often be far more suitable and effective than the traditional rib. You must consider the type of yarn you are using (e.g. thickness and/or elasticity); the type of fabric you are making (e.g. lace, woven patterns); the style of your garment and the fashion trends.

Machine attachments

Knitting machines are much easier to use now and all the attachments available are basically designed to make knitting a garment quicker and simpler. However, all these aids are really invidious traps! In reality they can stop us from experimenting and exploring the creative possibilities of machine technology.

Lets look at the traps more closely to see if we can avoid them.

I The tension mast
Although the mast ensures that we have an even feed to make a smooth and regular fabric, it can limit our use of colour or yarn as there are only two feeders. There are, however, several ways to escape being locked into producing a two yarn fabric.
(1) Cut the yarn just below the tension discs on the mast and tie in an alternative yarn. Then pull the new yarn through the feeding system. This will help you to avoid having to re-thread every time you wish to change your yarn.
(2) Practice hand-feeding the yarn straight from the floor in front of you into the carriage feeder. This way you can change your yarn at will.
(3) Ply several different fine yarns together to make your own multicoloured yarn.
(4) Make up your own ball of yarn by tying together in series lots of short lengths of various yarns. You can blend the colours and shades and tones to get a very interesting multi-coloured ball of yarn which you can then knit directly into the fabric.

II The punch card
This pattern aid is very easy to use but its ease is, in a way, a drawback as well. One reason people tend not to experiment with the punch card is because of the tension square. If you have made a tension square for your garment you are reluctant to vary the stitch or yarn because it means making another swatch in order to be able to calculate accurately the stitches and rows you will need for your garment. Don't be lazy! Do try sampling – that is using a technique widely used by designers.

Knit a length of fabric doing no more than twenty rows for each variation. Vary the knitting as follows.
(1) Use the same yarn and change the punch card.
(2) Use the same card and change the yarn.
(3) Vary the speed at which the card moves in the machine; row by row, once every two rows, or lock the card.
(4) Vary the stitch (tuck, slip, etc.). This cannot be done with all patterns. Check to see the card you are using is suitable for variation.
(5) Alternate pattern knitting with plain knitting.
(6) Vary the stitch size.
(7) Turn the card upside down or back to front.

III Pattern attachment
Although the pattern attachments are a godsend in that they truly enable you to create your own garments, too many people rely on designs and shapes they see in magazines. These tend to be the simplest type. You must approach your garment shapes more adventurously. Look at your garment shape as if it were a jig-saw puzzle or an origami puzzle. Once you have mastered drawing out your basic block there is nothing to stop you from cutting it up and knitting the separate pieces in all different types of yarn and/or stitch patterns or even in different directions. Then you will be able to make a very individual garment. Don't be trapped into knitting the easiest shape in the easiest way.

IV Time and Distance
This last category is perhaps the most difficult one to analyse. Because the machine produces the garment so quickly it discourages you from taking the time to stand back and assess your work. One tends to think that speed is a critical factor and if the garment is not produced quickly, it defeats the object of machine knitting. The opposite can be true. Use the speed of the machine to do what it does well – i.e. automatic patterning and combine this with hand-work such as cables etc. to make the best of both worlds. Because you have a machine this does not mean that any work done by hand is bad!

Also, because you are always viewing the work with the purl side facing you on the machine and because you are always 'on top' of it, you may find it difficult to judge the effect of your work. It is even more difficult to assess it if you have a ribber because the work always falls behind the ribber. Do try to get back off your swatches to get a better idea of what the finished garment will look like. Pin them up on the wall and stand back off them. It is also a good idea to use a design aid like a magazine photo mounted on a stiff piece of card with the actual garment cut out. You can place this cut-out over your swatch to get an idea of how your garment will look – but do view this from a distance. Get a perspective on your work and don't be in too great a rush. After all, the machine will produce your garment far quicker than you could hand-knit it, so don't begrudge a little extra time spent on the design stage to get it 'just right'.

2 The garment shape

When approaching the knitting machine to knit garments you may find that a magazine will have just the garment you wish to knit in just the yarn that you would choose. In which case it is a simple matter to knit your tension square, measure it and follow the pattern to produce your garment.

However, with experience I have found that the garment you want to knit is never quite like the one in the pattern. The yarn you have is not the yarn specified in the pattern, or you want to knit the garment in a tuck stitch and the pattern is for a Fair Isle garment. If you were sewing it would be a simple matter to add or subtract but with knitting, because you don't often apply the scissor method, it becomes a little more complicated.

A The pattern attachment

(1) With a full scale, full shape pattern attachment (Jones/Brother KL 113, 116) you can reproduce the diagram exactly as you are going to knit the garment on a pattern sheet which is marked in centimetre squares.

(2) With a full scale, half shape pattern attachment (Jones/Brother Built-In Knitleader, Knitmaster Knitradar, Toyota Knit Tracer) you can draw the shape out onto the graph or pattern sheet. You will draw only half the pattern, however, and knit it in a mirror image technique. All shaping carried out on the left side of the needle bed is reproduced exactly the same way on the right side of the needle bed. If you require non-symmetrical shaping, you must draw out *two* diagrams, one for each side of the needle bed. It helps to draw the diagrams in two colours. This makes it easier for you to follow while you are knitting.

You can draw the diagrams the same size as your finished piece of knitting. On the Jones/Brother built-in Knitleader you will have to do your tension swatch before you draw out your diagram; this is because the size of your tension swatch will dictate whether you need to draw the diagram out with the centre of the knitting at the left side or right side.

(3) With a half-scale, half shape pattern attachment (Knit Radar, Passap/Pfaff Forma) you will have to use a half scale ruler to draw out your diagram. All your drawings will be half the size of your finished piece of knitting. You can still use the diagrams in knitting magazines as the measurements given in the diagrams will be directly transferable.

B Calculating the garment shape

To calculate the number of stitches and rows you will need to knit the shape you require is a simple matter once you have knit your tension swatch. You can either use a calculator or the Knitmaster green or blue 'ruler'. Simple machines and older machines (before the advent of the pattern attachment) often used this technique. Sometimes you will find it the preferred method if you require regular shaping, such as side-ways knit skirts or raglan shaping.

Sources of patterns:

I Diagrams from hand-or machine-knitting patterns
Many continental hand-knit and machine knit patterns now come with diagrams. It is a simple matter to transpose these diagrams onto your pattern attachment; you are then free to use the yarn and stitch pattern of your choice to knit the garment. You can transpose these diagrams directly onto the sheets for your particular pattern attachment. You will either use an ordinary of half-scale ruler.

II Hand-knitting or machine-knitting patterns without diagrams
These patterns are a bit of a nuisance as you will have to work the shape out first and then convert it back into stitches and rows to decide how many you will need in your yarn and your stitch pattern. You can sometimes use a hand-knitting pattern to tell you how many stitches and rows you will require to reproduce it on the machine, but you must match the machine knitted tension square to the one achieved in the hand-knit pattern. You will often find that you will be obliged to alter your stitches or rows to knit the same shape.

If you have a pattern attachment the procedure would be reversed to the usual procedure you would use to knit the garment. Firstly, decide which ruler or stitch gauge you will have to use according to the number of stitches per cm specified in the pattern. If the pattern tells you how many stitches there are per inch (2.5cm) multiply the stitches by 4 and you will have the number of stitches per 4 inches or 10 cm. This will tell you which stitch gauge to use for the Knitmaster pattern attachment because the Knitmaster gauge is based on the number of stitches per 10cm and the green or blue ruler is not a ruler at all but it measures a constant number of stitches and automatically converts the variable measurement into the number of stitches in 10cm.

If you have a patterning attachment where the stitch gauge is dependent directly on the measurement of 40 sts. you will have to convert the number of stitches per 10cm (4in.). To do this you calculate the number of stitches in 10cm (4in.), and divide that number into 40. Then multiply the result by ten. This will tell you which stitch gauge to use.

$$\frac{40}{\text{No. of stitches in 10cm (4in.)}} \times 10$$
= measurement of 40 sts

Secondly, decide what number you will use in the row gauge of the pattern attachment. If the pattern tells you how many rows to the inch and you multiply by four you will have the number of rows to 10cm. This will tell you what row adjustment to use on the Knitmaster pattern attachment as this attachment is based on the number of rows in 10cm. The green and blue rulers measure a fixed number of rows and automatically convert that measurement into the information that tells you how many rows there are in 10cm (4in.).

$$\frac{60}{\text{No. of rows in 10cm (4in.)}} \times 10$$
= measurement of 60 rows

Thirdly place the correct ruler in your pattern attachment, adjust the rows to the correct number as in the pattern and feed in a blank pattern sheet.

Finally work the pattern attachment by hand moving it row by row, marking the sheet according to the knitting pattern. Thus you are drawing-out the pattern on the sheet as instructed by the knitting pattern.

III Dressmaking patterns
These patterns can often be traced directly onto pattern attachment sheets. If your attachment requires a pattern sheet which is not transparent, you will have to trace around the shape. If you have a half-scale attachment, you will have to measure the garment shapes and draw them out with the aid of your half-scale ruler.

Because knitted fabric is much less stable than woven fabric you won't require as much ease in some areas. For instance, you can lose some of the extra fabric required in the fitted sleeve head. Cut the sleeve head down until the circumference measurement is the same as the armhole plus 2–4 cm. Also, you will not always want to decrease and then increase on the bodice armhole shaping. You can alter the armhole line so that you will be shaping only under the armhole and you will not increase again as you come up towards the shoulder.

This would be for a more casual type of garment. If, however, you were knitting the garment in a less flexible fabric (such as a woven fabric) you might want to retain some of the give allowed in the sewing pattern. Yet if you were knitting a more traditional tailored garment you might find the extra shaping would give a more finished look to your knitting.

IV Drawing your own block
This is by far the most accurate way of designing your own garments. When you have finished establishing your own pattern block, which you have based on your own careful measurements, you can add, subtract and shape according to your fancy or the current fashion trend and you know

the garment will always fit you – even if you are a four-foot tall gorilla.

3 The basic block

The most important aspect of designing a finished garment is to be found in starting on a firm footing. There can be no firmer footing than *careful measurement*!

If you look at a lot of the Japanese books you will see that *underneath* the drawing of the knitted garment shape, there is a basic *body*. This is the basic shape of the person over which the garment will fit. Even if you are knitting very loose and sloppy fashions you must know what these 'bags' will hang on. You cannot add 'ease' until you know what you are adding it on to!

If you are constantly knitting garments for a few people you may wish to make your basic block and either knit it up, or, if you do a bit of dressmaking, cut it out of *very stretchy* fabric and sew it up. The second method is a bit quicker. Once you have made your knitter's equivalent of a *toile* you can make all the necessary basic corrections as to length and width across critical sections, e.g. upper arms, arm length, across upper back, etc. Do not be keen to add ease at this stage. This is not a wearing-out garment. This is only a *guide*. Do make it neat. The amount of ease you will add will vary greatly depending on a number of different circumstances.

The basic measurements

I Horizontal
(1) Chest: measured neat over basic undergarments (*1*).
(2) Across chest: midway between the top of the shoulder and the armpit. This measurement should be neat from sleeve seam to sleeve seam (*2*).
(3) Upper arm: just below the armpit over the thickest part of the arm (*3*).
(4) Wrist: the circumference of a

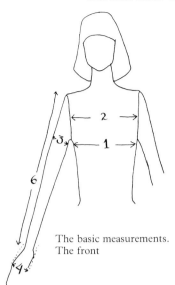

The basic measurements. The front

closed fist – after all the sleeve must fit over the hand (*4*).

II Vertical
(1) Body length: from the bone protruding at the base of the backneck/top of the spine to the waist (*5*). Garment length is, of course, optional.

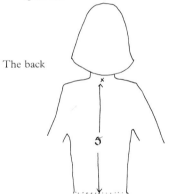

The back

(2) Sleeve length: from the bone at the top of the shoulder to the bone at the wrist (*6*).
(3) Armhole depth –
  (a) Method 1: place an article with a firm straight edge under the arm, e.g. a book or magazine. Measure from the back edge of the book, up over the shoulder and down to the edge of the book in the front. Divide by two (*7*).
  (b) Method 2: measure neatly around the armhole and up

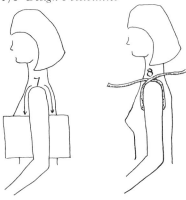

The armhole   The armhole

over the top edge of the shoulder. Divide by two (*8*).

III *Alternative cross-back/sleeve length measurement*

(*1*) Measure across the top of the back just below the top of the shoulder point (*9*). (You can subtract 1.5cm (½in.) from this measurement). This will give a looser fit.

The cross back

(*2*) Total garment width: for knitting sideways knit garments or garments with dropped sleeves, hold your arms out parallel to the floor. Measure from wrist bone to wrist bone (*10*). To get separate sleeve length subtract the cross-back measurement and divide by two (*11*).

These measurements will give an approximate toile, finer fitting adjustments can be carried out after the fitting. The basic pattern should then be drawn out in a form which can be

kept to be used again. If you need large sheets of inexpensive plain paper, I would suggest wall-paper lining paper could be used. If you want to keep the basic block in a more permanent way you might try Vilene (the non-stick variety!). Do try your measurements out before you knit the final garments. You can't alter knit-wear the way you can alter ordinary dressmaking.

Ease

When designing a garment the addition of ease is very important. Basically, my advice would be to think thick. If you look at a person wearing a garment in cross-section from the top down, you will see the body in the centre, an air gap around the body to allow for ease of movement and then the thickness of the knitted fabric itself.

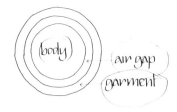

Cross section. The body in a garment

Another interesting indicator of the amount of ease that is now allowed in fashion garments is to look at hand-knitting fashion books (e.g. Pingouin, Phildar etc.). If you look at the pattern sizes, for example, for a bust size 86cm (34in.), the actual bust measurement of the garment may be 100 to 110cm. In other words an ease allowance of at least 20 per cent is added.

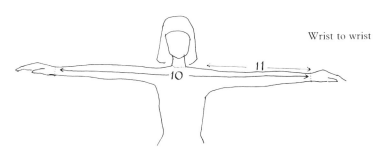

Wrist to wrist

The amount of ease that you will add to your basic block is governed by three basic factors:

1 Wearing Room – The amount of room that will be necessary when wearing the garment.
- The type of garment – e.g. tailored, sports wear, etc. A garment to be used in active sports requires more ease.
- What is worn under the garment – e.g. will it be a jacket, or will it be a dress to be worn only over undergarments?

2 The type of fabric used –
(*a*) The elasticity of the fabric.
- Will the stitch pattern be woven (very firm fabric) or will it be a tuck stitch or rib (very stretchy fabric)?
- Will the yarn be very stretchy, e.g. some types of wool or acrylic or very inelastic, e.g. cotton and silk.
- Stitch size: a small stitch size results in a very firm fabric with little give.
(*b*) The thickness of the fabric:
- Will the stitch pattern be 'thick', e.g. Fair Isle, as you are knitting with two yarns and making the fabric twice as thick.
- The thickness or texture of the yarn, e.g. smooth cotton or fluffy mohair.

3 Fashion trends –
This subject is the most difficult to define. Fashion is very fickle and what one person likes another dislikes. Often someone will say they like one type of garment but in reality the clothes they wear are much more conservative. People often tend to mislead themselves regarding their measurements as

	Fine yarn	Medium yarn	Thick yarn
I Bust/chest			
Tight	−6% to −2%	−4% to 0%	−2% to +2%
Medium	0% to +4%	+2% to +6%	+4% to +9%
Loose	+6% +	+8% +	+12% +
II Upper arm			
Tight	−4% to −2%	−2% to +3%	0% to +5%
Medium	0% to +10%	+10% to +20%	+20% to +30%
Loose	+20% +	+30% +	+40% +

well. Actual *size* isn't as important as just getting the correct measurements. One way of determining just what sort of measurements might be most appropriate is to actually go to a store and try on a garment that you find attractive and suitable. Take a small tape measure with you and actually measure the garment. This is as good a way as any to determine what dimensions you will need to knit to make the garment fit you the way you want it to!

Here is a table with some guide lines for ease allowance.

These are only the most general of indications and really should be taken with a pinch of salt. The most useful indication is really to measure a garment you like that fits you and proceed from there.

Necklines

The one subject we have not dealt with in our basic block is the neckline. There are various methods used to arrive at a suitably sized hole. There are two critical factors:

(1) The neck should be big enough to go over the head.
(2) The neck band should fit snugly around the base of the neck. These two factors can be difficult to reconcile. The neck must be extra stretchy where children are concerned as there is a particularly big difference between the measurement around the head and the diameter of the neck.

Generally speaking with a crew or round neck, the back neck is $\frac{1}{3}$ plus 1–2cm the total neckband measurement

and the front neck (from shoulder to shoulder) is $\frac{2}{3}$ minus 1–2cm the total measurement. Use one of these ways to determine the basic round neck line on the block and then if you wish to alter the style of the neckline, you can do so. The first step will be to determine the *back neck measurement*.

A Back neck measurement – There are several ways of deciding how big the back neck measurement should be.
(1) Take the mid-neck measurement and add on 3cm (1¼in.).

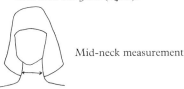

Mid-neck measurement

(a) $\frac{1}{2}$ the back neck = *mid-neck measurement* + 0.5cm (¼in.).
(b) If you are not shaping the back neck (i.e. you are dropping the centre back neck line by 2cm (¾in.)) then widen the back neck slightly.
(c) An alternative to the mid-neck measurement would be to measure the 'jewel line' – that is, to measure loosely around the base of the neck.

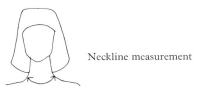

Neckline measurement

(2) Use the cross back measurement as a basis and divide by three to ascertain the back neck measurement. The cross back measurement is from shoulder point to shoulder point across the top of

the back. This is a bigger measurement than the one you would be using to establish the basic block as it does have quite a bit of ease.
(3) Use the neat cross chest measurement that you use as a basic measurement in making the block and divide by two.

B Front neck drop – The front neck drop should be half the back neck measurement plus 1cm (½in.). You can always use a tape measure or a cord to curl around your neckline to aid in measuring it.

4 Basic pattern drafting for machine knitting

Now that you have carried out all your basic measurements you can begin exploring the world of pattern making. You should start by drawing out your toile. This is a very basic shaped garment which will tell you if the essential measurements are correct and the garment will fit you. Any alterations will be made to the basic pattern after you have fitted the toile. It really isn't as frightening as it sounds, and you can cut the toile out of any stretchy type of fabric if you feel you don't want to be bothered to knit a garment, even in waste yarn. Once you have had the experience of making one sample garment this will give you confidence to go ahead and knit garments straight from measurements. It is good experience, however, to do a sample, even if you only do it once.

I The basic block

Bodice
A = $\frac{1}{2}$ the chest measurement (1)
B = Cross chest measurement (2)
C = Armhole depth (7) or (8)
D = Shoulder drop 2–4cm (¾–1½in.)

Sleeve
E = 2 × C
F = Sleeve length (6)
G = Wrist (4)

No ease has been added to the basic

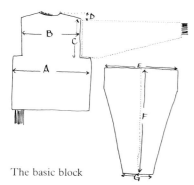

The basic block

block as this is designed to be the basis from which you will draw garment patterns and the ease will be added when you have taken the other factors regarding ease into consideration. If you wish to make this a garment that you would wear, you may add ease (10% or so) to A, but remember that you have done this, when you use the block in future.

II Dropped shoulder

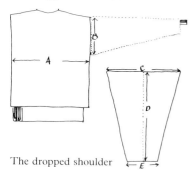

The dropped shoulder

Bodice
A = ½ Chest measurement
B = Armhole depth (7) or (8).

Sleeve
C = 2 × B
D = Sleeve length (11)
E = Wrist circumference
Ease may be added to your choice.

III Square armhole with a shaped sleeve cap

Bodice
A = ½ chest measurement (1)
B = Cross chest measurement (2)
C = Armhole measurement (7) or (8)
D = Shoulder drop 2–4cm (¾–1½in.)

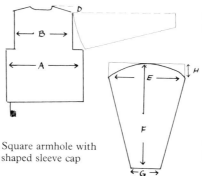

Square armhole with shaped sleeve cap

Sleeve
E = 2 × C
F = Sleeve length (6)
G = Wrist circumference
H = Shaped sleeve head 6–8cm (2½–3in.)

Ease may be added to your choice. The armhole may also be rounded off slightly to prevent a 'poking' at the bust line.

IV Set-In sleeve

Although this is quite a common pattern shape, it is rather tricky to do. You should master the simpler shapes before attempting this one. However, because of the stretchy nature of the knitted fabric, it is much easier to do a fitted sleeve head. You will need to have only the measurement around the circumference of the sleeve head approximately 2–3cm (¾–1⅙in.) longer than the actual measurement of the bodice armhole.

Bodice
(1) Use the basic bodice block. Add ease to the chest measurement at this point before you begin.
(2) Divide the armhole drop by three and curve the armhole in the lower third.
(3) Measure around the armhole. Note the measurement.
B = Armhole measurement.

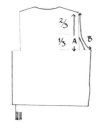

Bodice for a set-in sleeve

Drafting a set-in sleeve

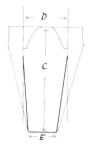

Sleeve
(1) Draw out the basic sleeve to get the length and the wrist.
C = Sleeve length (6)
E = Wrist circumference (4)
(2) Draw two lines parallel to the centre. D = Upper arm width. (3) (Add ease at this point.)
(3) Draw in the curved sleeve head. The line goes between the two lines indicating the width of D and touches the top of C. It is the same as 2 × B + 2cm (¾in.) in length. You could use a piece of string the correct length to help you draw this line.

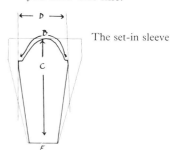

The set-in sleeve

V Raglan sleeves

Although raglan sleeves are simple in principle, it is the shaping at the top of the sleeve which can be difficult. It is much more attractive to shape the sleeve top where it becomes part of the neck line than to have the sleeve come to a point.

This pattern is also based on the basic block but is much more casual in

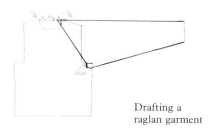

Drafting a raglan garment

fitting. A great deal more ease is allowed. The bodice and sleeve are drawn in one.

(*1*) Draw out the basic bodice and sleeve block with the sleeve in place. Do not draw in the shoulder slope.

(*2*) At the bottom of the armhole, draw a 2cm (¾in.) square.

(*3*) Divide the back neck into thirds. Mark it off with ⅔ in the centre and ⅙ at each side.

(*4*) Draw in the neck.

(*5*) Draw a line from the top inside corner of the 2cm (¾in.) square to the back neck at a point ⅙ from the outside edge of the neckline.

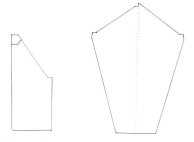

The raglan pattern

5   The tension square

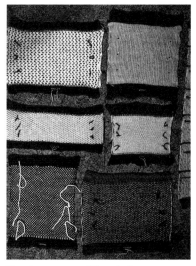

Tension squares. The stitch pattern varies but the yarn and stitch size are the same.

Once you have decided what you are going to knit you must knit a tension square. All good knitting is based on the accuracy of the measurement of your tension square! You must treat your tension square as you will treat your garment *before you measure it*. If you intend to wash the garment or press it you must wash or press the square. To measure your swatch accurately, smooth it out on a piece of sandpaper or a carpet tile.

When you are knitting on the machine, the needles are fixed in the needle bed at given intervals. The distance between the needles does not change. To make big and little stitches you alter the way the needles move – that is, you alter the distance the needles pull the yarn through the stitches to make big loops and little loops. The knitting is always under tension on the machine. This is why, when you remove the knitting from the machine, you must roll the swatch up lengthwise and give it a tug. This tug allows the yarn to relax. Consequently the stitches will gradually assume their natural shape. This happens more quickly with natural fibre than it does with acrylic fibres. This is why you *never* measure work on the machine and you always allow your swatch to rest before measuring.

When you are knitting a tension square you must bear in mind the type of garment you intend to knit. There are several important factors which you should consider in relation to your tension square:

The type of yarn

If it is a natural fibre you must wash it to test for shrinkage or removal of oil or both. If you are knitting in an oiled yarn you must remember that the oil tends to matt the fibres of the yarn. Once the oil has been removed the fibres are freed and tend to spread out, making the yarn thicker and fluffier. You must make allowances for the expansion of yarn and knit your initial tension swatch in a larger stitch than you might if it were not oiled.

If you are knitting in acrylic yarn you must decide whether you wish to flatten the fabric by pressing it or leave it more elastic by damping it with cold water, then allowing it to dry naturally pinned out flat. There is no law that says you must not press acrylic. If you press the fabric flat it will become a more stable and flowing type of fabric, which is perhaps less obviously a 'knit'.

The way the garment will be knit

If you are knitting a garment sideways you must remember that the yarn will be hanging on the body perpendicular to the ground. This means that the yarn is not looped on itself, but as you wear the garment, the yarn in each row straightens out and is not held supported on itself. This means, in fact, that you have a less stable fabric, i.e. a fabric that is more prone to 'dropping'. You may find your garment gets longer and narrower as you wear it. With sideways knit garments it is always a good idea to hang the swatch up with a small weight, such as a bull-dog clip, attached to one end for a day or two to allow the knitting to drop before you measure the swatch.

Elasticity

Some stitches are more elastic than others. Tuck stitch is an extremely stretchy fabric, but weaving is a very stable fabric. The weft (the yarns woven across the fabric) tends to hold it in place and prevent it from moving. Also, any stitch where you have yarns that are carried across any distance in the row tend to be less stretchy and more stable – e.g. slip stitch and Fair Isle.

Size

The size of the garment you are knitting is important. When you are knitting a smaller garment a small error in measuring the tension square may not make a great deal of difference. However, if you are knitting a dress or skirt this small error may mean a difference of 5–10cm (2–4in.) in a hem line. The golden rule is: the larger the garment, the larger the tension square! It is wiser, safer and more accurate to knit a tension square twice the number of stitches and rows you require, measure it and then divide the measurement in half.

The importance of a tension square cannot be overemphasized. It is a very good idea when designing a garment to knit small samples of the edges and finishing you intend to use as well. If you find they are not suitable before you have begun the garment it is a lot easier to change your mind and use alternatives than it is to cut off a hem that is floppy and pokes up afterwards.

It is naturally very difficult to count the actual stitches and rows in stitch patterns. With hand-knitting when you are calculating the tension swatch you are given a *fixed measurement*, and the variable is the number of stitches and rows; with machine knitting it is the opposite. Because it is far easier to mark the work while it is on the machine, the number of stitches and rows are fixed and the variable is the measurement of those stitches and rows.

There are basically two approaches to knitting a tension swatch, depending on whether you are trying to match a given measurement from a printed pattern you wish to follow or whether you are designing the garment from scratch.

Tension square to match stitch and row measurement in a printed pattern

(*1*) Cast on the required number of stitches mentioned in the pattern plus ten extra stitches on either side and knit ten rows in W.Y.
(*2*) Thread up with main yarn and, using the tension mentioned in the pattern, knit half the number of rows specified in the pattern.
(*3*) Using contrast yarn, mark the tenth stitch in from each end of the knitting.
(*4*) Knit the second half of the num-

ber of rows specified in the pattern.
(*5*) Remove the M.Y. and thread up with W.Y. Knit ten rows and cast-off loosely.

You can now measure the stitches and rows you have marked with W.Y. and see if the measurement corresponds to that specified in the pattern. If it does not you will have to decide whether to alter your stitch size. If the stitch measurement is correct, you may decide to use this tension size and to alter the number of rows you will knit when knitting the pattern.

Tension square for a pattern attachment or for calculating your garment

(*1*) Cast-on 60 stitches in W.Y. Knit six rows. Mark the tension dial number in the waste knitting by either:
  (*a*) knitting the same number of stitches by hand in a contrast yarn; or
  (*b*) transferring the same number of stitches to adjacent needles (making 'holes') but leaving the empty needles in W.P. Knit four rows W.Y. Remove the W.Y. and thread up with M.Y.
(*2*) In the stitch pattern you require, knit 15 rows. Mark the 21st needle either side of O with W.Y. markers. Repeat this marking on the 30th and 45th row.
(*3*) Thread up with W.Y. and go back to stocking stitch. Knit ten rows and cast-off loosely.

6 Calculating your garment

All calculations will follow the tension square. The swatch should be measured very carefully after allowing it to rest. Separate swatches should be knit if different parts of the garment are to be knit in different stitches.

Simple stitch and row shaping

(*1*) Take the number of centimetres you want to knit the (measurement of the width of your garment).
(*2*) Divide this by the measurement, in centimetres (or inches), of your tension swatch of 40 stitches. (This gives you the number of widths of your tension swatch that you need to knit to get the right width for your garment.)
(*3*) Multiply this number by 40.
(*4*) The result is the number of stitches you need to cast on.

$$\frac{\text{Measurement to knit (cm/in.)}}{\text{Measurement of 40 sts. (cm/in.)}} \times 40$$
$$= \text{No. of sts required}$$

(*5*) This same procedure may be followed to calculate the rows. You must use the measurement of rows in your tension swatch and multiply by 60 where you used 40 in the stitch calculation.

This whole procedure can be simplified by the use of the green and blue Knitmaster rulers. These rulers are not, in fact just measuring devices. They are combined measuring and calculating devices.

A table of common tensions in stocking stitch

Ply	Stitches 2.5cm (1in.)	Rows 2.5cm (1in.)	Tension dial
1	10	16	1,2,3,
2	9	14	3,4,5,
3	8	12	4,5,6,7,
4	7	10	6,7,8,
Double knit	6	8	8,9,10.

The green ruler

(*1*) Make a standard tension square on a standard gauge machine, as described above, carefully marking out 40 stitches and 60 rows.

(*2*) With the S visible on the green ruler, place it against the tension square, the S end just inside one of the stitches marked. The other end of the ruler, where the other stitch marker is, will tell you how many stitches there are in 10cm (4in.).

(*3*) With the R visible on the green ruler, place it against the tension square, the R end just inside the rows knitted in W.Y. The other end of the ruler, where the other section of W.Y. knitting is, will tell you how many rows there are in 10cm (4in.).

The blue ruler

This ruler works in the same way as the green ruler except that it is designed to deal with knitting done on a chunky knitting machine. This means that you can use it on tension squares knit on 8mm or 9mm gauge machines.

Your first step must be to knit a tension square, making it larger than

Measuring the stitches

the number of stitches and rows you intend to measure because this will enable you to measure more accurately.

(*1*) Start your tension square by casting on 30 sts. and knitting ten rows in waste yarn. Mark your tension by knitting the appropriate number of sts. at row 5 by hand in a contrasting yarn.

(*2*) Join the main yarn and in your chosen stitch pattern knit 30 rows, marking the 11th needle on either side of the centre 0 with contrasting yarn on row 10 and 20. This marks a 20 stitch interval.

(*3*) At row 30 break off the main yarn. This marks the end of your 30 row swatch. Join the waste yarn and knit ten rows. Cast-off.

Allow the swatch to rest. If you plan to wash or press the garment, do the same to the tension square. Use the blue ruler on this swatch in the same way as the green ruler.

To calculate the number of stitches and rows you require to knit your garment shape you must take the number of stitches or rows in 10cm and move the decimal point one place to the left. This will give you the number of stitches or rows in 1cm.

Then you can multiply the number of centimeters you need for your garment by this number and you will find out the number of rows or stitches you require.

Regular increasing and decreasing

(*1*) In order to calculate the frequency of your increases or decreases:
   (*a*) Determine the number of stitches you need to cast on.
   (*b*) Determine the number of stitches you need at the end of your piece of knitting.
   (*c*) Determine the number of rows you need to knit to get the required length.

(*2*) Subtract the smaller number of stitches from the larger number of stitches. This gives you the number of stitches you need to add/subtract to get your garment shaping.

(*3*) Divide this number by two (if this is a symmetrical piece such as a sleeve or skirt panel). This gives you the number of times you must increase/decrease.

(*4*) The number of rows you must knit represents the number of

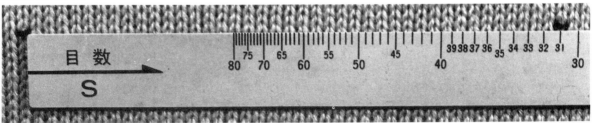

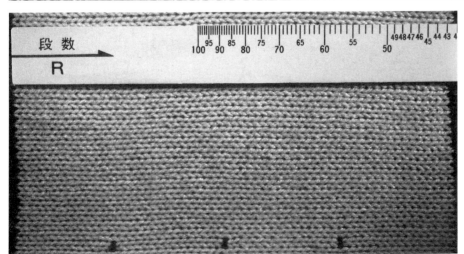

Measuring the rows

'chances' you have to do this shaping. You want to make the shaping as regular as possible.

(5) Divide the rows (the number of chances) by the number of times you must shape to finish up with the correct number of stitches. The result is the number of rows you can put between each increase/decrease.

(6) If the result of this sum leaves you with a remainder, this number represents the number of extra rows you have to knit to get the required length for your piece of knitting. You may wish to add these one by one regularly in with the rest of your shaping.

If this is all as clear as mud, there is a formula into which you can insert your numbers and without having to understand it, it will tell you (fairly painlessly) what to do.

THE MAGIC FORMULA I

$$\text{No of rows between shapings} + \text{1} =$$

No of shapings − Remainder	No of rows
	Remainder
No of times you shape regularly without an additional row	No of times you shape regularly with an additional row between shapings

Example one – decreasing/increasing evenly across the edge of a garment

You have to knit a sleeve, and you have cast-on 64 stitches. You need to knit 146 rows to make it long enough and you need 96 stitches at the end to make it wide enough.

How many rows between each increase do you need to have?

(1) Subtract your smaller number of stitches from your larger number. This will give you the number of stitches you have to increase.

$96 - 64 = 32$

As your shaping will be done symmetrically, that is at the same time on both sides of the knitting, divide this number by 2. This gives you 16. This is the number of times you increase 1 stitch at each edge of the knitting. You have 16 shapings to do and 146 opportunities to do them in.

(2) Now apply the magic formula above. The working is shown below.

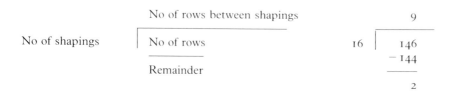

(3)

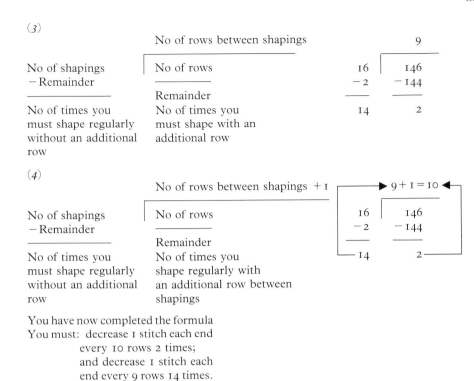

No of rows between shapings   9

No of shapings − Remainder	No of rows		16 − 2	146 − 144
	Remainder			
No of times you must shape regularly without an additional row	No of times you must shape with an additional row		14	2

(4)

No of rows between shapings + 1 → 9 + 1 = 10 ←

No of shapings − Remainder	No of rows		16 − 2	146 − 144
	Remainder			
No of times you must shape regularly without an additional row	No of times you shape regularly with an additional row between shapings		14	2

You have now completed the formula
You must: decrease 1 stitch each end
every 10 rows 2 times;
and decrease 1 stitch each
end every 9 rows 14 times.

THE MAGIC FORMULA II

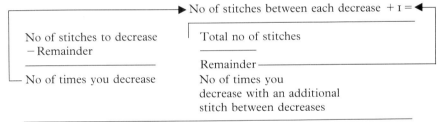

→ No of stitches between each decrease + 1 = ←

No of stitches to decrease − Remainder	Total no of stitches
	Remainder
No of times you decrease	No of times you decrease with an additional stitch between decreases

*Example two – decreasing evenly
across the row*
You have to knit a child's dress with
the skirt gathered on to a yoke. Your
skirt will be 172 stitches wide; when
you come to the yoke you will need
122 stitches. How many stitches will
you do between each decrease to make
the garment symmetrical.
(1) Firstly, subtract your larger
number from your smaller one to
give you the number of stitches to
lose evenly across the row.
172 − 122 = 50

You will have to lose 50 stitches
evenly across the row and there
are 122 opportunities to put 2 sts
onto 1 nd.

(2) Now apply the magic formula (II) as above. The working is shown below.

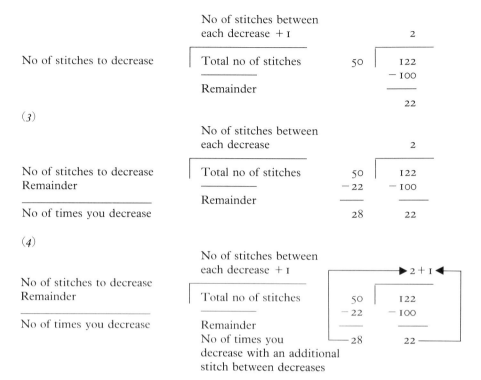

No of stitches between each decrease + 1

No of stitches to decrease	Total no of stitches	50	122
	Remainder		− 100
			22

(3)

No of stitches between each decrease

No of stitches to decrease	Total no of stitches	50	122
Remainder	Remainder	− 22	− 100
No of times you decrease		28	22

(4)

No of stitches between each decrease + 1 → 2 + 1 ←

No of stitches to decrease	Total no of stitches	50	122
Remainder		− 22	− 100
No of times you decrease	Remainder		
	No of times you decrease with an additional stitch between decreases	28	22

You have now completed the formula. You must remove the work onto W.Y. and replace stitches on 122nds putting:
2 sts. on a nd. every 22 times
2 sts. on a nd. every 28 times

Construction techniques

When you are knitting your garment you don't have to think of starting at the beginning, stopping when you reach the end and leaving the middle for in between. In fact, thinking this way can seriously limit your creativity. You are allowing the machine to dictate the shaping of your garment. There is nothing to stop you from starting in the middle and working outward or starting at the top and working downward or sideways. The only thing that you must remember is that all your bits and pieces must come together in the end, no matter how you go about constructing the separate sections.

If you think about the whole garment before you begin you will be in a much stronger position. This means that you must *not only* do a tension square for your basic fabric (or fabrics if you are planning to knit the garment in several sections using different stitches and/or different yarns in each section). In addition, it is very important that you also do samples, albeit small, of the edges and finishes you plan to use.

If you are planning to knit the finishings (edges, hems, etc.) separately and attach them to the garment *afterwards*, it is important to plan beforehand how you will attach them! This section deals with ways of attaching edges onto garments.

I Edge knitted at the beginning of the garment piece

Simple Edge – Knit the edge onto the beginning of the garment as an integral part of the knitting. This is the simplest, most straightforward and most commonly used technique. *Beware*, however, as it will not always achieve the desired effect.

Edge with increasing – Knit the edge and remove it onto waste yarn. Replace the edge on the needles increasing evenly across the row so that you will be using *more* needles to knit the body of the garment.

It is not possible to knit an industrial 2×2 rib, (a 2×2 rib at half pitch), remove the work onto waste knitting, then replace each stitch onto a separate needle on the main bed. The rib simply will not stretch enough to enable you to do this.

II Edge knitted separately

When you are knitting the edge separately and attaching it to the garment afterwards you must think about this before starting the main knitting. You must decide whether you will:

- start (or finish) the main knitting with waste knitting;
- start (or finish) the main knitting with a closed-edge cast-on or cast-off;
- knit the garment sideways.

III Methods of attaching the edge

Knit onto the garment
Rehang the garment back onto the needles and knit the edge onto the knitting. Finish off either casting-off or folding over to the wrong side and catch stitching down.

If you wish to knit an industrial rib (2×2 half-pitch rib), when you rehang the garment replace two stitches onto every third needle on the main bed. Push the ribber up and selectively hook each of the doubled stitches onto one ribber needle – a tricky procedure.

Attached onto the garment on the machine –
(1) Knit the edge desired and arrange it on the main bed with the right side facing you.
(2) Pick up the garment onto the same needles and *either* pull the stitches of the garment through the edge *or* knit the stitches together with a large row.
(3) Cast-off the two pieces together.

Graft by hand –
(1) Knit the edge and remove the work onto waste knitting.

(2) Graft the last row of main yarn loops onto the first row of main yarn loops on the garment. If you are using this method to attach an edge onto a sideways knit garment, you will sew the edge on using the grafting stitch on the last row of main yarn loops on the edge but just sewing onto the edge of the knitting.

The main advantage of this technique is that you can decrease evenly across the row of the main part of the garment when the edge of the garment is knit using waste yarn. Place the last row of main yarn of the garment back onto the machine decreasing evenly across the row. Remove the piece with another section of waste knitting and then graft the edge on. The main advantages are that the join is extremely elastic, flexible and invisible.

Using the linker –
(1) Use a cast-on cord or a row knit in sewing cotton between the main knitting and the waste knitting on both the edge in question and the main knitting.
(2) Carefully replace the last row of main yarn loops on both sections onto the linker pins.
(3) Link off.

Sewing machine –
There is no law that says you cannot put two finished edges (either cast-on or cast-off) together on the domestic sewing machine. The industry has been doing it for years!

Back-stitch –
(1) Knit the edge and remove it onto waste knitting.
(2) Place it against the garment onto the right side and back stitch through the last row of main yarn loops.
(3) 'Pocket edge' – If you are dealing with an edge you wish to conceal (i.e. cut and sew) you will have to consider your edging very carefully because you will want to enclose the cut and sew section. There are several edges listed in the appropriate section and there are various ways of attaching

them depending on your preference. You may find that your hand sewing is not sufficiently competent to give you the finish you require. Don't worry; the methods of attaching the edges on the machines will give you a professional finish. They only require a little practise.

With all these techniques do a small sample before you begin. Make sure you know how to achieve the effect you want. A little time spent now will save such a lot of disappointment, time and heartache later when you have finished the garment and find the edging curls-up or flutes outward and has to be removed and replaced.

7   The skirt

When making basic decisions about knitting a skirt you have four main measurements to consider, two of these are fixed, the first two horizontal measurements, the other two are determined by taste and fashion.

- Waist
- Hips
- Hem width
- Length

The skirt

I The straight gathered skirt

The simplest type of skirt to knit is a straight square skirt. This would be a gathered skirt rather like a peasant dirndle skirt and works extremely well if the fabric is not too heavy. You would firstly decide on the width and

Simple dirndle skirt

length required. The waistband would be knit separately and added after the pieces had been removed from the machine. This type of skirt, being straight and square lends itself to patterned borders. You can also use the basic idea to knit a gathered wrap-around skirt by attaching the skirt pieces onto a long tie-piece. If you are knitting for a very slim figure, you can knit a skirt without gathers.

II A straight skirt with hip-waist shaping

Skirt with a yoke

If you want to knit a straight, fitted skirt you will have to do some shaping between the hips and the waist to avoid unsightly gathering around the waist band. There are several alternatives.

(1) Decrease evenly across the row between the hips and waist by removing the work from the machine and replacing it on fewer needles.
(2) If the main part of the skirt is knit on a single bed, you could use the ribber for the yoke, transferring some stitches and knitting the piece between the hips and the waist in a ribbed and therefore narrower fabric.
(3) You could use graduated stitch size to make the knitting narrower.

(4) You could remove the skirt from the machine onto waste yarn when you reach the hips and knit the yoke in sections, decreasing on each section thus, in effect, inserting darts across the width of your skirt.

III The A line skirt

This is a panel skirt. You must decide on the number of panels you require. More panels (more vertical divisions) will result in a slimming effect. The hems on a panel will look better if the sides are shorter than the middle.

'A' line or flared skirt

This can be achieved by partial knitting. Also remember that if you are knitting a decorative border at the hemline, then you will have to insert your partial knitting above the border. You can shape the edges by decreasing regularly as you knit the garment or you can knit it upside-down, increasing regularly. If you knit it this way you will find it easier to alter to length.

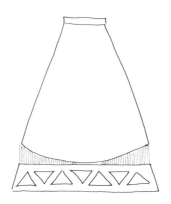

Knitting a border on a flared skirt

You can also use an increasing or decreasing stitch size to help in shaping the garment.

These are the basic skirts. You can vary them by adding patterned areas, or decorative finishes.

8 Pleated skirts

Pleated skirts can be knit on a single bed machine or a double bed machine. There are various techniques to master in order to achieve pleated effects. Firstly I will consider the skirt knit from hem to waist (sideways pleat effects will be considered with sideways-knit skirts).

One of the characteristics of pleated skirts is that the panels cannot be shaped at the edges by increasing or decreasing as this will effect the pleats. All shaping must be carried out evenly across the width of the fabric. This can be done by one of the following methods.

Altering the stitch size –
The standard procedure for doing a tension square is to knit the square using 3 different tensions.
(1) Start the square with W.Y.
(2) Change to M.Y. and knit: 20 rows M.T.; 20 rows M.T. − 1; 20 rows M.T. − 2
(3) Knit W.Y. and remove from the machine
(4) Measure the 60 rows. Calculate the number of rows you will require for the length of your skirt as follows

How to calculate the number of rows for the length of the skirt –
$$\frac{\text{Length of skirt}}{\text{Length of 60 rows}} \times 60$$
$$= \text{No of rows to be knit}$$

Divide this number of rows by three. Knit one third at M.T. − 1; and one third at M.T. − 2.

Altering the needle arrangement –
You can transfer stitches at regular intervals across the needle bed and

remove the empty needles to N.W.P. This will give you a thinner fabric. This is easiest to do if you are knitting some type of double-bed or ribbed fabric.

I The single bed pleated skirt

Single bed pleats can be achieved automatically with the help of the punch card, but you must remember the pleat repeat is determined by the stitch repeat. These skirts are best knit, therefore, on punch cards with a 24 + stitch repeat.

(*1*) A needle left in N.W.P. will give you the negative pleat (that is the pleat that folds inwards).

(*2*) A needle tucking on alternate rows will give you the positive pleat (the pleat that folds outwards). This tuck can be achieved by punching one row of a card and locking it in the card reading mechanism.

After you have completed the knitting of the skirt you can remove the panels and replace them onto the needle bed, doubling up the stitches to form the pleats before adding the waist-band.

II The double bed pleated or ribbed skirt

Ribbed skirts – These are the most clinging type of skirts and should be made and worn with caution. They can be shaped easily by making the fabric more ribbed, e.g. altering a 6 × 6 rib to a 3 × 3 rib. The skirt must be planned in advance if ribs are to be altered and separate swatches for each rib needle arrangement must be made to ensure the correct length is achieved.

'Flat rib' skirts – This type of rib is a less clinging sort of fabric but gives the appearance of a ribbed skirt. The needles are arranged so that all needles are working on one bed and selected needles are working on the second bed. The shaping (above the hip) can be done as in the ribbed skirt above by transferring stitches and pushing empty needles back to N.W.P.

Full needle rib skirts – These skirts are not as flowing and can only be done effectively with a *very fine yarn*. Because you are using most needles on both beds, you will have a thicker fabric. It is much more difficult to shape by removing needles to N.W.P. and it is more common to shape by altering the stitch size.

III Sideways knit skirts

There are several ways to achieve pleats in sideways knit skirts.

(*1*) You can knit panels/rows in thick/thin yarn.
10 rows – two strands
2 rows – one strand
10 rows – two strands
2 rows – four strands, etc.
(This is also called shadow pleating, and you can experiment with the number of rows in the intervals.)

(*2*) You can knit panels altering the stitch size:
10 rows T. 4;
2 rows T. 10., etc.

(*3*) You can use patterning to achieve pleats:
(*a*) Insert card one into the card reading mechanism and lock it or use a 1 × 1 needle selection on a manual machine.
(*b*) Knit a number of plain rows.
(*c*) Knit two rows in tuck stitch.
(*d*) Repeat the number of plain rows.
(*e*) Knit two rows in slip/part/ empty stitch.

9 The sideways-knit skirt

When you knit a garment sideways you are dealing with knitted fabric in a totally different way to a garment knit from bottom to top. When fabric is knitted to hang on the body horizontally, the loops of yarn hang onto each other. This means that although the fabric is not particularly stable, the loops can be pulled tight; each loop is only pulling or being pulled in relation to its neighbour.

If you knit so that the fabric hangs on the body vertically, the loops of yarn no longer pull on their upper or lower neighbour. The yarn just wiggles along in a line from top to bottom and there is nothing to 'hold' the loops in shape. So as gravity acts on the fabric it has a far greater potential to drop. The strands of yarn merely tend to straighten out. For this reason the tension square must be knitted and measured in a different way.

The tension square

(*1*) Knit the tension square at least twice the normal tension square size.

(*2*) Leave the square to settle by hanging it up attached to bulldog clips at both bottom and top. The reason for the extra clip at the bottom is to simulate the extra weight of yarn or knitting.

(*3*) When measuring the square don't pull it lengthwise as you would for a normal square but stroke it gently sideways. It will give entirely different results than if you were to measure it in the normal way.

The garment shape

The garment will be knit in sections. The sections can be rectangular in shape. Wedge-shaped sections achieved by partial knitting can be inserted between the rectangles to give the fabric shaping without seams.

A Measurements –
(*1*) waist measurement
(*2*) hem circumference;
(*3*) length.

B Then calculate from the measurement of the tension square –
(*1*) number of rows required for the waist;
(*2*) number of rows required for the hem circumference;
(*3*) number of stitches required for the length.

C *The panels (sections) –*
You must decide how many panels you will require in your skirt. The shaping or partial knitting wedges needn't go right up to the waist – they can be inserted with the major part of the extra knitting at the hem, thus giving the skirt a fluted look. Remember the following points.

(*1*) You must decide on the width and size of the wedge.

(*2*) You may shape both sides of the wedge or only one side of the wedge. The shaping is achieved by partial knitting and you may put needles into H.P. gradually and then knit the whole lot back to W.P. or you may return them gradually to W.P. row by row thus giving you a wedge with shaping at both sides.

D *The pattern —*
(*1*) With the information you have so far, you may simply draw the shapes you wish to knit on your patterning attachment for the machine and knit the garment or

(*2*) You may indulge in the 'juggling process'. The advantage of the juggling process is that if you wish to have patterned knitting, your decision beforehand on the number of rows you will knit in each panel will give you more control over the number of rows in the pattern knitting.

> You must remember that every short row in your shaping panel represents two rows of knitting. The number of panels can be odd. The number of stitches in each shaping can be odd and can vary. The number of rows at the hem and waist in each panel *must* be even.

E *The juggling process –*
(*1*) Divide the number of rows to be knit at the waist by the number of panels. (Adjust the number of rows to be even.)

(*2*) Divide the number of rows to be knit at the hem by the number of panels. (Adjust the number or rows to be even.)

(*3*) The number or rows in the hem of each panel minus the number of rows in the waist of each panel = the number of rows available for each shaping.

(*4*) Decide on whether you will have shaping on both sides or only one side of the wedge. If you want to have a double-shaped wedge the number of shaping rows must be divisible by four (the number of times you will knit short rows). If you want a right angle wedge the number of shaping rows must be divisible by two (the number of times you will shape).

(*5*) To calculate the number of stitches in each shaping you must decide on how deep your dart will be, i.e. will it just be at the bottom of the skirt or will it extend up to the hip or waist area. Divide the number of stitches you wish to include in the dart by the number of times you will shape. This will give you the number of stitches in each shaping. This does not have to be consistent or even and can be done using the magic formula.

10 Planning the garment

You now have a library of machine knitting techniques and a simple system of achieving your own garment designs. You must pull together all the threads and use your knowledge.

Do lots of tension swatches and sampling, trying out different colour combinations/stitch combinations. If the garment will be made up of more than one type of fabric do a separate tension swatch for each type of fabric. *Measure the swatch carefully.* If in doubt, do a double-sized tension swatch.

Do separate sample swatches for all trimmings and edgings required to ensure you will get the effect you want.

Plan your campaign of attack carefully and decide what order you will carry out the knitting to make sure you don't waste time and effort. For example, you could knit the body first, join the shoulder seams, and then pick up and knit the sleeves down towards the cuff. This will avoid the problem of joining the sleeves on later.

Keep a record of all garments made.

(*1*) Weigh the yarn before and after making the garment. This will give you a perfect record of how much yarn was used in each garment.

(*2*) Note the stitch sizes used and the measurement of all the swatches.

(*3*) Note the stitch patterns used.

(*4*) Make a note of any special techniques used.

(*5*) Make a note of the measurement of the person for whom the garment was made and the measurement of the garment itself.

(*6*) If possible attach a small tie of the yarn used.

After you have completed the garment it will have to be presented or given a proper finish. You must decide how the fabric will be treated. If it is oiled wool, or wool, or a mixture of fibres the garment should be blocked.

(*a*) For wool or natural fibres you must follow this routine.
- Wash the garment in hand-hot water with a mild soap or detergent (to remove the oil if it is oiled).
- Roll the garment in toweling (and press the roll to remove excess moisture).
- Lay the garment out flat on a gauze 'sweater drier' to dry or
- Lay the garment out on a blocking board and pin it out with 'U'-shaped upholstery pins (obtainable in haberdashery stores) and press or steam it with an iron.

(*b*) For man-made fibres you must.
- Wet the garment thoroughly (or wash it), pin it out to dry carefully and leave it at least overnight.
- If you decide to 'kill' the fabric, steam it with a steam iron. This will change the nature of the fabric and result in a more flowing but less elastic texture.

To make a useful blocking board sandwich together a piece of hardboard and a piece of foam. Make a cover out of checked or gingham cotton fabric by sewing a turned over edge around the fabric and inserting a cord to pull it tight over the foam square. The checked fabric will give you a grid to line your garment pieces up against. It is wise to make the board big enough to block the length of a skirt. When not in use, it can be slipped under the bed.

VIII Appendix

1 Foreign knitting magazines

Knitting Fashion Monthly
The Silver Knitting Institute
5–9–16 Shinjuku
Shinjuku-ku, Tokyo 160
Japan

Nihon Vogue Co. Ltd
3–23 Ichigaya-Honmuracho
Shinjuku-ku, Tokyo
Japan

Hello Knit
Shiroki Co. Ltd
10–18, 3 Chome
Nishiki, Nakaku
Nagoya, 460
Japan

Rakam
Rusconi Editore
Via Vitruvio, 43
20124, Milano
Italy

Macknit
The Knitting Machine Studio, Inc.
42 Hillside Ave.
Englewood, N.J. 07631
U.S.A.

Knitking Magazine
Knitking Corp.
1128 Crenshaw Boulevard
Los Angeles, California, 900019
U.S.A.

2 British knitting magazines (and subscriptions available in the U.K.)

Modern Knitting (Knitmaster)
P.O. Box 175,
Kingston-upon-Thames
Surrey KT2 6HA

Brother Fashion (Jones/Brother)
Jones/Brother
Shepley Street
Guide Bridge
Audenshawe, Manchester M34 5JD

Macknit (American)
from
Metropolitan Sewing Machines
321 Ashley Road
Pardstone, Poole
Dorset BH14 0AP

Machine Knitting World
1/2, East Market Street
Newport, Gwent NP9 2AY

Other foreign publications can be obtained from

The Knitting Neuk
32 Ashley Road
Aberdeen, AB1 6RJ

British Publications available at newsagents

Machine Knitting News
Machine Knitting Monthly

3 Yarn suppliers

Atkinson Yarns
Canal St
S. Wigston, Leics LE8 2PP

Argyll Wools Ltd
P.O. Box 15
Priestley Mills
Pudsey, W. Yorks LS28 9LT

F.W. Bramwell & Co. Ltd
Holmes Mill
Greenacre St
Clitheroe, Lancs BB7 1EA

T. Forsell & Sons Ltd
Blaby Rd
S. Wigston, Leics LE8 2SG

Patsy Yarns
P.O. Box A24
Union Mills
Milnsbridge, Huddersfield HD3 4NA

Schaffhauser Yarn
Smallwares Ltd
17 Galena Road
King St
Hammersmith, London W6 0LU

Scheepjeswol (U.K.) Ltd
P.O. Box 48
7 Colemeadow Rd
Redditch, Worcs B98 9NZ

Texere Yarns
College Mill
Barkerend Rd
Bradford BD3 9AQ

H.G. Twilley Ltd
Roman Mill
Stamford, Lincs PE9 1BG
(Telephone 0708 52661, 01–821 7430)

4 Comparative settings for pattern knitting

Passap	Jones/Brother	Knitmaster
Back Bed and/or Front Bed	Main Bed / Ribber	Main Bed / Ribber
AX (with pushers)	←TUCK→ / PR : P : PR (with card)	←TUCK→ / O : ∩ : O (with card)
BX (with pushers)	←PART→ / PR : R : PR with cd on BB only	←SLIP→ / O : – : O (patterns with card on back bed only)
CX (all needles)	←Free Move/KNIT→ / ←KNIT/Free Move→ (all needles)	←Free Move/KNIT→ / ←KNIT/Free Move→ (all needles)
DX Tubular tuck (with pushers)	←Free Move/TUCK→ / ←TUCK/Free Move→ (patterns with card on back bed only)	←Free Move/TUCK→ / ←TUCK/Free Move→ (patterns with card on back bed only)
EX (all needles)	←TUCK/KNIT→ / ←KNIT/TUCK→ (all needles)	←TUCK/KNIT→ / ←KNIT/TUCK→ (all needles)
FX (with pushers)	←TUCK/KNIT→ / ←KNIT/TUCK→ (patterns with card on back bed only)	←TUCK/KNIT→ / ←KNIT/TUCK→ (patterns with card on back bed only)
GX	←Free Move→	←Free Move→
HX (with pushers)	←Free Move/SLIP→ / ←SLIP/Free Move→ (patterns with card on back bed only)	←Free Move/SLIP→ / ←SLIP/Free Move→ (patterns with card on back bed only)
N	KNIT / ←N/N→	KNIT / I/I
Hold	HCL:H / HCL ←H H→	Russel Levers ←I I→ / Russel Levers ←I I→
Knit	HCL:N / HCL ←N N→	Russel Levers ←II II→ / Russel Levers ←II II→

EX/FX on one bed, N on the other will give English rib, on both beds will give fisherman's rib.

Passap do not have a system to knit two colours simultaneously in one row. Fair Isle is accomplished by using a set-up to knit first two rows in one colour, then two rows in the contrasting colour, thus passing the carriage across the bed four times for every two rows accomplished. It is basically a slip stitch technique and uses a BX setting on both locks with pushers.

5 Free move setting for different machines

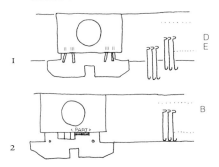

Jones/Brother push button machine
1 Holding cam lever III: needles in *E* do not knit; needles in *D* are pushed to *E*.
Holding cam lever II; only needles in *E* do not knit.
2 Part buttons pushed in: needles in *B* do not knit

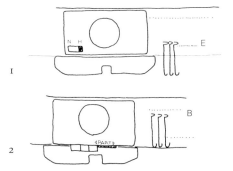

Jones/Brother automatic machines
1 Holding cam lever; needles in *E* do not knit
2 Part buttons pushed in: needles in *B* do not knit

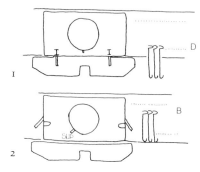

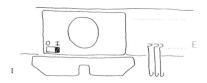

Knitmaster
1 Russell levers: levers to I: needles in
   D do not knit
2 Pattern dial to slip: side levers
   forward.
   Needles in B do not knit

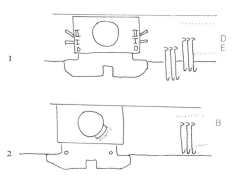

Toyota 858
1 Side levers to II: needles in E do not
   knit.
   Needles in D pushed to E and do not
   knit
   Side levers to I: needles in E only do
   not knit
2 Pattern dial: needles in B do not knit

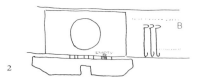

Toyota 901
1 Lever to I; needles in E do not knit
2 Pattern dial to empty; needles in B do
   not knit

Index